Advance praise fo
Radicals, Rabbis and Peac
Conversations with Jewish Critics of Israel

I'm grateful to have lived long enough to cherish such, truth telling, unacceptable and yet crucial as it undoubtedly is, both. (I turn 84 this year). It has been a long uphill climb since '72, when I spoke for the Palestinians—and paid up. Admirable ecumenism! The denunciations could be heard on the moon; right, left, center, Jewish, Christian. I was compared to Rev. Charles Coughlin, a clerical Jew baiter of the '30's! Someone estimated that 100 articles appeared after my speech; 90% at the least, were hostile (One of the very few who stood with me was Sylvia Heschel, widow of Abraham of blessed memory, my friend and co-founder of Clergy and Laity Against the War in Vietnam).

Since that time, I've been 'practicing diaspora' as a way of life.

Permit me to thank you with all my heart for your book. It is a ray of piercing truth, amid the darkness that lays claim to our world, from Tel Aviv to Washington, For me, indebted as I am to the prophets from Isaiah to Jesus, you have illumined the human vocation (whether of unbeliever. Jewish. Muslim, Christian); to labor on behalf of justice and peace, to stand with the victimised; 'the widow and orphan and stranger at the gate', to oppose war and its vile tactics—occupation, bombing, sanctions, slaughter of innocents - war, the creator of widows and orphans, of generational hatreds, of a ruined creation - untended wounds on the planet and the body of the human family.

The book is simply indispensable, given the welter of outright lies, slants, omissions that sum up our 'unmediating media' regarding the ongoing tragedy of the Palestinian people. To you and the noble minority who people this book, thanks are due from those who seek the truth, ever endangered and dishonored by the mandarins of untruth.

—Daniel Berrigan, S.J.

Radicals, Rabbis And Peacemakers: Conversations With Jewish Critics of Israel is an important book. Its value is to be found in the many diverse opinions which are presented, many of which contradict one another. Few readers will agree with all, and many may agree with none, of the views expressed. The myth which is shattered by this book is that Jews, somehow, share the Zionist vision of Israel as a state which is the "homeland" of all Jews, who remain in "exile" outside of the borders. This has always been a minority view, both historically and among Jews at the present time. In our country the vast majority of Jews view themselves as American by nationality and Jews by religion. They reject the idea that the State of Israel is in any way the fulfillment of biblical prophecy or is the legitimate object of their own loyalty. While sympathetic to the many displaced people who have found a home in Israel, they lament the fact that for many in the organized Jewish community, Israel has replaced God as the proper object of worship. Seth Farber is to be congratulated for gathering together so many interesting men and women and for sharing their divergent views with us."

—Allan C. Bloomfeld, editor of Issues, the quarterly journal of the American Council for Judaism.

The principal theme of this book is that Judaism is a religion of universal values, which does not assume a nationality and unquestioned loyalty to a political sovereignty. Hence, peace in the Middle East requires the application of Judaism's commitment to truth and justice and the repudiation of Zionism's commitment to Palestinian dispossession, dispersion, and oppression under the present occupation. Farber has intensively interviewed Jewish individuals and remarkably all, including Farber, reject categorically the claim by Zionism and the state of Israel that all who profess Judaism as their faith...endorse all policies of the state of Israel. Forceful, insightful and brutally honest.

—Naseer H. Aruri, Chancellor Professor (Emeritus) University of Massachusetts, Dartmouth, and author of *Dishonest Broker: The US Roles in Israel and Palestine* (South End Press, 2003)

This book is must reading for Muslims who may still not realize that the conflict in the Middle East is not between Islam and Judaism or between Muslims and Jews, but between the Zionist Israeli state and its sponsors on the one hand and their victims, the Palestinians, on the other. The editor and the contributors are a highly reputable and credible group of Jewish scholars and activists who actively endeavor, even struggle, from within the Jewish community to expose Zionism for what it is and rescue the Jews, the and the world from its claws.

—Dr Azzam Tamimi, Ph.D., Director, Institute of Islamic Political Thought, Co-editor with John Esposito of *Islam and Secularism in the Middle East* and author of *Rachid Ghannouchi: A Democrat Within Islamism*.

Seth Farber has earned our deepest appreciation for his book, Jewish Critics of Israel, which presents his interviews of several of the most courageous Jewish American critics of Israel and political Zionism. While the leading Jewish organizations in the United States have increasingly operated as mere extensions of the Jewish state of Israel, offering uncritical support to Israeli violations of the human, civil and political rights of the Palestinians, it is important to note that a growing minority of American Jews have been actively engaged in opposing the illegal and inhumane Israeli Occupation of Palestine. Indeed, some of them view Jewish support for Israel as the worship of a new 'golden calf,' a betrayal of the deepest values of historical Judaism. Now thanks to Seth Farber, we can listen to some of the leading Jewish American critics of Israel as they make the moral, legal and political case against the Israeli Occupation of Palestine and propose solutions that will allow the Jews and Palestinians to live in peace in two separate states or a single bi-national state. I can hope that his book will be read widely, and that it will persuade more Americans—Jews and non-Jews alike—to recognize the just demands of the Palestinians for an honorable existence in their own country.

—M. Shahid Alam, Professor of Economics, Northeastern University, Boston, Author of *Is There An Islamic Problem* (Kuala Lumpur, IBT Books, 2004)

These deftly probing interviews with committed U.S. Jewish Middle East peace activists and intellectuals offer unsparing analyses which carry the ongoing and recently intensified debate over Israel/Palestine to a new level, making this book required reading for anyone seriously interested in an enduring resolution to the Israel-Palestine conflict.

—Terri Ginsberg, Ph.D., Jews Against the Occupation (JATO), co-editor of Perspectives on German Cinema

All those who are perplexed by the continual "Middle-East Conflict" meandering through the minefields of big-power diplomacy will be grateful to this compilation of current Jewish dissidents. Not only are such views lacking from the popular media but the Jewish political culture itself has lacked the voices of prophetic dissent since the Nazi Judaeocide (the Cherbun / Holocaust). The Zionist parties of the time sought to preserve their members for the sake of their State to be and so sacrificed the Jewish Ashkenazi people themselves together with the majoritarian Jewish movement of the Bund in Poland. The Jewish Bundist leadership was likewise either eliminated or assimilated into the Communist Party and the Jewish Partisans absorbed into the Red Army leaving the Jewish People leaderless and so subject to the Zionist parties alone. This work serves to restore the political diversity that is natural and necessary to not only the Jewish People but to anyone who needs to understand the current impasse imposed by ideological concerns.

—Abraham Weizfeld Ph.D., Jewish People's Liberation Organization

RADICALS, RABBIS & PEACEMAKERS

Conversations with Jewish Critics of Israel

Seth Farber

Common Courage Press   Monroe, Maine

Library of Congress Cataloging-in-Publication Data is available from
publisher on request.
ISBN 1-56751-326-3 paper
ISBN 1-56751-327-1 hardcover

ISBN 13 paper: 9781567513264
ISBN 13 hardcover: 9781567513271

Common Courage Press
121 Red Barn Road
Monroe, ME 04951

207-525-0900
fax: 207-525-3068

www.commoncouragepress.com
info@commoncouragepress.com

First printing
Printed in Canada

For my parents who modeled the Jewish liberal values that constituted the matrix for my radicalism, and in memory of my grandfather Benjamin, the dedicated little Jewish doctor and jokester.

Acknowledgments

I am grateful to Robert Molteno who read my proposal and sample chapters at Zed Press in 2003 and recommended Greg Bates of Common Courage Press. Because of space limitations several interview could not be included. For their time and astute insights I thank Rabbi Michael Robinson, Professor Avi Bornstein (author of the seminal book *Crossing the Green Line*), and Professor Yakov Rabkin (author of the French language: *In the Name of Torah: A Study of Judaic Opposition to Zionism*). I strongly recommend Rabkin's essay in *Tikkun*, July-August 2002. (It can be read at www.one-democratic-state.org/articles/rabkin.html). I originally intended to include in the appendix the section of Dr. Rabkin's article titled: Abrahamia. Brief interviews or correspondence with Allan Brownfeld, Rabbi Daniel Goldberg, Rabbi Everett Gendler (see his important article on Rabbi Aaron Tamaret, an early 20th Century Orthodox rabbi who opposed political Zionism—it can be read at the website of the American Council for Judaism, Fall 2003) and Henry Siegman helped to clarify my thinking.

I am grateful to the following for advice: John Mahoney of Americans for Middle East Understanding (www.ameu), Dr. Anthony Gronowicz, Nita Renfrew, Harold Channer, Dr. Ray Russ, Joe Dubovy, Professor John Rempel, Richard Cummings and Cheryl Rubenberg (author of several excellent books, including The Palestinians: In Search of a Just Peace), John Baldwin, Laura Levine, Beth Strisik, Dr. Deniz Tekiner, and Russ Hermann who suggested I write a book on the Mideast. For encouragement and/or emotional support I am grateful to Dina Dahl, my parents, Pat, Sal, Justin, Miranda, Pasquale, Steve Apodacca, Elizabeth Prasad, Angelina, Dennis Brown and Steve Pearlman.

CONTENTS

I should much rather see Jews living together with the Arabs on the basis of living together in peace than the creation of a Jewish state... [M]y awareness of the essential nature of Judaism resists the idea of a Jewish state, with borders, an army, and a measure of temporal power, no matter how modest. I am afraid of the inner damage Judaism will sustain—especially from the development of a narrow nationalism within our own ranks.... We are no longer the Jews of the Maccabee period. A return to a nation in the political sense of the word would be equivalent to turning away from the spiritualization of our community which we owe to the genius of our prophets.

—Albert Einstein in *Ideas and Opinions*, 1954

We declare before world opinion...and before the Arab world, that we shall not agree...to the rule of one national group over the other. Nor do we accept the idea of a Jewish state, which would eventually mean Jewish domination of Arabs in Palestine.

—David Ben-Gurion, 1931 (cited in Chomsky, 2003, p. 34)

Preface

Jewish Critics of Israel

Supporting the Palestinian Resistance: The Challenge to the Idolatry of State-Power

Jewish critics of Israel? Probably to the average American this sounds like an oxymoron. The instinct of many *Jewish* Americans is to lash out against Jewish critics of Israel as 'traitors" within their midst, as "self-hating Jews," Jews who are ashamed of their Jewishness—even as Jewish anti-Semites who must be exposed as such for the good of the Jewish community. Both individual Jews and Jewish organizations have denigrated Jewish dissidents. Henry Seigman, senior fellow at the Council on Foreign Relations, a former head of the American Jewish Congress for 16 years, and a refugee (as a child) from the Germans in World War II recently told *The New York Times* (Siegman, June 13, 2002) that American Jewish organizations have confused Judaism with "uncritical support" for Israel and "the actions of Israeli governments, even when these governments do things that in an American context these Jewish organizations would never tolerate." Siegman, who was a student and close friend of the late Rabbi Abraham Heschel, believes that "social justice," "the prophetic passion for truth and justice" used to be central to Jewish faith, but that now the ideology of the Jewish state has become a "surrogate religion," a substitute for Judaism. Thus from Siegman's perspective it is not surprising that critics of the state of Israel are treated as heretics. Siegman stated, "If you do not support the government of Israel then your Jewishness, not your political judgment, is in question" (*The New York Times,* June 13 2002). Thus in contemporary America ironically worship of Israel—nationalism—has become a substitute for Judaism, a religion which holds that idolatry, including the sacralization of the nation state, is among the most serious sins, an act of sacrilege.

The persons interviewed in this book are representative of the small but vocal minority of American Jews who have dared to oppose in one way or another the actions of successive Israeli governments, and to challenge the mythology that currently masks the abuse of power by the Israeli state. Many of the members of this minority do not consider themselves religious, some are even atheists, many speak deliberately in purely secular terms, yet almost all of them believe implicitly or explicitly that they are obligated to register their dissent in the name of, and at least partially for the sake of, their Jewishness itself.

Some dissidents not only criticize Israel, they "take the side" of the

Palestinians whom they see as the victims of the state-power of Israel—and of its American patron. They compare Israel to the South African apartheid government. Adam Shapiro, a young Jewish activist from Brooklyn, has spent much of the last two years of his life in Occupied Palestine braving the wrath—and sometimes the bullets—of the Israeli Army. He garnered national and international publicity when he and several other comrades in the Palestinian solidarity movement smuggled into Arafat's besieged compound in Ramallah, hoping their presence would protect Arafat (and other Palestinians in the building) against assassination by the Israeli Army. Newspapers in New York City denounced Shapiro as "the Jewish Taliban," despite Shapiro's commitment to non-violence. Many pro-Israeli Jews were so enraged by Shapiro's pro-Palestinian sympathies, as reported in the newspapers, that they deluged Shapiro's parents with angry telephone calls and death threats. The Shapiros were forced to flee their home in Brooklyn—temporarily—and seek refuge with relatives in upstate New York.

The ranks of Jewish critics of Israel have been growing in the last decade. In the summer of 2004, the International Court of Justice (the "World Court") has declared (July 9, 2004) that the infamous Israeli Wall–ostensibly a security measure–was a violation of Palestinians human rights and must be dismantled. The Israeli government can build a wall on Israeli territory but not on occupied land. The Court rejected Israel's argument, endorsed by the Bush Administration and the Democrat Presidential nominee John Kerry, that the Court has no jurisdiction in the matter of the Wall. On July 27, the General Assembly of the UN agreed with the ICJ opinion, by a vote of 150-6 with 10 abstentions. (Of course the US and Israel voted against the Court.)

As the violence against Palestinians reached epic proportions under the government of Ariel Sharon (a former terrorist himself), the protest against the Occupation of Palestine gained momentum. While Jewish (and non-Jewish) students sign petitions and go to marches in order to protest the policies of Israel, some young (and sometimes older) Jews—like Shapiro—joined the International Solidarity Movement (ISM) and traveled to Palestine to live with Palestinian families.

The International Solidarity Movement (ISM) was founded by a Palestinian activist strongly influenced by Gandhi's philosophy of non-violent resistance. In the late 1950s and 1960s young American Jews went down to Mississippi and Alabama as part of the civil rights movement to demonstrate again segregation and Jim Crow laws, to help integrate the South. Today many young Jews, disturbed by Israel's violation of the civil and human rights of Palestinians, go to Palestine to act as "human shields" (as the ISMers have been termed by journalists)—they use their own bodily presence in an effort to deter attacks on Palestinians, to protect them from being shot or killed by the Israeli Army, known as the Israeli Defense

Forces (IDF). Thousands of Palestinians living in the occupied territories have been randomly shot by the IDF, but Israel has a policy—not always adhered to—of not shooting "internationals," presumably in order to avoid the risk of adverse publicity or diplomatic conflict. This policy was breached in the weeks before and during the Bush Administration's war on Iraq—mid-March and April, 2003: Three internationals were shot by Israeli soldiers, including an American college student, Rachel Corrie, who was deliberately murdered by the IDF on March 16, 2003—run over twice by a bulldozer. (The Israel government dismissed it as an "accident" despite preponderant evidence to the contrary.) Another one of the victims, Tom Hurndall, has suffered massive brain damage and was in a coma for months before dying.

The ISM has been relatively successful—the presence of American and European acting as "human shields" and international witnesses in all probability reduced the numbers of Palestinians who were shot or killed by the IDF and helped to publicize the plight of the Palestinians to the rest of the world (although to a much lesser degree in the United States where the media routinely censors information detrimental to Israel's reputation).

On college campuses Jews were active in the movement in 2002-3 to pressure their universities to divest from Israel in protest against the occupation of Palestine, and its failure to comply with United Nations resolutions. The President of Harvard, Lawrence Summes, incensed by a divestment petition signed by 70 Harvard professors, gave a speech in September 2002 in which he claimed that the divestment movement (despite the large percentage of Jews involved) was "anti-Semitic in effect, if not intent." Summers' statement was widely reported in the press but few University officials publicly follwed suit. Yet evidently the Right was preparing for an attack. At the time of this writing (March 2005) it has become clear that the leaders of the Jewish establishement, including AIPAC, ADL and Hillel (it is notable that their views do not represent the opinions of most American Jews, the majority of whom do not belong to any Jewish organization) have joined forces with officials in the Bush administration in an effort to suppress criticism of Israel in University classrooms. Legislation currently pending before the Senate (it passed Congress) would subject government-funded academic programs to monitoring by a government appointed board, including representatives of the CIA and FBI—ostensibly to protect "homeland security." Daniel Pipes, a well known author and neo-conservative "authority" on the Mideast, who was appointed by Bush in August 2003 to the United States Peace Institute, has spear-headed the crusade to silence scholars critical of Israel. As Professor Joel Beinin of Stanford University noted: Having failed to win in "the marketplace of ideas," the neo-McCarthyites seek to use the power of the state to suppress wayward thinking." (Beinin 2004, p. 113). Renowned Palestinian-American scholars at Columbia

University critical of Israeli policies were the first to come under attack. (Ginsberg, March 14, 2005). The premise of new McCarthyism is that criticism of Israel constitutes a threat to the US—thus raising the ante set by Summers.

This book consists of interviews or conversations with 8-10 individuals, a mix of scholars on Israel-Palestine, political activists and spiritual leaders. The boundaries between the categories is obviously permeable. Almost all of them (one or two of the interviewees resist such categorization) are critics of *political* Zionism–the theory that a Jewish state, or Jewish political sovereignty in Palestine, is/was the solution to the "Jewish problem" however it was/ is conceptualized. (It should be noted that Jewish dissidents are not opposed to "cultural Zionism," a theory more popular in an earlier era, which posits that Israel. will be the focal point for Judaism or a revival of Jewish culture. Martin Buber was a cultural Zionist who repudiated what I have referred to as *political* Zionism—he was an advocate of a bi-national state.) Considering the complex variables involved in the Mideast some of these critics may accept a Jewish state as a necessary evil at present or as a transitional form that must be temporarily accepted but they regard a Jewish state (or a Christian or Islamic state) as inherently undemocratic, and contrary to the universalism proclaimed by the Enlightenment.

Introduction

The Return of the Jewish Prophetic: The Support of the Palestinian Resistance

This book, this compilation, is intended to be an affirmation of the moral and spiritual tradition of Judaism—or at least of certain aspects of this tradition that probably most Jews, most Americans, agree constitute a valuable legacy. It is based on my conviction, shared by most of the individuals interviewed in this book that this legacy (however one may interpret it) was betrayed, and is currently threatened with extinction, by the policies of the state of Israel, and in particular its violation of the human rights of the Palestinian people. It was betrayed also by the American Jewish establishment which gives active and unqualified support to Israel, and by many American Jews who have generously given their support to Israel and been willing to turn a blind eye to the considerable evidence that Israel's actions over the last few decades are those of a racist state engaged in a brutal military Occupation in violation of fundamental principles of international law. For various reasons discussed in this book most American Jews are reluctant to even consider the argument that Israel belies the ethical ideals of Judaism at its best—of prophetic Judaism—and instead have endowed Israel with mythic status as the political embodiment of Jews' eternal innocence and goodness (see Ellis, 1990). The memory of the millions of Jews killed in the Nazi Holocaust helps to sustain the dominant cultural metanarrative that features Israel as the heroic agent of a victimized people's redemption—despite the fact that the Israeli Zionists' record of actually rescuing European Jews from extermination was far from exemplary (see Schoenman, 1988; Brenner, 1983).

The persons interviewed in this book are members of the minority of American Jews who have vocally and/or actively opposed the policies of Israel. Many of the members of this minority do not consider themselves religious, some are even atheists, many speak deliberately in purely secular terms, yet most all of them believe implicitly or explicitly that they are obligated to register their dissent in the name of, and at least partially for the sake of, their Jewishness itself. This of course does not mean that they do not also believe that Israel should be opposed in the name of post-Enlightenment liberalism. The universalist principles of the liberal tradition resonate with virtually all of Israel's critics, and they constitute the almost exclusive moral basis of the critique of Zionism and Israel formulated by renowned scholar Norman Finkelstein, a "devout atheist."

Although Jewish critics of Israel are frequently labeled as traitors to the Jewish community, as "self-hating Jews," there is a measure of irony in the fact that those Jews who will brook no criticism of Israel, who rationalize and defend Israel's policies in virtually every instance, who treat the state of Israel as an object of idolatry that must remain protected from moral doubt or criticism, are—however unwittingly—themselves arguably unfaithful to their heritage as Jews. The constant refrain that Jews who criticize Israel are self-hating Jews seems to be based on a misunderstanding of what it means to be Jewish. Do Jews who are proud of their heritage use it as a cloak to defend or deny the mistreatment of people who are not Jewish? Do they refrain from protesting when Jewishness (with all its connotations of high ethical standards and abysmal martyrdom) is used to bestow a halo of sanctity upon actions that are unethical? Does the affirmation of one's Jewish identity require the subordination of universal values to tribal loyalty? Is God's covenant with Israel a promise of privilege rather than a call to service? If the answer to these questions is negative, on what possible grounds can criticisms—even those that are mistaken—of the policies of Israel be equated with anti-Semitism, or with self-hatred? Norman Finkelstein, whose mother and father were survivors of the Warsaw Ghetto and (respectively) of the Auschwitz and Maidanek concentration camps, sees it differently: "Far from an expression of 'self-hatred,' denouncing Israel when it merits denunciation signifies remaining faithful to the memory of Jewish suffering" (Finkelstein, 2003).

But—some readers may object—even if criticisms of Israel are not necessarily anti-Semitic, why should this book, or any book, make Israel the *focus* of criticism? Are not the Palestinians equally guilty? This question will be answered in the course of this book: In order to understand the argument against the policies of the Zionists within Israel, it is necessary to understand the history of the conflict in the Mideast. A few comments are in order here however. While unequivocally condemning suicide bombings as crimes against humanity, most of the persons interviewed here would argue that Israel bears a greater responsibility than the Palestinians for resolving the current debacle in the Mideast. Why? In the first place it is Israel's founders who deliberately in 1948 deliberately expelled the Palestinians from their homes, thus transforming 3/4 of a million people into refugees (see Benny Morris cited in Ari Shavit, 2004). It is Israel that seized additional Palestinian territory in 1967 and began an unending Occupation. Furthermore the Palestinians could not bring an equal number of bargaining chips to the table when they entered into negotiations in the 1990s—the most salient fact about the Israel-Palestine conflict is the gross disparity between a dispossessed largely impoverished people living (many in refugee camps) under continuous military Occupation and a wealthy country with a high standard of living, a powerful State, the fourth largest military in the world and the unwavering support of the world greatest superpower. It is not the enfeebled Palestinians who refuse to compromise. (The myth that Barak made a "generous offer" at Camp David is refuted later.)

The idea that the responsibility for peace is *equally* shared derives much of its force from the premise that Israel's policies have been motivated primarily by a desire to protect the "security" of its citizens, that its military policy is primarily defensive, that the Palestinians are the aggressors. Thus Israel is seen as the innocent victim that—at worst—responds "excessively" to Palestinian aggression. (This is another variant of the dominant cultural narrative or myth of Israel's eternal innocence, as Marc Ellis has demonstrated.) But it is the contention of the contributors to this book that the policies of the Israeli government are jeopardizing the safety of its own citizens, as well as maintaining the Palestinians in an unending state of misery, subjugation and humiliation. The lack of security of Israeli citizens—who have themselves has been jeopardized by Israeli policies—rests largely with the successive Israeli governments, all committed both to retaining possession of the illegally occupied Palestinian territories and continuing the establishment of more and more Israeli settlements on this land–and possibly expanding territorially. Since the Israeli government is democratically elected, the people of Israel bear some responsibility for these policies—but it should be noted that Israelis seem unwilling to face the fact that the representatives they keep electing are willing to sacrifice their lives, the lives of ordinary Israelis, rather than to negotiate a peace agreement with the Palestinians based on an exchange of land for peace. (The majority of Israelis support ending the Occupation of the Palestinian territories.)

The occupation has been characterized by "a severe and prolonged regime of unreported and illegal practices of torture and… confinement" of Palestinians (Lustick, 2002a) and recently by an ongoing and largely successful effort by Sharon to destroy the infrastructure, not merely of terrorism, but of the entire Palestinian civil society (see Margalit, 2002). Neither Israel's occupation of the Palestinian territories nor the efforts to quash the resistance provoked by its own policies have succeeded in making Israelis even slightly safer. In fact, as Rabbi Michael Lerner has commented, "despite Sharon's protestations against Palestinian violence, it is precisely this violence that his policies seek to encourage, because it is those acts that provide him with the legitimation to avoid negotiations and to expand the West Bank settlements in defiance of the world's insistence that Israel give up the West Bank and Gaza" (Lerner, 2002b). Professor Lev Grinberg of Ben-Gurion University aptly noted, "[W]e are stuck in the same thirty-five-year-old problem: Messianic-nationalists and a war-craving military elite run our government, and they are currently supported and encouraged by the extremist conservatives of the Bush administration" (Grinberg, 2002b). Considering Israel's power and the fact that the policies of its government have been detrimental to the security of its own population, it is clear that Israel has the ability, if not the will, to negotiate a peace settlement with the Palestinians that would provide justice for Palestinians and security for Israelis.

Lev Grinberg gives another reason to focus upon Israel. While the suicide bombings have justifiably been condemned, the acts of Israeli state-terrorism have been minimized if not entirely ignored or justified by the American media and government. In fact the United States gives more aid to Israel per year than any other country—averaging (according to Richard Curtiss in Washington Reports on Middle East Affairs) approximately $23,240.00 dollars per American taxpayer each year, approximately 2 billion dollars. And yet the terrorism of the Israeli government is in many ways more reprehensible than the suicidal bombings of desperate individuals. The former is the direct responsibility of Ariel Sharon, Shimon Peres and other representatives of the "democratic" state of Israel. Unlike Palestinian terrorists they are not held responsible for their crimes: State terrorist policies are the "cold and 'rational' decisions of a state and military apparatus of occupation financed and backed by the only superpower in the world." (Grinberg, 2002a). Grinberg asked passionately in the spring of 2002: "Who should be arrested for the targeted killing of almost 100 Palestinians? Who will be sent to jail for the killing of more than 120 Palestinian paramedics? Who will be sentenced for the killing of more than 1,200 Palestinians [now close to 3,000] and for the collective punishment of more than 3,000,000 civilians during the last eighteen months? And who will face the International Tribunal for the illegal settlement of occupied Palestinian lands, and for disobeying UN decisions for more than 35 years? When is Sharon going to be defined as a terrorist, too?" (Grinberg, 2002a) Thus it is partially because Sharon and the state of Israel are rarely held morally accountable—and certainly face no legal consequences—for their terrorist acts, unlike individual Palestinian terrorists, that most of the criticisms of the persons interviewed here focus upon Israel, and upon its primary patron and enabler, the US government.

There are other reasons for the focus (the seeming one-sidedness) of this book—despite the fact, for example, that the Arab governments, if not the Palestinian people, bear a major share of responsibility for the plight of the Palestinians. We are Jews and Americans, and thus it is our primary responsibility to hold our own government and "the Jewish state" accountable for their actions. The American government ostensibly represents its citizens and takes actions in our name. Israel claims to represent all Jews (and according to its laws all Jews are Israeli nationals) and thus its actions are also performed in our name. It is particularly morally incumbent upon us to protest atrocities that are committed by those who claim to represent us—who act "in our name." It is this sense of heightened responsibility that is the impetus behind much of the writing and of the activism of the persons interviewed in this book.

There is a final—and for some of us important—reason for criticizing Israel; this was alluded to in the first few paragraphs above. What is ultimately at stake in the deeds of "the Jewish state" is the Jewish spiritual tradition itself. Our faithfulness to our heritage—our obligation to preserve it—requires that we protest against Israel, which implicitly (if not explicitly) claims to be devoted to and acting in accord with the Jewish tradition! But in fact both Israel, and influential American Jews who for the most part have become uncritical apologists for Israel, are betraying Judaism. Boas Evron, a secularist himself, observed that "the cult of the Jewish state has seduced [American Jews] to whore after strange gods," and that "the moral identification with power politics is tantamount to idolatry" (Evron, 1995, p.253).

Marc Ellis, the Jewish theologian (see Chapter 10 below), has asserted in his books more forcefully than any other contemporary writer/ witness that American Jews' uncritical support of Israel is destroying the spiritual core of Judaism itself, driving a dagger through the heart of our identity as Jews. Jews' relationship to Israel has displaced their relationship with God, and the vicarious identification of most American Jews with the state of Israel has eclipsed their recognition of their identity and vocation as the *people* of Israel who are bound by an ancient covenant to the God of all nations. This vocation entails the obligation to criticize, with the unflinching insistence of the Biblical prophets, the community of Israel when it acts in violation of God's will—of universal norms of justice. Ellis writes, "[T]he covenant remains today in a struggle for life in the heart of every Jew, religious and non-religious alike. It is murdered or given life as the other, the Palestinian, is banished or embraced by the Jewish community" (1999, p91). And on a more despairing note, which is at the same time a prophetic call to action, Ellis writes a few years later, "What the Nazis had not succeeded in accomplishing—the undermining at a very fundamental level of what it means to be Jewish—we as Jews have embarked upon. I witnessed this [in 1988] in the hospitals and in the streets [of Israel/Palestine] where Palestinians, struggling to assert their own dignity, were being systematically beaten, expelled, and murdered by those who had suffered this indignity less than fifty years earlier " (2002b, p156). These actions can be accurately described as a suicidal abnegation of Jewish identity, as a manifestation of Jewish self-hatred, precisely because of the fact that with all Jews' "flaws and limitations as a people" it is not possible "to consider Judaism without justice." Ellis buttresses his point, in characteristic fashion, with an image and a rhetorical question "Is it possible to be Jewish with helicopter gunships at our center?" (2002b, p.48).

Over the last few years there has been a marked increase in the numbers of Jews prepared to criticize Israel. I believe that this constitutes *a return of the Jewish prophetic*. (See Ellis, 2003 for discussion.) For years after the 1967 war the Jewish prophetic had been stifled–at least in terms of Jews' willingness to publicly criticize Israel's policies, particularly the oppression of the Palestinians.

The fundamental principle of the Jewish prophetic is the identification of God's will with the human striving to realize universal ideals of justice. The prophetic thus entails a willingness to criticize one own country, tribe, people, co-religionists for thwarting the realization of these ideals. The great Jewish prophets—including Jesus—were essentially critics of their own society. As Isaiah stated, "Cry aloud, do not hold back, let your voice resound like a trumpet; declare to my people their transgression, and to the house of Jacob their sins" (Isaiah: 58,1). The people I have interviewed in this book have declared to our people our sins. Some of them have risked their lives defending Palestinians in the occupied territories. They *are* prophets: They have heeded the prophetic call—which is always to seek God's justice, not to subordinate the good of humanity to the maintenance of tribal or national allegiances, not to commit the sin of idolatry and worship the State as God and master.

Not all of the persons interviewed here would use these terms. Norman Finkelstein, a self-proclaimed "devout atheist," would probably contend—if he had to give an opinion—that one can as easily be a Jewish fascist as an atheistic or Christian fascist. If Jews are perpetrating terrible crimes against humanity (as they are in Israel), it is neither because of their adherence to Judaism or because of their disloyalty to Judaism or God, but because they have become corrupted by power. If Jews, religious or not, have a better historical record over the centuries on that score—violence, inquisitions, murderous crusades—than Christians or Moslem or atheists it is only because throughout most of their history they have not occupied positions of power. Marc Ellis, a religious Jew, could hardly disagree with this conclusion—as a critic himself of the baneful effects of the empowerment of Jews.

But he would undoubtedly add to this the wry observation that Finkelstein's relentless critique of state-power (of Israel and its imperial patron, the United States) and of American Jews' cult of Israel is unwittingly an affirmation of the Jewish tradition at its best. His denunciation of the crimes of the state places Finkelstein the atheist—-along with, to pick an outstanding example, the great incorruptible secular Jew Noam Chomsky—in the position of "paradoxically embodying the most ancient of Jewish traditions, the refusal of idolatry" (2003, p169). And yet what is idolatry if not self-hatred–that is, the denial or refusal of the self's authentic identity? That is to say it is the hatred or denigration or violation of our own moral heritage, of the higher spiritual ideals that are embedded in Jewish culture—in our collective imagination–and contribute to our Jewishness, as well as to our humanity. It is the Jews of conscience who speak in this volume who are, often unwittingly, salvaging the Jewish covenant, who are acting in accord with the spirit of the great Jewish prophets.

Introductory Chapter

Noam Chomsky:
Binationalism: Then and Now

Noam Chomsky needs no introduction: Professor Emeritus of Linguistics at Massachusetts Institute of Technology, he is most well known for his analyses and critiques of State power and US foreign policy. Once famously referred to by The New York Times as "the most important intellectual in the world," The Times has ironically maintained their policy of not publishing articles by him (recently they made an exception); his searing critiques of corporate and state-power fall too far outside the limits of mainstream thought. His lectures are typically attended by thousands of people. His most recent book on the topic discussed herein is entitled *Middle East Illusions* and contains essays published in his 1973 anthology *Peace in the Middle East.*

SF: First I'm interested in your intellectual connection to Ahad Ha'am. Generally he's known as a cultural Zionist, not a negation of the Diaspora type who thought all Jews should go to Palestine but one who thought the center was in Jerusalem, in Palestine...

NC: A spiritual and cultural center.

SF: ...would revitalize—I believe he called it—Jewish national culture, and part of that for him I think for him was the prophets. How did you relate to it? What did you embrace in his work at the time?

NC: Well, just to be clear, you're asking me to reconstruct experiences from over sixty years ago, so they're going to be not very authoritative, but I remember impressions. I mean, I read his work in Hebrew and with a lot of interest, partially together with my father with whom I used to read Hebrew, partially on my own, and there...it certainly had a formative influence in my way of thinking, not only about Zionism but about a lot of other things, for example, interpretation of the Bible, which I studied the way any kid studies it. But he had interesting perspectives which I think are important. For example, one of his essays if I remember correctly was about what he called "the two Moseses:" the historical Moses, whoever it was, if it even existed, or is some construction from a set of oral traditions; and the cultural Moses, who is a creation of a cultural tradition and plays a certain role in it right up to the present, whether or not any such human being ever existed or if any of the stories are any more than a compilation of imaginative reconstructions and some historical events drawn from different folk epics and so on and so forth. So that one Moses is the topic of archaeology, and the other is the topic of cultural history, and he argued that they're equally real, just in different realms. And the cultural Moses is the one who's part of his development of his form of cultural

Zionism, a creation of a cultural and spiritual center in which the cultural Moses has whatever role he has, and the same with the rest of the created tradition of thousands of years.

SF: And what would be the positive effect of that revitalization...?

NC: He was interested in Jewish survival, and it was, at the time he was writing, not a matter of imminent catastrophism—nobody predicted the Nazis—but there were a lot of other processes going on which were undermining traditional Judaism. Traditional Judaism was a kind of medieval construction which was the entering in various ways into the modern age. Part of the Jewish community was being assimilated into Western culture, especially in Germany—that's the part we know about— Einstein, Freud, etc.—but also within Russia. I mean, a very large percent—I don't know exact numbers—but a substantial percentage of the Russian intelligentsia and the business leaders, political figures, and others, even under the czar, were people who had been sort of drifting away from the Pale of Settlement and into the urban centers and becoming part of world intellectual culture within the Russian environment. The same was happening in other countries. And of course there was a huge emigration to the United States at the time, which was going to dismantle a substantial part of the core of the Eastern Europe-based traditional Jewish community.

SF: What was the positive effect that he thought that would have?

NC: Well, he thought the cultural Zionism...my recollection and understanding at the time was that he thought that a cultural center in Palestine would be a sort of unifying element and would contribute to development and creation of a form of contemporary Judaism which would be fit to the modern age and which would draw from tradition and which would bring people together through these connections and enrich their own lives and interactions and so on.

SF: Did he emphasize prophetic Judaism?

NC: Yeah.

SF: Oh, he did?

NC: He did. I mean, prophetic Judaism is, of course, a fairly late construction. In the Bible, the prophets were mostly driven into the desert and jailed and so on and so forth. But the message of prophetic Judaism became an ideal of what we would I guess call dissident intellectual life that he certainly wanted to see revived.

SF: In that way, he was like the early Reform movement, people like Elmer Berger who thought that the prophetic Judaism was the height of Judaism as compared to the Torah...

NC: Rabbinic.

SF: Yeah.

NC: Well, partly the Torah. I mean, the main Jewish tradition for thousands of years was neither the Torah nor prophetic Judaism but Rabbinic Judaism, which is something quite different.

SF: Talmud.

NC: And the modern movements did want to leave the tradition of Rabbinic Judaism pretty much behind. You know, they maybe drew elements from it but didn't want to be bound by it, especially under the rule of authoritarian rabbis and so on and so forth. And yes, prophetic ideals fit with enlightenment ideals, and...

SF: So at that time, presumably you considered.... You know, I've interviewed people—Adam Shapiro, who says he's not Jewish. He accepts—I don't know if he got it from there, I presume he did—he accepts the idea of Jews as a distinctive worshiping community which was Reform Judaism's original idea as well as Elmer Berger's idea, and since he's an atheist, he says he's not Jewish. At that time and today, you would still consider yourself Jewish?

NC: Yeah, to me, it's much...I mean, I've been an atheist ever since I was a child. That's not so unusual within the Jewish tradition. I mean Judaism even as a religion was a religion more of practice than of belief. I mean you do say things like, "I believe" ("Ani ma'amin") and so forth, but what really counts in Judaism is practice, performing the actions that you're supposed to perform—well I don't perform those either (past a certain age—I did when I was twelve and thirteen). But it's just a community, it's a historic cultural community. And yeah, I feel very much a part of it.

SF: So, you wouldn't say that Judaism is incidental to your identity?

NC: How could it be? I grew up in it. I've lived a good part of my life in it. I've been closely involved with the Jewish community in Palestine, later Israel since childhood, with the history of Judaism and Jewish culture. It's part of my life.

SF: It's integral to you...

NC: I mean, I don't see anything problematic about that. It's just a lot of different factors that enter a person's life.

SF: Well, it's certainly...the people I interviewed, some of them felt very close to Judaism, and others, like Norman Finkelstein, felt it was pretty much incidental.

NC: Those are perfectly fair individual choices.

SF: Do you consider yourself a Jew in the sense of the influence of the Jewish prophetic tradition? You've often been called a prophet.

NC: Well, I think there are a lot of.... First of all that it's just marvelous literature, and a lot of what appears in it I think is very uplifting. And, you know, a lot isn't.

SF: You've also been accused, of course, by your political enemies or adversaries of being a self-hating Jew.

NC: Well, that's a concept which developed pretty much since 1967, and it's a political concept. It's a way of trying to fend off criticism of the policies of Israel. In fact that was sometimes made pretty explicit.

SF: What do you find most resonant in Judaism that you identify with today?

NC: Same as a child. I mean, the historical, cultural tradition, always alive, being recreated in new forms. I find a lot of that stimulating and exciting.

SF: What, a kind of iconoclasm?

NC: Well, that's one element of it. The prophetic tradition basically comes down to the call on the authorities to act morally and decently, the call on the population to keep to basic and fundamental moral principles: ensure care for those who need care; ensure justice; fight for freedom; don't be misled by, in those days, kings who are leading the country to disaster by their wild geo-political fantasies and so on. That's the prophetic tradition, that's very much alive today. We just call it dissidence.

SF: Do you think Heschel's presentation in his two-volume book on the prophets is pretty accurate? I don't know if you remember it.

NC: It was so long ago, I can't really comment. I must say that the interpretations were of much less interest to me than the original material. So yes, I studied the...I knew the original documents, I didn't care very much about the modern interpretations.

SF: Do you think it fructified your own political radicalism? Your readings?

NC: Well, it's very hard to introspect about what were the causes of.... It's something from which I draw in my own thinking and experience but in whatever private ways there are. And I can't tell you that I'm doing this because I read Amos last night (to mention my favorite prophet).

SF: I better get to binationalism. First, before 1948.... Until I carefully read Cohen's book, I assumed that no Arab was interested in binationalism. And then I looked over your book and your 1969 essay that was reprinted, and of course you point out the powerful influence of the binationalists, but in terms of even people who are critical of political Zionism—for example, Zachary Lockman, the guy who wrote the book on Jewish-Arab cooperation—he says that Aharon Cohen was naive. Well in certain ways, he was naive...

NC: With Cohen we must read with care. He was a very committed ideologically—I think at that time he was a loyal communist, not the Israeli Communist Party, but as a kind of a Stalinist. A large part of Hashomer HaTzair, which he was connected with, was very Bolshevik in character. So in the days when I was growing up, Hashomer HaTzair in the United States and pretty much in Israel was split into a Stalinist and a Trotskyist movement. That's one of the reasons I never joined it. When I went to Israel to a kibbutz, the kibbutz was originally

Buberite but straight Stalinist. It's hard to imagine it, especially because of the timing—that was 1953, after Stalin's latest, last outburst of fanatic antisemitism, but they remained pretty loyal.

SF: The interesting thing that Cohen...

NC: That colors a lot of what he writes. You've got to take it with care, a grain of salt.

SF: But he does give...well there are certain things that seemed incredibly naive that just reflected the prejudices of the time, for example, the idea that Jews have a historic right to Palestine.

NC: He was a committed Zionist. He never concealed that. So if you want to learn more about Arab-Jewish cooperation, interesting places to look would be in the work of the Jewish Communist Party, which really was committed to Jewish-Arab cooperation in a way much beyond Hashomer HaTzair. And so, for example, they wanted...they were opposed to the concept of Jewish labor and worked together with...

SF: Yeah, that's one thing that seemed to be missing in the...

NC: Well, you find it in the Jewish Communist Party. I mean, I don't know that literature very well, but there are some interesting things. There's, for example, a book you might look at—it's not really on this topic—it's by Leonard Trepper. He's a fascinating person. He was a Russian Jewish communist who went to Palestine, I think in the 1920s, maybe even as an emissary of the Communist Party (I mean, I read this a long time ago, and I don't want to swear by my memories). He writes interestingly about the activities of the Jewish Communist Party in Palestine in the 1920s, very anti-Zionist and very much involved in Jewish-Arab working-class cooperation. He then went on the Germany, where he became the head of something which was called the Rote Kapelle (the Red Orchestra), which was the Soviet espionage system inside Germany, and he in fact warned Stalin, sent Stalin tons of warnings about the fact that an invasion was coming, and Stalin never believed it. And of course the invasion came, and they were destroyed. He was finally picked up by the Gestapo in 1944, I think, and sent off to a concentration camp, and then he was liberated by the Russians, and they sent him off to the Gulag. It's an incredibly interesting story, I think it's called *Great Game*, or something like that. And one piece of it is about the Jewish Communist Party in the 1920s, which was pretty interesting. I didn't know much about it. There must be more literature on this that I don't know. But they were really committed to Jewish-Arab cooperation.

SF: But you supported Hashomer HaTzair at the time?

NC: Not really. As I say, I could never really. I was kind of sympathetic to them, and I agreed with them about a lot of things, but I never...I couldn't really join with them, simply on straight political grounds. They were all Leninists.

SF: You described...you said on WBAI that you thought the establishment of Israel was "a tragedy"; you qualified that characterization because you were relieved the displaced people would finally have somewhere to go. But you opposed the creation of the Jewish state.

NC: I think the creation of a state as a Jewish state was a serious mistake. I remember at the time—not only I, but my closest friends and the older people around me, the old Avukah people and so on regarded it as almost a tragic day when that happened.

SF: What about it? Did you have in mind any of the dire consequences?

NC: I took it to be implicit in the very concept of a Jewish state. I thought then, and think now, that it is wrong in principle to establish a state that is not the state of its citizens, but rather—as the High Court later defined it, though it was clear enough from 1948—the sovereign state of the Jewish people, in Israel and the diaspora. Hence it is my state as an American Jew, though it is not the state of non-Jewish citizens. For the same reasons, I would oppose moves to turn the US into the sovereign state of the white (Christian, whatever) people, and I object to Islamic states, etc. It's a matter of principle, quite apart from the consequences.

SF: Some binationalists at the time predicted that Israel would inevitably become militaristic and expansionistic.

NC: I don't think that was inevitable. The Jewish state could have moved to a political settlement in the early 1950s, and that might have succeeded; it chose not to. That was certainly possible by 1971, and we know that the possibility was rejected in favor of expansion.

SF: What did the idea of a binational state have going for it as opposed to the idea of an ordinary secular state? Many binationalists were criticized because...

NC: There are various.... These are not alternatives. I mean, a secular state could be a binational state and in fact should be.

SF: I meant...

NC: A single...?

SF: Yeah.

NC: Well, look. There are various ways for democratic communities to be organized. Let's put aside the defects of democracy and think of them as ideal. So there's a kind of an American model in which everybody's an American citizen, period. There's no... I mean, there are, but in principle there shouldn't be...other divisions. An alternative to that is, let's say, the Swiss or Belgian or Spanish model, and in fact a model which is evolving all over Europe—England, too—in which the state is the state of its citizens, but it's more complex. There's also regional autonomy, cultural autonomy, and so on. So in Spain, there's regional autonomy, a fairly substantial amount of it, different languages, a lot of self-government in particular areas. In Belgium, it's not even regional...well, it's partly regional because of population distribution...but it's basically cultural. It's a binational state which is essentially cultural. In the old Ottoman Empire, which in many respects... I mean, nobody wants to reconstruct the Ottoman Empire...but in some respects, they sort of had the right idea, in my opinion. The local autonomy was carried pretty far. In a particular city, the people who wanted to consider themselves Greeks ran the Greek affairs, the Armenians, the Armenians' affairs, and so on. But those are obvious...and the Ottoman Empire was no democracy, but those are a variety of ways in which democratic societies could be organized; the United States is a little bit unusual in the world, because most of the world is sort of multi-ethnic and multinational. The U.S. is unusually homogeneous, but that's because in the United States, the indigenous population was wiped out. In Europe, the indigenous populations remained. So there's an element of homogeneity in the United States which...a kind of homogeneity—I don't want to suggest that there's homogeneity here: there's racism and ethnic conflicts and all sorts of things. But they come from different roots; they're not from the indigenous population. Now in the former Palestine, the heterogeneity results in substantial measure from immigration from abroad, and a recent one. But the effect by the 1940s was very much...was in my view more similar to the European system—say Belgium or Switzerland or whatever, or Spain today—than to the American system. And there are simply two separate communities. There's no way of overlooking that. They have different languages, different cultures, different practices. They see themselves as having a different created history, different aspirations. And in that condition, I think what's required is one of these other models, not the American model of a single state.

SF: What do you say to a Palestinian who says that the Jews had no right to go to Israel in the 40s and 30s, even before Hitler, and demand that they become... and expect that they would become a majority, that they should have gone and they were welcome in Palestine and Arab countries, but they should have become citizens of all the various different countries including Palestine?

NC: I can't and don't argue that they are wrong. I mean, I agree with Native Americans who say that the colonists had no right to come here. I don't see a lot of point in these discussions, but I can certainly agree with them. I agree with Mexicans who say that the U.S. has no right to be sitting on half of Mexico conquered by violence.

SF: Do you think the binationalist movement was more practical in the 40s, at the time, in the 30s, even before Hitler? WWII gets into other complications that would take too long to discuss.

NC: It's very hard to know what would have...what could have been if people were committed enough to it. But it's...I mean, I felt since the time I was a child—I don't lay a lot of weight on my judgments—but looking back, it seems to me there really were possibilities, and it could have been much more constructive than what happened. Whether that would have been possible in the wake of the Holocaust and everything else that was happening in the world, I don't know, but it seems to me it would have been, and I feel then now as I felt then that it was an ideal worth standing up for.

SF: Cohen says—which it seems to me he gives copious examples of—that the obstacle to a negotiations and a collaboration with Arabs was Ben Gurion's and his whole clique's unwillingness to agree to political parity and not—you also quote this—and not as Cohen put it "the oft quoted complaint that there is no one to talk to in the Arab camp"—which is astonishing you wrote that in 69, Cohen said it in the 30s, but of course that's what the Israelis are saying now: "There's no Palestinian to negotiate with.!" I think it was Labor Zionists' alibi for not negotiating–then and now.

NC: Look, they were not going to get a lot of warm welcome from the Palestinian population, that's for sure. But if there had been really honest efforts to move towards some form of integration and not a separate Jewish economy...I mean, first of all, you can understand the motivation behind the Jewish economy; the fact of the matter is that the Jews coming in from Europe could not compete with Arab workers any more than if I went to Guatemala and tried to live on a farm, I couldn't compete with Guatemalan peasants, you know, you just can't. And they didn't want to hire them as hired labor; they didn't want to be South Africa, and they wanted to develop the basis of their own society. So putting all these things together, it led to the Jewish labor, the boycotts, and everything else, which were wrong, but understandable. Now if there had been other approaches, which may have been possible, and if there had been real class collaboration, serious collaboration between Jewish and Arab working classes of a kind that Cohen a little bit describes, and Kalvarisky describes and others, maybe that could have led somewhere else.

SF: What kind of economically feasible binational state could you have had in the circumstances of the 1930s?

NC: Well, the Palestinian community was largely feudal, but it was becoming...could well have become part of a more modern, industrial world, and there were elements that wanted to be.

SF: Without...that would just obviously...

NC: I mean, it's kind of like asking, how could you have an industrial economy in the United States when Black farm workers, who are virtually slaves, were pouring in from the South to the North in the mid-twentieth century with the mechanization of agriculture. Well, that's what sensible social policy should be about. Or you could ask the same about Europe. I mean how could Europe ever be unified with Spain, Greece, and Portugal being semi-backward, semi-modern societies. It was done with compensatory funding and other kinds of development, which led to pretty successful outcomes.

SF: So that could have been done, with the Zionists giving up the...

NC: Giving up the hope of dominant political power, a hope I don't think they should have had anyway. Was it feasible? Well, you know, it's very hard to say.

SF: They would have had to give up...even before Hitler, the binationalists would have had to give up the idea of getting a majority in Palestine, which some were willing to compromise on–and some were not.

NC: Yeah, it might have been that.

SF: Wouldn't they have had to give up the idea of buying all the arable land from absentee landowners and kicking the fellaheen...

NC: Which they should have done anyway. But first of all, it wasn't that much. By 1948, I think they owned six or seven percent of the country.

SF: According to Farsoun, it was twenty-five percent of the arable land.

NC: Could be, yeah.

SF: So you don't agree with...

NC: I mean, the notion of arable land itself is an ambiguous notion. With more modern technology...is Southern California arable land? I mean, that's one of the main centers of American food production, but it's basically in a desert. They made it arable land by technology. So there was more land that could be shared by two groups and put to good use.

SF: Yes but the technology that was used in California–was anything like that available in the 1940s?

NC: The technology that developed southern California was not only available at the time, but also had been used. Furthermore, it's not the right question. If a tiny fraction of the R&D resources/efforts that later went into high tech industry from the 1950s (via the Pentagon primarily) had gone to, say, desalination and other sustainable forms of development, the technology could have been available when needed.

SF: Obviously you don't agree with people like Michael Lerner who described the eviction of Arabs off the land and the "no Arab labor" policies as a necessary form of affirmative action for Jewish people.

NC: Well, I understand what he's saying, and I think you can understand the motivations for it of the kind that I mentioned, but I don't think it was justified.

SF: What about Pappe's idea that the urge for co-habitation came from below, and that the drive for colonialism *and* nationalism came from above, and that he never uses the word, "binational," but he seems to be hinting at a binational political solution as well.

NC: I just don't know enough about the nature of what was happening inside that society at the lower levels to even have a judgment. There's very little information about it. Actually, he's one of the first people to have written about it. There's very little in the way of written sources to go back to, because these were... this is essentially a peasant society. So you have to...it's hard work to find out what was going on. I just don't know enough to have a judgment.

SF: That's the only place I've read that statement. You said that in 67 and 73 that a binational state once again became, or became, an option.

NC: I think it did. In fact, I felt then, and I still feel, that Israel could have instituted first a federal arrangement moving on towards closer integration and some form of binationalism that would be alongside of accepting a general peace settlement with the Arab states, which was possible, certainly by 1971 but maybe even before, and I think would have been accepted, in fact favorably accepted by the Palestinians. Actually similar proposals, I learned much later, were being floated by Israeli military intelligence and the military authorities—not the same, but similar—but rejected by the political echelons.

SF: You mention that military authorities...

NC: I didn't know that until I read Gazit's memoirs, who was the head of the...

SF: The one you cite in your book?

NC: Well he's the same guy but...

SF: Peled?

NC: Oh, Mattityahu Peled, that's different. He's completely different. Shlomo Gazit is very much part of the system, in fact pretty hawkish, but he was the head—he's a general—he was the head...he ran the military administration in the Occupied Territories from about 67 or 68 until the mid-1970s, and he wrote his memoirs in Hebrew. They came out in English a couple years ago. And in it he describes proposals which I hadn't known about, coming from the military intelligence and the military authorities for varying degrees of autonomy in the Occupied Territories, which could have been the basis for a kind of federalism. He says they were just dismissed by the higher political echelons, by the Labor Party. He thinks this was a tragic error which led to all kinds of catastrophes later on, and it was my feeling, too, but I didn't know about his proposals. But it seems to me that those were feasible options. There was no resonance whatsoever among at least the elite elements, including the doves, and I think it was a sad, sad mistake at that time, even mention of the notion was total anathema and caused absolute hysteria. And now it's being accepted, so you can read about it in the *New York Times* and so on, but I suspect that the reason is that it's now understood to be unfeasible, so therefore we can talk about it and look humane.

SF: Yeah, you've said that. Why do you think it's more unfeasible now than it was in 67?

NC: Now there's no basis for it at all. For example, by the mid-1970s,

Palestinian national rights became a leading issue. Since then, there's been thirty years of attempts to—blocked by the United States—to create a two-state settlement. The end result of that has led to rising conflict and antagonism. Israel no longer has the kind of authority over the Territories that could have allowed it to institute a sensible form of federalism and then back off to its own section. The conditions are just totally different. I mean maybe it's still feasible, but it would have to go through—I think maybe it still is—but it would have to go through stages. And the first of those stages I don't see any alternative to some two-state settlement.

SF: That's the same thing Phyllis Bennis said. But many of the people who are now talking about a binational state, at least some of them—I'm assuming many—have given up on the idea of achieving even a two-state solution. You still think that's possible?

NC: I think they're giving up on a binational state if they don't accept the two-state solution, because that's a stage towards it. Now look, we have to make a distinction here between what we might call proposals and advocacy. So you can propose that everyone live in peace and love each other, but that doesn't become advocacy until you give...until you lay out a plausible procedure for getting there. Now I think we can propose a binational...most people are proposing a one-state settlement, which I don't think is even the right end, but if we propose a binational state, that's easy. But if we advocate a binational state, we're going to have to talk about how to get there, and I simply don't see any way to do it as the world now exists, there and in the international community, except by going through some form of two-state...

SF: How do you see...you've said in your interviews you actually envisaged, a movement in the United States putting pressure on the legislature and the executive to pressure Israel. Hard to imagine competing with AIPAC!

NC: There isn't any pressure, but there certainly could be. A large majority of the population is in favor of it. It's just the way U.S. democracy works, the population is excluded. So I mean, right now, according to the latest polls, the percentage of the population who thinks that the U.S. should be tilting towards Israel is seventeen percent, but you could say the same about just about any other issue. A large majority of the population is in favor of the Kyoto Protocol; that doesn't have any effect on policy.

SF: And do you expect it to have any effect?

NC: It depends on whether a democratic system can be reconstructed in the United States. Right now we're very far from that.

SF: It seems further from it than we were ten years ago, or four years ago.

NC: It just means more work.

SF: One thing in your interviews with Stephen Shalom and other people, you said when you were questioned that the refugees outside of the Occupied Territories certainly shouldn't give up the right of return, but you said their American supporters should support programs like the Geneva Accords that require them to give up the right of return.

NC: No I didn't. We should not accept a proposal that requires them to give up the right of return.

SF: Oh you don't think it does?

NC: The Geneva Accords are, in my opinion, a basis for negotiation.

SF: Oh is that how you would...?

NC: Yes, that's what I said. In fact, if you look back, I think I said they're a reasonable basis for negotiation. There are elements of them that I don't think are acceptable.

SF: Oh, so you would agree, then, that the American anti-occupation left should not support the sacrifice of the right of return on the part of the...?

NC: Well, we have to be a little cautious here. I think the right of return should be maintained, but the expectation that it will be implemented is completely unrealistic. And to advocate that is just to cause pain and disaster to the refugees. Now it may be that that right can be implemented, but only over a long period of reduction of violence, integration and so on within Palestine, maybe it can be implemented.

SF: Well the left could at least call for the right and say that the implementation is negotiable?

NC: I mean, I think that the Native Americans have a right to this country. They shouldn't give it up. But that's not going to be implemented.

SF: Nor should American supporters of the Palestinians advocate that they give it up or...

NC: Not give up the right, give up the illusion. They should not pretend that it's realistic; it isn't. It's just deeply immoral, in my opinion, to block efforts that might ameliorate the conditions of suffering people, that might ultimately lead to the realization of the right, because you want to stand on what you call principle. That's not principle, that's immoral.

SF: So ultimately, if possible, you would like to see a binational state or, you mentioned, a regional...

NC: Ultimately I would like to see the optimal solution, which is no state at all, in fact not for that region but for most of the world. Kind of roughly the Ottoman system.

SF: Kirkpatrick Sale the green theorist speaks of "bioregionalism"—I don't know if you...

NC: I don't care what you call it. I mean, it's just a typical anarchist point of view.

SF: Let me return to a point. Cohen argued, and Magnes made the same kind of charges in his letters, that the Labor Zionists continually put up obstacles to negotiations with Arabs that could have led to a binational state–or at least to an outcome less catastrophic for Palestinians than what occurred in 1948. When the Palestinian Arab Adil Jabr and the Zionist binationalist Haim Kalvarisky drew up a program for bi-nationalism in 1940-1 which they wanted to present to Arab leaders for discussion, Kalvarisky first showed it to Ben-Gurion at the end of July 1941. Ben-Gurion got angry and called it "an abomination." A few weeks later, Sharett, Ben-Gurion's right-hand man and future Prime Minister of Israel, wrote the draft was not acceptable unless it was revised to include a Jewish state. Cohen concluded that the "bottleneck" to negotiations with Arabs was Ben-Gurion's refusal to accept a bi-national Palestine based on political parity. Of course this was not known at the time because Ben-Gurion publicly favored binationalism until the early 1940s. The obstacle was not–I quote Cohen– "the oft heard complaint that there is no one to talk to in the Arab camp." And you seem to agree above that cooperation from below could have been forged with Arabs, although in your 1973 book unlike Cohen you don't impugn Ben-Gurion's sincerity as a bi-nationalist, but attributed the undermining of Labor Zionism's belief in bi-nationalism to the trauma of WWII and the Nazi holocaust. I just also want to add that most American leftist scholars on this issue——like Lockman–argue, on the basis of what I think are false premises, that "there were no left-wing forces within the Arab community ready to compromise with Zionism, of whatever variant" (p.288). For one thing I think this overlooks the fact that the Jews had the upper hand. Cohen writes that when it became clear Axis powers were losing, Arabs' desires for accommodation became stronger; he comments that "it was again made clear that had relations been methodically and consistently nurtured , it would have been possible to work out a definitive working basis for agreement after the war" (p.123). In other words it was not naive to posit that had Zionist centrists supported bi-nationalists' efforts, unforeseen kinds of opportunities could have emerged. But as usual ethics took to a back seat to power politics.

NC: As I said before, I think we have to treat Cohen's account with a degree of skepticism. The fact is that we don't know what could have happened if there had been a commitment to genuine accommodation——perhaps, as I believed at the time, along the lines proposed by the League for Arab-Jewish rapprochement, socialist binationalism based on Arab-Jewish working class cooperation. Realistic? We cannot know.

SF: And do you believe, like most people that I spoke to, that Jews have a particular obligation to protest the crimes being committed against Palestinians?

NC: If people regard themselves as related in some manner to what is happening there, they do have a particular obligation, for two reasons. For one thing, because they're Americans. And all Americans have that obligation, since the U.S. is deeply implicated in the crimes. So that's one thing. If, in addition to being American citizens, they also feel some connection to the Jewish world...

SF: Which you do?

NC: Which I do. Then there's an extra obligation.

SF: Let me end with a quote from your old mentor. In 1920 Ahad Ha-am heard of an act of Jewish terrorism committed against Arabs; he had witnessed these kinds of abuses before. He wrote, "My God... Is *this* the goal for which our fathers have striven and for whose sake all generations have suffered? Is *this* the dream of a return to Zion which our people have dreamt for centuries: that we now come to Zion to stain its soil with innocent blood? Many years ago.... I stated that our people will willingly give their money to build up their state but they would never sacrifice their prophets for it. .... I apparently erred. The people do not part with their money to rebuild their national home but, instead, their inclination grows to sacrifice their prophets on the altar of their "renaissance': the great ethical principles for the sake of which they have suffered, and for the sake of which alone it is worth while to return and become a people in the land of our fathers. For without these principles, my God, what are we and what can our future life in this country be...?" (Cited in Kohn, p. 831)

Chapter 1

Steve Quester

Steve Quester is a member of Jews Against the Occupation, a graduate of Columbia University and an elementary school teacher. At 41 he has been a social activist since college.

SF: I don't know how many founders there were of JATO...

SQ: I'm not a founder, no.

SF: You're not?

SQ: No, Dena, Daniel Horowitz... I joined JATO in May of 2001. It was formed in, I don't know, maybe October of 2000?

SF: Well, you know a lot of people I've met in JATO have seemed to defer to your authority or your knowledge.

SQ: I'm outspoken.

SF: What made you join Jews...I know you were in Israel as a child, so you had some sort of...

SQ: An *explicitly* Zionist education.

SF: You're kidding?

SQ: I was sent to...in 6th grade I was sent to the religious school at Temple Emanuel, which is the big synagogue on 5th Avenue. It was the third religious school I'd been to, because we'd moved around. But I hadn't been to religious school in a few years, and the 6th grade curriculum, at least with this particular teacher—it was just a Sunday morning program, the curriculum was very explicitly Zionist. Right-wing Zionist. You know, we were eleven years old...

SF: Right-wing Zionist?

SQ: Oh, yeah.

SF: You mean like...Like Menachem Begin was considered a hero or something?

SQ: The teacher used to hand out pamphlets that showed the borders of Israel, the post-June 1967 borders of Israel, so the state of Israel, the Sinai Peninsula, the Gaza Strip, the West Bank, and the Golan Heights were all presented as one country with no internal borders. And there'd be arrows pointing at this entity from all sides, and it would be... as to how Israel needs defensible borders and cannot give up any of these territories.

SF: Listen, you said this was Temple Emanuel? Isn't that...

SQ: It's a Reformed temple with very conservative politics.

SF: I didn't realize their politics...

SQ: But I bought it, I bought the whole thing hook, line and sinker. And you know, it was reinforced—my mother would just drop little anecdotes about how Israelis care so much for human life that when there's a traffic accident, it's the top story on the news, or they care so much for human life that there are no swings on the playground because children can get hurt, and Golda Meir was such a moral person that when she was brought to Victoria Falls in Rhodesia on a state visit and they said, Okay, whites this way, blacks that way, she said, "Well, I don't need to see these falls" and refused to go. I mean, these are all the little tidbits that my mother gave me...

SF: Where do you think your mother got the stories from?

SQ: I don't know... So I grew up very pro-Israel. I did not remain a right-wing Zionist because I was, you know, left in every other way, so that wasn't sustainable at all.

SF: That's the whole idea of Alan Dershowitz' new book—how good the Jews were, and they were morally so sensitive—Israelis cared...

SQ: I was certainly taught that the Arabs were told to leave by the Arab governments in 1948 to aid the war effort, and the Jews begged them to stay but... that all we wanted to do was just live there in co-existence, the Arabs kept attacking us, we never started it. I was taught that whole thing. And I believed it.

SF: Were you parents...was your father into this whole thing, too?

SQ: My father died when I was nine.... So the summer before my senior year in high school, I went to Israel.

SF: You were still in Emanuel high school?

SQ: Emanuel is just a Sunday school. I went to public school. And, so, I went to this two-month program called High School in Israel, which I paid for myself. I had some savings, which really go me all pumped up about wanting to live there, and it was all this history program, history taught from the Zionist perspective. And then I spent my junior year in college at Hebrew University, and there I started seeking other perspective. I had the opportunity to travel up to the town of Tira, which is a Palestinian town outside of Haifa, and to meet people who talked about their own experiences in 1948....

SF: Really? What year were you there?

SQ: 83-84. I was at Hebrew University...

SF: What college were you in here?

SQ: Columbia.

SF: You were an undergraduate at Columbia.

SQ: Yeah. You know, I had the opportunity to meet Palestinian students and talk with them, and really.... What my Zionism turned into was a passionate advocate for Jewish-Arab co-existence within Israel. That was going to save Zionism, the Jewish state concept, in my own mind. So after college...

SF: Save Zionism and not end the Occupation.

SQ: No, I *was* then anti-Occupation. So I applied and was accepted for an internship for two years after college in a group called Interns for Peace, which works with Palestinian-Israelis and Jewish-Israelis and gets them together for social events. They meet each other...

SF: That has nothing to do with the group that Adam Shapiro mentions, Seeds for Peace?

SQ: No. But it's a similar kind of premise. You know, get them together, let them know each other, humanize the other. It's an apolitical program that only worked inside the Green Line [in Israel]. So I did that for two years, but continued to evolve in my own political thinking and decided I wasn't a Zionist and I didn't want to live there and came back here and didn't really do much from 1987 forward. You know, when the Intifada broke out in 1987, I'd just moved back to New York, and I just really didn't think very deeply about Palestinians are taking their destiny into their own hands and rising up against the Occupation. My first thought was, I'm worried about my ex-boyfriend, because he was in the army at the time.

SF: In the Israeli army?

SQ: Yeah. So I was worried he was going to get hurt. And I basically withdrew from Middle East politics except for, you know, some conversations, until the Al-Aqsa Intifada broke out. I went back to visit Israel once in 98. From what I saw and what I heard, I was convinced that Oslo was this wonderful thing, that there was going to be freedom and peace. I didn't think through the refugee issue at all.

SF: You mean the refugees from 1948 who were outside Palestine?

SQ: Yeah. But it was also clear to me that during the Camp David talks in 2000 that Arafat was absolutely correct to reject this bum deal that he was being offered, and I was sort of felt like, "Okay, so they're going to keep negotiating, and this is going to take a long time to hammer out, but it will turn out okay." But it didn't turn out that way. When Sharon went up on the Temple Mount with all those police officers, I said, "What a fucking bastard." And then the Intifada erupted, and Israel started gunning down unarmed demonstrators which, you know, they hadn't done before. The Occupation has always been brutal, but they hadn't done that before.

SF: One reads about the Israeli Army in the early 90s breaking multiple bones of rock-throwers—often little kids—during the first Intifada.

SQ: Yeah, that was Rabin's thing. And I mean they killed people too, but it wasn't...

SF: I read that in 1989 that Palestinians were beaten and not able to get physical rehabilitation for injuries so they ended up crippled and being brain dead because of being hit in the head with nightsticks and all that kind of thing.

SQ: I'm sure horrible things were done, but it wasn't on the scale of the behavior of the Israeli army in late 2000. It was a different level.

SF: And actually in 2000 when it started was before the suicide bombing that time, right?

SQ: No. Suicide bombing started after the Baruch Goldstein attack, which would have been 96, I think. So I was really galvanized by what I was hearing in the news, and then when the suicide bombings started one after the other, I was like, Okay, now everyone's got to understand how horrible the Israeli behavior is. Look, these Palestinian kids are blowing themselves up—they really have to be driven to insanity, but of course that's not how it played out. So, I just went out and I bought myself a little Palestinian flag pin and wore it around all the time.

SF: You mean like a....

SQ: Just by myself. It was just like an act of solidarity. And I was really clear in my mind that I would not want some pin that had the Israel and Palestinian flags. It was about solidarity with people who were getting creamed by this big army. And then when I heard on WBAI about the upcoming Chanuka action of Not in Our Name, and the person who was speaking about it was Naomi Braine of Jews Against the Occupation .... I was very excited, and I know Naomi. So I e-mailed Naomi and she put me in touch with Chloe or Jesse, but I just didn't get around to coming to a meeting, and then it was time for the Israel Day Parade, and I just couldn't believe, in the Spring of 2001, with the Intifada going on, that they were going to go forward with the Israel Day Parade. I was just horrified. And I said, I e-mailed either Jesse or Chloe, and I said, you know, there has to be a response. And they said, as a matter of fact, we're planning something. And they had these wonderful coalition meetings. So before I ever went to a JATO meeting, I went to all these coalition meetings with all these people from Al-Awda [Palestinian liberation group] and all these other groups and JATO at NYU, and we planned the first Salute to a Free Palestine demo. And then my first JATO meeting was the first meeting after the Salute to Israel Parade. It was the meeting at which that demo was discussed and how did it go. So that's how I sort of got to where I got to.

SF: Actually, at this point, JATO affirmed in the points of unity the acceptance of the right of return for Palestinian refugees from 1948, didn't they?

SQ: Absolutely.

SF: Was that there from the start?

SQ: Yes. And it made perfect sense to me. . . Because I had known from many years...I knew from reading Edward Said when I was in college that the Universal Declaration of Human Rights says everyone has a right to leave their home, and everyone has a right to return to it. It was as simple as that.

SF: Were you religious at all?

SQ: No, sort of. In a Reformed kind of way.

SF: I wasn't Bar Mitzvahed, so...

SQ: I was Bar Mitzvahed ... I took it very seriously

SF: My parents were Zionists, but they're not religious at all. My mother is sympathetic to the Palestinians. My father's kind of naive about this issue. He blames everything in Israel on Yasser Arafat.... But they never went to synagogue—

not even on the holy days.

SQ: I instituted the lighting of Sabbath candles in my home for a few years when I was a teenager. That had never happened before.

SF: You believed in God?

SQ: No, I don't think I did. I just wanted to try out some of the ritual. You know, we're an American Jewish family. We have Passover Seder, we go to synagogue on Rosh Hashanah… That's about it. You know, in college, I took classes with Edward Said, which were not about Palestine at all, they were about Joseph Conrad. Said was a scholar of modernist novels. He's known for this whole other thing. He was the great Conrad scholar, the way that Noam Chomsky is known for this whole other thing, this whole theory of genetic grammar in the human brain. It's very interesting; he doesn't always talk about politics. But anyway …he was just very nice to me and I really looked up to him. I also studied with Arthur Hertzberg. I took a class on the history of Zionism.

SF: Hertzberg was rather ambivalent.

SQ: He is **a** Labor Zionist.

SF: A while ago, he wrote this thing in the NY Times that some people thought was progressive, but I thought it was terrible. The first part was, the Israelis should be punished by the US cutting grants if they won't dismantle the settlements, and the second part was, the Palestinians should be punished—if the terrorists do suicide bombings—by cutting off the humanitarian aid that was being given. It would have starved them to death, collective punishment. Do you know the piece?

SF: Hertzberg nonsense. So, you know, whatever, it was a very interesting reading list. I'm very glad I took that class. I think all Palestine activists should take Hertzberg's class on the history of Zionism. I read all these Zionist thinkers, and then he had us read the history of the conflict prior to 1948, from Jewish, British, and Palestinian perspectives. And the Palestinian perspective was *The Arab Awakening* by George Antonius. It made a very big impression on my, that book.

SF: I read online some things about your trip, the horrible things you saw, and you went-—two trips?

SQ: I've been there 3 summers—in Palestine with the ISM.

SF: Actually let me quote this from Said. This is from the first book he wrote on Palestine, *The Question of Palestine,* written in the late 1970s. He says it's one of "the most frightening, cultural episodes" of the century, this almost total silence about Zionist treatment of the native Palestinians. "Any self-respecting intellectual is willing today to say something about human rights abuse in Argentina, Chile or South Africa…. Yet when irrefutable evidence of Israeli preventive detention, torture, population transfer, and deportation of the Arabs is presented, virtually nothing is said." Anyway, what struck me is, is that *is* one of the most frightening cultural episodes of the 20th century, this almost total silence. It is so bizarre in

America, the things you see, only suicide bombings, nothing about what Said described... But then when I read your descriptions it seems like sadism on the part of the Israelis. So this whole thing about purity of arms on the part of Israelis is a joke. Obviously following orders from above, but *with gusto*, they seem to enjoy tormenting Arab Palestinians. One guy wrote a book about it, apparently. Have you read that book that came about the checkpoint syndrome?

SQ: I heard about it, yeah.

SF: I think someone had a review about it on the JATO listserve; that's where I read about it. He was a basically nice guy, but when he got on that checkpoint, he became a bastard, and he described how he...

SQ: I saw that at the Qalqilyah checkpoint. I saw this soldier. She was really nice to me and this activist from San Francisco, Nura Furi. And we're like giving her this cock-and-bull story about why we need to get into Qalqilyah, because they're not letting foreigners into Qalqilyah at all. They don't want them to see. Oh, we have to go see Nura's aunt, and she lives in Qalqilyah, I'm American. This young soldier, she's really sweet to us, and as she's talking to us, some kid, a Palestinian boy, shows up leading his donkey.

SF: You mean like 12, a real boy?

SQ: Yeah, and she turns around and she says, Excuse me for a moment. And she turns around and she screams at him, and she curses him out, and she hits him with a stick and tells him to turn around and treats him like a piece of shit, and then she turns around and continues her conversation with us, and she's perfectly sweet. And it was so clear, it's like, you are humans, he is not. And it's racism, but it's a very convoluted kind of racism. Because I was with Nura, who is of Arab descent. This soldier herself was very dark-skinned, but it was like, "These two Americans deserve respect, and that Palestinian boy deserves abuse," and that was clearly what was in her mind. And she didn't even think to hide it from us, you know, it's just so ingrained.

SF: To what extent do you think it's them being indoctrinated that the Arabs are all antisemitic Nazis?

SQ: Everything. Absolutely. It's what they get taught. And look, in the States we get taught that, too. We were never taught about Arabs growing up.

SF: Well they never talked about Pal...even now they don't like...I tell people, liberals I'm writing the book, they say "Be careful not to be taken in by the Arabs, the Arabs!" They always say "the Arabs." They don't mention the Palestinians. It's easier just to talk about the Arabs.

SQ: Right.

SF: And instead of the Palestinians, you get the image of the Arab regimes, and the king...

SQ: Well that was the whole notion of Zionists from the very waning years of the 19th century forward right to 1948: you know, we've got to get these Arabs out of Eretz Yisrael so that it can be filled up with Jews. And so, you know, we should make some deal with somebody to resettle them in Iraq, to resettle them in Syria. It's not going to make a difference to them, they're just Arabs…

SF: Oh yeah, one Arab country is like another.

SQ: There was explicitly, you know, it's in black and white. That's explicitly what they said and what they thought about it. And they expected to get cooperation from Arab leaders. And it was like, oh, they figured Syria and Iraq would want more Arabs to come and settle there as a bulwark against the Persians and the Turks.

SF: You described in your reportbacks and journal…it seems the purpose is preventing the farmers from going to their farms. The UN report by Jean Ziegler, UN Special Rapporteur who spent a week in the territories in July 2003–and the Israeli government let him because in the past he had been sympathetic to Israel—talked about a policy of deliberate starvation of Palestinians by the Israeli government, the prevention of deliveries of aid from the UN, the entering into the houses and brutalizing the inhabitants. When you were in Palestine you saw all that?

SQ: We, in Nablus in the summer of 2002, a group of us from JATO would go around to all the occupied houses in Nablus where the army would be using a home as their base, and all the many residents of the home would all be imprisoned on the first floor, and they'd often…we'd be in phone contact with these families, and they'd be saying, "Bring us food, bring us milk for the babies." They wouldn't be allowed out to get anything, so we'd go and sometimes you could talk your way in. Because there's a very—Israeli soldier behavior is very diverse. There are some that are calm and some that are very brutal; they seem to have a free hand from their commanders.

SF: Most people are not calm, are they?

SQ: I don't know. Many of them…seem, when you're face to face with them, fairly calm.

SF: With the Palestinians face to face with them?

SQ: Look, what is it, the Heisenberg principle? The thing that's observed is changed by the observation? I can only tell you what I saw when *I* was present, when an international was present, so that's always going to calm things down. So sometimes we could talk our way in and we were able to bring food into the home. Sometimes we were not at all. They didn't care, they wouldn't let us in—They threatened a bunch of JATO people with arrest if they didn't leave the property. We came with this one truck driver they had arrested; they'd taken his truck because he shouldn't have been out driving after curfew, and it was full of fruit. They know there was a fruit shortage in Nablus; there'd been a curfew for a long time. And we came up and we just said, "Give the guy his truck back." Ho hum, maybe tomorrow. And we said, "The fruit will be ruined by tomorrow, it's sitting here in the sun and people are hungry." They were like, Fuck you. The guy did get his truck back eventually, but not until the fruit was ruined. At one point, at one house, they arrested Erica [a JATO member from NYC] and they arrested Seith from Oskar Camp, and an ISM coordinator, a young man. And Erica they just took her, so they drove her off to the settlement of Ariel and put her in the police station. Him, Seth, they put inside the occupied house, and then they let him go. They let Erica go to; she went to Jerusalem. He walked home in the dark under curfew. He could have been killed.

SF: What's his background? American? Palestinian?

SQ: No, he's from Oskar Camp; he's a Palestinian refugee living outside of Nablus. His family's from Jaffa. And all they were doing was attempting entrance into an occupied home. I saw in the spring of 2002 in Bethlehem, I witnessed Israeli soldiers holding Palestinian ambulance workers face down on the pavement, guns to their heads. They had responded to a scene where the Israeli army had shot into a civilian car, which they did a lot. And this was while curfew was supposedly lifted for a few hours.

SF: They just shot randomly?

SQ: Yeah, they just shot, you know, so an ambulance came to the scene to see if they'd hurt anybody, and they just made all the ambulance drivers lie face down, so a bunch of us internationals—this is right outside of Azah Camp—a bunch of internationals came out of Azah Camp, surrounding a Palestinian doctor from the camp who was scared shitless to be leaving the camp with all the soldiers there. So we totally surrounded him and just walked and tried to find out, and there was no injured person. Whoever had been in the car had fled, the car that was shot up. So we stood out there until they let the ambulance workers go. We just stood there. And eventually they did. They made the ambulance workers go around and look for whoever had fled at gunpoint and they finally let them go. And then we blocked the entrance of the camp. Now the entrance of the camp, it's just an alley. It's not like a gate or anything, it's just an alleyway, and then you're in the camp. We stood across the entrance of the camp as the soldiers came up the road because on the way down, they had all pointed their guns into the camp as they'd pass by, and the street was full of children. You know, you're a kid living in a refugee camp, what are you going to do? You're going to sit on the road and play with the rocks. That's all there is to do. Little children, kids in diapers. So on the way back, we're like, "We don't want them fucking pointing their guns at these little kids." So we blocked the entrance…

SF: Would they have fired?

SQ: Absolutely. They do all the time. They were firing not at such close range, but they were firing down that alleyway *every day* when I was there in April 2000. They killed a 14 year-old girl in March of 2000…

SF: Just randomly?

SQ: She just stepped out of her doorway. So we stood there and this one soldier took up position while his comrades went up the street, just pointing his gun. And so we stood in his way, and we were talking to him: "Don't shoot, these are just children." And he was trying to point his gun so it was in between us pointing at the kids. So we're kind of swaying back and forth making sure the gun was always pointed at us, because we know he doesn't want to shoot us. And then his comrades left and he left and that was the end of it. But this was a time when many, many Americans, the entire American public, not just committed Zionists, really believed that Israel was fighting terrorism. So I would tell the story; I would say, "Exactly how was the Israeli army fighting terrorism by aiming their weapons into this street full of children? Please explain that to me." And it's not like the soldiers were afraid that there were armed men in the camp, because they knew *perfectly well* that all the armed men in all the camps had gone inside the Church of the Nativity when the invasion started. And the reason we know that they knew and were confident of that was because there were these tanks and APCs they used to circle around the camp (Azah Camp is very small) just terrifying everybody all night long. But then, when they weren't doing that, they'd open up the hatch at the top of the tank, go sit on top of the tank out in the open to smoke a cigarette. *Now would they do that if they thought there were armed men inside the camp waiting to pick off Israeli soldiers? They knew perfectly well they were shooting at unarmed civilians.*

SF: You made some analogy between them and the KKK in one of your diaries.

SQ: Well that business—it was the night riding—really reminded me of the KKK. I remember when I came back (I was only there a week that first time), and I live right on Third Avenue, so I hear trucks and buses pass by all the time, and every time I heard one, I jumped. Because when you hear that sound in Palestine, it's a tank or an armored personnel carrier. And they would just drive around and around and around the camp, and they'd shoot at the houses that were on the edge of the camp, and it reminded me…

SF: They'd shoot at the houses with people in the houses?

SQ: Yeah.

SF: So people would just lie on the floor…to try to…

SQ: Some of the homes on the edge of the camp were abandoned. The 14 year-old girl who was killed on the main road in the middle of camp, she had originally lived in one of the houses on the edge of the camp, and they had had to leave it, because it got shot up so much. She was living with relatives in the central road. So that just driving around reminded me of the nightriders. You know, the Klan would come with torches on horses and ride around African-Americans' homes, whooping it up, then just ride off into the night, just to terrorize people.

SF: Wow. And of course, the Israeli army's supposed to exemplify "purity of arms," the greatest most humane army in the whole world they claim. That's what Alan Dershowitz says too…

SQ: Tohar HaNeshek (purity of arms) is a lie. It has always been a lie. It's always been…

SF: How do you convince an American Jew that that's not true? Even those who oppose the Israeli settlements are proud of the Army.

SQ: Before it was the Israeli army, when it was the Hagganah, including the Palmach as well as the Irgun and the Stern Gang, it was always an army that's main purpose was to terrorize civilians. They dealt with some civilians who would pick up their rifles and resist, and many, many civilians were just in the way. And they were doing ethnic cleansing at the turn of the 20th century. It was just on a smaller scale. That's what that army is for; it's for moving around civilian populations that are undesired.

SF: So now the purpose, at least of the higher ups, is to get them out, to make them move away, to ethnically cleanse them—that's what you said at your reportback?

SQ: Yeah, I don't think they have a comprehensive plan.

SF: The higher ups?

SQ: Israel. Since 1967. Certainly recapturing the rest of what they call the western land of Israel was the plan since the turn of the 20th century. In 1948, they got what they could; it was always the plan to take the rest. So they did. But in 1967…

SF: Unlike Ben-Gurion's reputation as being against the Occupation and non-expansionist…

SQ: He was on record from the 1930s forward, saying, when the Peel Commission came out, saying, Look, we'll take what they give us, and we'll take the rest when we get a chance. He said it. So it was a Labor government, it was Golda Meir and Moshe Dayan, these were Labor Zionists who took the West Bank and the Gaza Strip.

SF: Of course people like Hertzberg and Lerner don't like to admit that, do they?

SQ: Hertzberg? He'd never admit it in a million years. But in 1948, they really exploited their opportunity as far as moving out as many Arabs as they could. In 1967 they did not. They expelled about 200 thousand Palestinians, which, in the context of the population of the West Bank and Gaza Strip isn't that many. And I think maybe it's because that war was so short. They won so fast they didn't have a chance. There was no fog of war in which to hide. It's hard to say... They've just had no plan. Look, like Finkelstein says, other than capitulation, they have two options… The Israelis: Apartheid or ethnic cleansing. They seem to have been unwilling to fully embrace either one. Rather, they pursue this kind of strange amalgam of both, and it's obviously not working for them.

SF: I've had this idea, it's somewhat speculative, that Sharon has been hoping that Bush will get in again, attack Syria—that's what the neocons talk about, attacking Iran…I mean, they're crazy…I've read some of their stuff, excerpts from Frum's book and a lot of their other documents, and…

SQ: It could happen.

SF: And then they'd have their opportunity to get rid of the Palestinians.

SQ: Maybe they will.

SF: Maybe he has that dream.

SQ: I don't know…

SF: …of complete ethnic cleansing.

SQ: They have to decide (the people outside Israel) what's in their own imperialist interests. What the plan has really been since Allon in 1970, right to the Apartheid Wall today, is to enclose Palestinian population in a northern and a southern enclave within the West Bank entirely surrounded by Israeli controlled territory. What I don't really get is, then what? Then you have these two big jails with millions of people in them, but it's not like they can leave…

SF: How many people are in those jails now? Thousands, right?

SQ: Well, all of the West Bank is a jail…. I'm referring to the idea of walling in the central northern West Bank and the central southern West Bank, so that East Jerusalem remains Israeli, so that the areas of the West Bank adjacent to Israel remain Israeli, so that the Jordan Valley remains Israeli, and you have these two isolated islands of Palestinian population. But I don't really get what's their plan, like what's the next step. Now you have these two isolated islands with millions of people in them, what do you do? Unless you're going to build gas chambers and kill them all, and I don't think that's the Israeli plan. Maybe then you make it easy for them to emigrate, because obviously they'd be starving in some places. I don't know, it's very bad.

SF: Why the brutality. I mean, they could control them without that degree of brutality, right? The shooting of children, the arbitrary things some of which you've described?

SQ: Well, you know, they've controlled them pretty well from 67 to 87. And in 87, the Palestinian civilians said, Fuck this, we're tired of being steadfast and waiting for the Arab armies to liberate us, and we're taking matters literally into our own hands. So then they couldn't be controlled, with or without the shooting of children, they couldn't be controlled. So then Clinton and Rabin came up with Oslo as a way of controlling them, and that was pretty successful for ten years.

SF: You mean, Arafat as the controller, the PLO as the policemen, of the Palestinians…

SQ: They brought him in. They brought him in. Do you know where Yasser

Arafat was before Oslo? He was in Tunis, suffering Israeli air raids, having had to evacuate Beirut because the Israelis forced him out. So he was a nothing. He was a nothing, and the Israelis were negotiating with the leaders of the Intifada, people like Hanan Ashrawi in Madrid in 1991, the Israelis were giving these ridiculous offers, and the Intifada leadership said, "No, there's no agreement; we're not accepting these offers." And so in 1992, they brought this doddering old man from Tunis to Oslo, and they were like, Sign here. And he was like going to sign fucking anything, because it turned him from a defeated nobody in Tunis to the president of Palestine sitting in Ramallah. So Palestinians were controlled during Oslo by holding up this image, this sort of promise of freedom: just play along, you don't need to throw rocks at our soldiers anymore, it's all going to be fine, we're talking, we're negotiating, there's going to be freedom. But of course, that was never the plan, and it all fell apart in 2000, and now, Seth, there's no controlling the territories, not with shooting children, not without shooting children. You can't control a population of millions of people who want their freedom. This is the Palestinian civilian population is completely mobilized against the Occupation. Is the mobilization effective? Not particularly. Is it strategic? No. Is it coordinated? Absolutely not. The Intifada's a mess. But they are mobilized from the youngest child to the oldest person, everyone is against the Occupation, and everyone is taking action against the Occupation...

SF: Well what would they do except throw rocks? It's the only Hamas and the Islamic Jihad and those groups that do the suicide bombings.

SQ: You know what the Shebab [the young men] do in Jayyous now, the young men? This was a big rock-throwing town during the last Intifada, including our host who is a respectable teacher now—he was a kid during the last Intifada. Now there they're not so big on throwing rocks. The Shebab go and cut the fence at night. They're forever cutting holes in the fence so they can bring the sheep out to graze, and then the jeeps come in and shoot up the town in retaliation...

SF: This happened on your last trip.

SQ: It's happening all the time. So it's like acts of resistance, acts of resistance. Every single day.

SF: It doesn't threaten the Israelis—I mean their security. It only threatens their sense of absolute power, though, right?

SQ: It threatens their sense of absolute power... They were in the mayor's house the other day, the soldiers, threatening him. The mayor of Jayyous.... Jayyous and Budrus...that were cheap labor.... They cannot keep them under control. Those days are over. That's why they have stopped using cheap Palestinian labor. Sometimes they let a trickle of laborers through, but mostly, that's what the importation of foreign workers is for. They just don't let the Palestinians work in Israel anymore. Someone else has to wash the damn dishes. When I lived in

Israel, it's sort of like in New York: look in the kitchen of any restaurant, cheap or expensive, and you'll find Central Americans washing the dishes. Cheap menial labor. And when I lived in Israel it was Palestinians, always, always, but that's no longer the case.

SF: What was the threat to the Israeli soldiers. Besides the suicide bombers who…. The Israeli army doesn't really care about the death of civilians, anyway. Tanya Reinhart in her latest book says for Sharon and the military it doesn't have a major impact

SQ: They don't care. I mean, Sharon…it's clear that Sharon does everything he can to provoke suicide bombings at opportune political moments. The reason for this raid in Gaza—for the last, what was it, two days ago? They killed fifteen people? —The reason for that is to make sure that there's a suicide bombing to coincide with the beginning of the hearings at The Hague this past February 23. (UN hearings in The Hague to discuss whether the Israeli wall violates international law.)

SF: So what can they possibly do in the territories to threaten the Israelis control? How do they constitute a threat to Israel?

SQ: Who?

SF: Ordinary Palestinian people.

SQ: By refusing to be controlled. They constitute a threat. They won't go along anymore. It is a population in revolt. No one can govern without the consent of the governed. The worst tyrant in the world needs the consent in order to oppress them, and the Palestinians have simply withdrawn their consent.

SF: So what do you think would happen if the army wasn't making all these raids at night and shooting children and so on and so forth?

SQ: I think Palestinians would be mobilized in huge street demonstrations like we saw in South Africa.

SF: Along the lines of non-violent…

SQ: The bulk of resistance has always been non-violent. There are demonstrations every day in the West Bank. When I lived in Qalqilyah this summer, there were demonstrations I think at least weekly inside Qalqilyah City.

SF: Okay you were with Palestinians…how could you go there and not be terrified after the murder of Rachel Corrie…yourself being killed, obviously?

SQ: By the Israeli soldiers?

SF: Yeah. As you said later, clearly they had made a decision they weren't going to kill any more internationals, but you had no way of knowing that when you went there this past summer—certainly the things you described…they could or they would kill you any moment.

SQ: We were careful and we were scared. What else can I tell you? You stand in front of them with their guns cocked, and you just…that's what it is to be a non-violent activist…

SF: But you were scared…

SQ: You like trust in the faith they won't shoot, that your action will shame them into putting their guns down, but you don't know that for sure, you never know that.

SF: Of course, you were a non-violent activist in Act-Up…

SQ: In Act-Up and in the Campaign for a Free South Africa.

SF: But you never thought you were going to get shot or seriously injured in any of those demonstrations, right?

SQ: Well, yeah, right. But I'm an American. I've learned non-violent resistance from the African-American struggle of the 1960s, when they stood up to guns and dogs and fire hoses and lynch mobs, and people did get killed. That's what I've been brought up to admire. That's what I've been brought up to think is the way you change things…

SF: Brought up, not by your mother?

SQ: Absolutely. Absolutely.

SF: Even though she's still such a strong Zionist?

SQ: Sure.

SF: Ora said her father was very liberal about Black civil rights. You know her story?

SQ: Yeah.

SF: But as far as Israel goes, it's like fascistic…

SQ: But that's been true of American liberals for a long time, and it's cracking now. But certainly in the 1960s…

SF: American Jewish liberals.

SQ: American liberals. Do you remember the Weavers singing Tzena, tzena, tzena, tzena…? It's like, that's what the American left believed in the 1960s. It believed in civil rights, in non-violent civil disobedience, and in support for Israel. Somehow that was like standing up for the underdog, somehow that was like standing up against the legacy of European fascism. It was muddle-headed thinking.

SF: Yeah it was, and then I remember reading recently that Daniel Berrigan gave a speech back then in 1972 that was very critical of Israel, and he was attacked by a whole spectrum of people on the left…of being antisemitic. So when you said, Brought up, you mean people like your mother brought you up to be activists for justice…

SQ: Absolutely.

SF: How old is she now?

SQ: My mother will be 68.

SF: So she was too old to be in the civil rights movement, but she admired it?

SQ: She was like many Jews of her generation. She was this suburban liberal who brought up her kids to be liberals. It didn't take entirely—my brother's a Bush supporter.

SF: Your brother's a Bush supporter?!

SQ: He's not only a…he's like a Bush worshipper.

SF: Is he is a businessman or what?

SQ: Yeah, he's surrounded by this. He is a very successful businessman, so he's surrounded by people with these attitudes. He married a Republican, her parents are Republicans.

SF: We were talking about the KKK. Aren't Palestinians living in terror? How do they cope with that?

SQ: The rate of mental illness in the Occupied Territories is astronomical. People are…they have something akin to Post-traumatic Stress Disorder, but you can't call it Post-traumatic Stress Disorder because they're not post-trauma. It's just traumatic stress disorder.

SF: How does it manifest itself?

SQ: In terms of your day-to-day interactions with people, you'd never know. Because people are so welcoming and hospitable and kind and thoughtful and they engage in—Palestinians are very well educated—wonderful conversations. But if you talk to any physician in Palestine, they'll say that they just have people streaming through their hospitals who are just completely falling apart. All the time. Just from the stress, there's nervous breakdowns. The children especially are extremely traumatized.

SF: What, they scream and have nightmares and that kind of thing?

SQ: I guess. You know that they still go to school, they still study for the tawjihi, which is the very, very hard high school exit exam.

SF: These gates they're putting up—they don't let the farmers go to their fields—you say it's completely arbitrary where the Israelis incorporate Palestinian land?

SQ: Yeah. At this point…

SF: And you didn't even think it's in order to get the land.

SQ: No, I don't think it's to get the land. I think it's to keep the land out of the hands of the Palestinians so that they have no choice but to emigrate. I think it's to kill their livelihood.

SF: So these are the orders from the top…

SQ: It's like this: when the United States, when the FBI closes the bank account of a drug trafficker, they don't do it because the FBI wants the money. They do it because they want to prevent the drug trafficker from doing the business. Well, when Israel takes all that land and those wells, it's not because they want the land and the wells; they have plenty. It's because they want to prevent Palestinian farmers from engaging in the business of farming—so that they starve.

SF: The other thing I wanted to ask you about: they shoot ambulances all the time—we've talked about some of these things—and then they claim because the ambulances…everything they claim, as you know, is a security measure, right?

SQ: There was one instance in I think March of 2002 where they claimed to have found a bomb belt inside an ambulance.

SF: Oh, this only happened once, actually?

SQ: It only happened once. And I believe that it was just a set up, that they just planted the bomb belt in there, because—or some facsimile of a bomb belt—because it was suspicious just how quickly the Israeli news media were there. It's like, they find this thing in the search of an ambulance, and like immediately, all the Israeli TV stations are there, and they're holding up what they claim to be a bomb belt for the Israeli news media to see. So I think it was just a set-up.

SF: Why is this attack on ambulances then? Is it just pure sadism, or once again to make it as difficult as possible or a combination?

SQ: A combination.

SF: And something about Rachel Corrie's diary…she said they're making it as impossible for Palestinians to live but she says you can't even call it ethnic cleansing because they can't get out of there anyway. So a lot of areas, they can't get out, right? They can't leave Gaza to get to some other Arab country or whatever. So it's not even that—Rachel Corrie said it's just pure genocide, just to kill Palestinians.

SQ: Maybe that's the plan. Maybe the plan is genocide. Maybe the plan is to force people to emigrate but to do it with Israeli permission. One of the things that the Israeli army is very good at is, rather than going out and looking for people that they want, they get people to come to them. So that's what a checkpoint is about. You drive up and you proceed to an intersection, they say this is a checkpoint, anyone who wants to leave Jenin to go to Nablus today, we have to check your IDs. So they know how to create a situation where all the Palestinian men will walk up to the soldiers and hand them their IDs. That's very convenient, trapping people inside Raffah, so that the only way for them to get out is for them to go to the Israeli authorities and request permission to emigrate. It's the same kind of thing. They force people to come to them and hand over their papers and invite scrutiny.

SF: It sounds almost like a psychological, absolute control…. How is this… for some reason, it's not true around the country, but like half of JATO are—when I was growing "gay," was the correct term but most people in JATO say "queer."

SQ: The term is "queer," because "gay" is a restrictive term. "Queer" is broader.

SF: Would a less radical liberationist use the word "queer"?

SQ: Yes.

SF: It's broader because it includes transgender, that kind of thing?

SQ: Yes.

SF: Okay, so half the people or more in JATO are queer? Isn't that just coincidental or something?

SQ: No.

SF: I mean, it's not half the people that are in the anti-Occupation movement.

SQ: Among Jews it is.

SF: Is it really?

SQ: Absolutely. And in Israel too.

SF: How do you explain it? I've never seen any discussion of it.

SQ: It's easy to explain. If you're queer, and you're out about being queer and you love yourself as a queer person, in order to get to that point, you have to first figure out—and this is a difficult process; for some people it can take years—that everything you have been taught about gender since you were three years old was a fucking lie. Now someone who has successfully gone through that process is—thinking specifically about Jews here—it's going to be much easier for them to realize that everything that they have been taught about Israel since they were six years old is a fucking lie. Whereas for straight Jews who've never gone through this process of realizing that they've been systematically lied to by all aspects of the society, it's much harder for them to let go of all the lies they've been taught about Israel. That's why the Jewish anti-Occupation movement is so queer in the United States and Israel.

SF: So you know that, as a matter of fact, half the anti-Occupation movement is queer?

SQ: It is certainly what I've observed, the people that I have met in ISM. It is my impression that Jewish Voice for Freedom is a very queer organization.

SF: OK but why the anti-Occupation movement. There are a lot of worthy causes. You don't find half the Jews in Earth First are queer. Or in the Green Party. Lots of Jews in NYC in Green Party but half of them are not queer. Or getting rid of Rockefeller drug laws. Why do radical queer Jews pick anti-Occupation specifically as an outlet for their radicalism? Do you think it opposition to the machismo of Israeli society?

SQ: I have no idea. You should talk to Emmaia about this.

SF: Anyway, we find most Jews tend to liberal except about Israel.

SQ: Except for the ones who aren't. I mean, that's a very dangerous generalization. There are conservatives all over the place.

SF: Yeah, I'm just making a generalization. Well you'll find more Jews who vote Democratic, if that's any index.

SQ: That's true.

SF: But when it comes to Israel, they're worse than the general population, wouldn't you say?

SQ: I see.

SF: Although I was surprised to see it's not as bad as I think. Most Jews do not support Israel, they don't care?

SQ: Yes. Most Jews don't care about Israel.

SF: So it's just the ones that care are just a small anti-Occupation group and a larger group of fanatical pro-Zionists.

SQ: You have fanatical pro-Zionists of many different stripes. You know, those fanatical pro-Zionists could be reformed Jews giving an award to Ehud Barak, congratulating themselves with a humanitarian award, congratulating themselves for being big liberals. Or those fanatical Zionists could be the American Friends of Beth-El holding dinners to bygones for Western settlers. There ardent Zionists of many different stripes.... And they might even be anti-Occupation, but they still buy into all these myths, such as Ehud Barak is a peacemaker.

SF: What about being Jewish? I mean, it must obviously mean something to people in JATO, unlike someone like Finkelstein, who sees... certainly considers himself an atheist who would not want to participate in any Jewish cultural activities.

SQ: Yes, see I do want to participate, and since...

SF: Would this be true of most people in JATO?

SQ: Yeah, that is true of most people in JATO.

SF: It doesn't necessarily have to do with...

SQ: I like Jewish culture, I like the Yiddish language, I like that I know Hebrew, I'm interested in Jewish history, I like having Jewish friends, I like Jewish humor.

SF: It has nothing to do with any Jewish religious or spiritual?

SQ: I'm an atheist. There are lots of people in JATO who have a spiritual bent. I'm not one of them. ... When JATO has a Shabbat service on its retreat, I'm one of the people who leaves the room. I'm just uncomfortable.

SF: Oh. but what about all the other people that participate?

SQ: You know, there's a group of us who leave and a larger group that stays and participates.

SF: And they consider it a religious or a spiritual thing?

SQ: Or cultural. You have to ask each individual.

SF: Do you think...is there, because you're Jewish, they're something about being Jewish—obviously you consider yourself Jewish?

SQ: Yeah.

SF: That you feel a greater obligation to oppose the Occupation?

SQ: Absolutely. Because organized Jewish communities in the United States and around the world are so effectively mobilized in support of Zionist oppression of Palestinians, I think that it's the responsibility of any Jew who like, gets it, who understands what's going on to mobilize in solidarity with Palestinians, to try to attempt to be some sort of counterweight to this international Jewish project of dispossessing Palestinians from their land.

SF: Do you feel in some way that it's something worthwhile, that there is something worthwhile—obviously, since you consider yourself Jewish, you must consider something worthwhile about Judaism that should be preserved and that's in danger of being destroyed by the whole Zionist project.

SQ: Every culture is worthwhile, and I inherited Jewish culture, and it's part of who I am, and it's something that I find meaning in, not separate from any other culture—it's no different from any other culture—it's just a calling, that's all. And is it in danger from Zionism? I think Jewish communal life is badly distorted by Zionism and has been for a hundred years. But I'm not anti-Zionist to save Jewish communal life; I'm anti-Zionist because of standing in solidarity with Palestinians. It's not to save the Jews but to save the Palestinians.

SF: Do you feel a greater responsibility to defend Palestinians than to defend any other group that may be oppressed in the world?

SQ: I'm an American, I have a responsibility to defend everybody who's oppressed.

SF: By Americans.

SQ: But you can't do everything. But you know, I have an activist focus. There was a time in my life when my activist focus was Apartheid. There was a time in my life when my activist focus was AIDS and HIV. Right now my activist focus is Palestine. But I applaud activists, Jewish or not, who are working on all those other issues, because they're all important, and something that's so important about the anti-globalization movement is people doing the real work of linking all these issues together. So if she's over there working in Chiapas, and he's over there doing anti-police brutality work in New York, and I'm over here working in solidarity with the Palestinians, that we're talking to each other and we're linking up those struggles as part of the same fabric of oppression.

SF: With the secularization of Judaism in America, a lot of it has just become...even Norman Podhoretz said that Israel has become the new religion of the Jewish people, and he's one of the main practitioners, you know Podhoretz...

SQ: Well, yeah, it is...

SF: What would hold Judaism together if it wasn't for the...what would keep them from being assimilated, what would hold them together as a distinct group? There's no longer, except for those small groups that are kind of religious there is no longer a distinctive religious way of worshiping and set of views, etc.?

SQ: I'm sorry, I there's a lot more to Jewish culture and Jewish religion than some fascist colonial ideology. I think that if it weren't for the obsession with Israel, American Jewish life would be much richer. I would be a more active participant. From the time I moved back to New York…well, from the time I left the field of Jewish education in 1989, until the time I joined JATO in 2001, I had no Jewish community. None. I had no Jewish affiliation. That was because you basically had to be a Zionist and swallow a lot of Zionist crap to participate in Jewish communal life. I think that Jewish life would be a lot richer if they would take the fucking Israeli flags off of the bema, the altar, in every goddamned synagogue. I mean, what the hell is that about? They have an Israel flag and an American flag on every bema. And I'm like, burn 'em both, man, this is supposed to be a house of God; what the hell are they doing?

SF: You know, Marc Ellis calls it Constantinian Judiasm. You know the analogy…

SQ: Sounds right to me.

SF: Christianity…Christians gave up the…well the martyrs who were representing Christ became legitimatized by Roman Empire. Why do you consider being Jewish part of your identity? Is it the prophetic heritage?

SQ: I was brought up in the Reform tradition of prophetic universalism, but I am motivated just as much by Gandhi's Hinduism, King's Baptism, Malcolm's Islam, or Emma Goldman's and Mikhail Bakhunin's atheism as by the Jewish tradition of justice. I was taught (even as I was being taught to negate the rights and the existence of Palestinian victims of Jewish nationalism). It's an ethnic thing for me. A belonging thing. I care about being part of a Jewish community, because I'm Jewish. Sorry if this is syllogistic; it's the best I can do…. Please exhort your readers in your book to read the words of Palestinians. They should read your book, and when they're done, they should read books written by Palestinians, because I think there's a very bad habit, even on the real Jewish left, of Jews talking to other Jews about the Middle East and thinking that they've just finished the conversation. I think that that new anthology that's out, *Wrestling With Zion*, to me it's a symptom of that. There's so many brilliant Palestinian voices out there: Mahmoud Darwish, Nur Masalha, Hasan Khamhani, and it's just so important…Edward Said…it's so important for people to hear those voices and to hear those words.

SF: Most Jews who read Palestinians are Israeli because Americans don't learn about it.

SQ: Nur Masalha is brilliant, absolutely brilliant.

SF: And Naseer Aruri.

SQ: I haven't read Aruri yet. Mahmoud Darwish is the poet…

SF: Oh you're talking about literature now.

SQ: Yes that's important. For American Jews to read Palestinian poets and novelists.

Palestine Journal

July 2, 2003

I feel privileged to have the opportunity to participate in this Palestinian-led non-violent resistance movement. I am often greatly distressed by the ways in which ordinary people in the U.S. and all over the world suffer due to the exercise of military and economic power by the powerful few, and in ISM I have a chance to stand in solidarity with Palestinians who are confronting that power and exposing its brutality. The oppression of Palestinians by the Israeli army and government is done in my name as a Jew, and with my cash as an American. I feel a strong responsibility to resist that oppression, both by engaging in Palestinian-led non-violent direct action in Palestine, and by telling Americans what I saw once I return.

I will strive to remain safe while I'm over there. Each of us in ISM determines her own risk threshold; the heroic actions that Rachel Corrie, Brian Avery, and Tom Hurndall took are past my personal threshold. I don't get in front of moving vehicles, nor do I go outdoors when there is live fire if I can help it. I may be turned away from Israel at the border, I may be arrested and deported, I may be struck by an Israeli soldier, but I believe that I can spend these next seven weeks in Palestine with ISM without getting shot or run over.

I have heard concern expressed over danger to ISM activists from Palestinians. There is none. No international solidarity activist has ever been harmed by a Palestinian.

July 21

On Monday, we traveled from Tel Aviv to Jayyous, a West Bank farming village close to the pre-1967 border. We had to travel to an Israeli roadblock where trucks have to back up to each other on either side of the roadblock and their cargo has to be hand carried from one to the other. We got into Jayyous, where we met almost all the men, women and children of the town, as well as about 40 internationals, for a march initiated by the farmers.

Jayyous lost 90% of its land when the war of 1947-1949 ended, and the village found itself on the Jordanian side of the armistice line with its land on the Israeli side. (That land had been slated to be part of the Arab state of Palestine in the U.N. 1947 Partition Plan, but was captured by the new state of Israel in the war.) When Israel occupied the West Bank in 1967, more land was confiscated to build illegal Israeli settlements nearby. Now, with the construction of Israel's "Separation Fence" (which we are calling the Apartheid Wall), they are being cut off from 70% of what's left. Farmers have one gate in the fence through which they may pass to get to their fields, but when internationals aren't present to monitor, they are often detained and/or beaten by the private armed security guards hired by the contractors who are building the fence for the Israeli government.

First, we attended a lecture in the municipality by a Qalqilya hydrologist about how the Oslo Agreement maps and the location of the Apartheid Wall have nothing to do with security and everything to do with stealing access to West Bank aquifers. (Millions of Palestinians in the West Bank have limited access to fresh water for living and for agriculture, while hundreds of thousands of Jewish settlers in the same territory have watered lawns and swimming pools.) Then the people of Jayyous, with international accompaniment, marched through the olive groves to the fence. The women and young men of the village chanted for a while as we watched the construction equipment completing the fence that cuts through Jayyous's lands. Some nearby soldiers watched, and some of the security guards joined them, but the men of the village made sure that the youngsters kept their distance. On the way back, some of the boys had slingshots to throw stones at the security guards who stood menacingly in the distance as we passed, but they were not permitted by their elders to engage even in this symbolic act of violence. The march ended without the soldiers gassing, beating, arresting or shooting at anyone, a testament to the discipline of the Jayyous organizers as well as the effect of international accompaniment.

Back at the municipality, the mayor thanked us for our support, and explained that the Israeli decision to cut them off from their land and therefore their income is an attempt to force them to abandon their homes. I agree. The fence is part of a policy of ethnic cleansing, in which parts of the West Bank are slowly being emptied of their indigenous Palestinian population and replaced with Jewish settlers, many of them from the United States.

We proceeded from Jayyous to nearby Qalqilya, through the Azun roadblock and the Qalqilya checkpoint. Again, we made it through the checkpoint with our Israeli-American member coming under special scrutiny and pretending not to know Hebrew. (Israelis are penalized by the government for participating in pro-Palestinian actions.) We joined up with the crew of Americans and one Brit already here. And met our local coordinators.

Qalqilya is a town of about 50,000 Palestinian Muslims that sits right on the Green Line, next to the most densely populated part of Israel. It's surrounded by rich agricultural lands, and appears to be a busy, though not particularly prosperous, trading center....

This morning, four of us spent two hours watching Qalqilya Checkpoint. There was nothing out of the ordinary—just the usual humiliations of men being forced to wait for an hour in the sun while the soldiers hold their IDs, and then being allowed to pass...Everyone we've met in Qalqilya has been warmly welcoming, and we've received official invitations to events as well as lots of public thank yous. We're being treated a little like a delegation to be feted and not as participants in non-violent resistance, but we're working toward a more active relationship with the community.

July 24

I was awakened at 3:00 yesterday morning by Jihad, a young man who spends time with us internationals. He was alarmed that Israeli army jeeps had entered the city, and a couple of internationals walked him home. We then bolted our door, and I didn't sleep very well as I waited for the alarm to ring at 5:00. At 6:00 I saw a jeep driving right near our apartment, and quickly ducked inside.

I was up at 5:00 for attempt #3 to go out with the farmers—successful this time!! There were no soldiers or security at the farmers' gate, and we high-tailed it into the fields west of the fence. We ducked behind some trees as construction vehicles and security sped past, and were not spotted.

We were horrified, however, to see that the Israeli army had dug a trench between the gate and the road from Qalqilya, and piled the dirt and boulders up before the trench. Passage into the lands outside of the fence, impossible by car, truck, or tractor for months, is now impassable by donkey as well. Farmers must bring in their crops on foot. Some of the trees immediately west of the fence and its attendant jeep road had been destroyed by a tank or a bulldozer.... Mohammad from the Peasants' Union took us around the lands of Qalqilya and Jayyous all morning. We passed many dried up fields and abandoned greenhouses belonging to farmers who just can't get through the security at the gate. We encountered numerous roadblocks; many dirt roads within this agricultural area have been rendered impassable by the Israeli army. Some of the lands are on the other side of a settlement bypass road put in during the Oslo process, and no Palestinian agricultural roads are allowed to intersect with this Israeli-only West Bank highway built on confiscated Palestinian land.

Farmer after farmer told us about the assaults on their livelihood caused by the fence. One man has a property that was cut in half by the fence. He used to go from one olive grove to the next by walking a few meters. Now he has to walk half an hour to the farmers' gate, and half an hour back. Another has a number of farm vehicles at home. He can get none of them onto his land. He has to bring in his crops by donkey cart, and then unload them by hand onto a vehicle at the roadblock. Some farmers have taken to sleeping in the fields during the week, because the way home has now been made so circuitous and long. To make matters worse, Israel has declared economic war on Palestinian areas during this Intifada, no longer allowing Palestinians to export, and using roadblocks and checkpoints to impede commerce within Palestine.

Qalqilya was once the breadbasket of the West Bank, with exports to Jordan and Iraq as well. Now, all produce goes to market in Qalqilya, at a fraction of the price....

Back in town, we visited a house that had been visited during the night by the Israeli army (hence the jeeps we saw). There were eleven people in the house: 3 women, one 13-year-old boy, and the rest little girls (one a baby). We saw hundreds and hundreds of bullet holes in the house outside and inside, including in one of the women's dresses in her closet. It's a miracle that no one was shot or killed, and I can't imagine how frightened the children must have been. One little girl (I can't say how old she is; I usually underestimate the age of Palestinian children because they look so small. Perhaps it's malnutrition?) was eager to show us the damage, and they all welcomed the attention. The teenage boy lay in a fetal position on a mat, must have had his stomach stomped on by Israeli border guards in an attempt to force him to say where they can find the man they were looking for. They never found the wanted man, so they took another man from the family, 26 years old, neat him, and arrested him. He may be facing 6 months of administrative detention now; under Israeli law, no charges have to be laid for administrative detention to occur....

July 25—Aug.4, 2003

At 3:00 last Friday morning, I was awakened by Kevin, a member of the ISM Qalqilya action group, and a local photojournalist I'll call Ragheb, and told that the Israeli army had again entered Qalqilya. Four of us went out to see what was happening. After the shocking attack on a house earlier in the week, we felt that it was important that we be present, albeit at a distance, visible, and out of the line of fire, in the hope that international witnesses might inhibit the Israeli army from their worst excesses.

We proceeded to the main street, and spoke to a few people who were out. An old man said to me, "Why do you want to drink from that cup?" Others called out, "Thank you for what you're doing." Some young men told us that the soldiers had been firing into the air.

A jeep and an armored personnel carrier (APC) entered the road from a side street. Both were completely enclosed, with tiny reinforced windows so that it was impossible to see the human beings inside. The APC stayed at a distance, and the jeep stopped with its bright lights on us for a long time. Then they sped away.

We continued down the street in an attempt to find the house(s) being raided. The jeep and APC returned, and stopped a block away. We're pretty sure we were visible to the jeep. A few shots were fired. A volley of machine gun fire followed, and in the dark we couldn't tell if the gunfire was directed at us, at the buildings opposite the vehicles, or in the air. I said, "This is how Brian Avery got shot." We got out of sight of the army, and returned to our house. We continued to hear sporadic gunfire as the two vehicles sped up and down the street. On Friday evening, we all had a long talk about going out at night when the army is in town, and decided that we would only consider going out if we had specific information about where the army was and what they were doing. Marwan, our local coordinator, said that there's nothing we can do if the army has come to arrest someone, but if they're planning to demolish a house, we might be of use.

On Friday afternoon we visited two of the houses that were raided. In the first, the wanted man was not present, and we saw the usual scenes of gratuitous destruction, although the house was not riddled with bullets like the one we saw previously. As usually happens in these situations, there were children in the family who were eager to take us from room to room to show us the damage and to bring us spent shell casings. The family had "Peace Now" stickers in almost every room, and the soldiers had tried to rip one of the stickers off the wall.

The adults in the family told us that a large number of jeeps and soldiers had shown up, and that the entire family had been made to stand outside for hours. Apparently, the one jeep and one APC we saw shooting up downtown were distractions designed to keep folks scared and in their houses. I wonder if the soldiers were wearing white sheets.

At a second house that was raided we were invited to stay and drink tea and coffee. Their son was taken, and they didn't know where. We gave them the number for HaMoked, an Israeli human rights organization that tracks Palestinian detainees.

In the news in the United States, we hear about the three-month cease-fire. It seems to be that the Palestinians are the only ones holding their fire....

On Saturday night, Basem, an ISM volunteer, invited the men among us to celebrate his having passed the tawjihi, the extremely rigorous end-of-twelfth-grade comprehensive set of exams. The party was in what looked exactly like a Brooklyn wedding palace, and was absolutely packed with deliriously happy young men dancing to traditional Arab music. At one point, they began chanting as they danced "kus uchtak yaa Sharon" (fuck you, Sharon). They were thrilled when we joined in. After the party, we went for a midnight swim at one of Qalqilya's 2 pools—men only, of course.

On Monday, while four from the Qalqilya action group (including Dena and

Eric from JATO) were participating in the "break the gate" action in Annin, outside Jenin, that got international attention, another four of us (including me and Ryan from JATO) met up with David and Nirit from JATO, other internationals from ISM, Boston to Palestine, and others, and activists from Jayyous in another delivery of supplies to the Bedouin family trapped outside the Jayyous fence. The army stayed away, realizing, I think, that they had provided the media with unfavorable photo ops the week before. The delivery went off successfully, but it was incredibly sad to see an old woman from the family standing at this enormous fence, waiting for handouts. She allowed the media to interview her and photograph her, and while she was talking to them I saw that she was crying....

On Wednesday, international activists arrived in Qalqilya from Ramallah, Jenin, Tulkarm, Jerusalem, Nablus, Jayyous, and elsewhere to participate in the Qalqilya face of the week's Wall actions. None were allowed through the checkpoint. Some snuck through the checkpoint when soldiers were otherwise occupied. Some crawled under a farmers' gate in the fence. Some snuck through another gate. Some stayed overnight in a nearby village after failing to get in (and nearly getting arrested), and succeeded upon trying again early in the morning. And some were unable to enter at all. Ady (JATO) and Tim from our action group were also able, with help from arrangements Marwan made and accompaniment from Ragheb, to get 8 big helium tanks (!) into town.

Thursday was the big day—the payoff after approximately one million planning meetings with everyone in Qalqilya from the mayor on down, and with each other, after creating a giant banner ("No apartheid wall" in English, Hebrew and Arabic) designed to fly 15 meters above the ground, after filling countless balloons with oil paint to fling at the wall (and then discovering that oil paint corrodes latex—oops), and after browbeating the press from Tel Aviv to Toronto (they usually wanted to know if there was going to be bloodshed). We marched from the municipality in the center of town—50 internationals, and Qalqilyans from the Prisoners' Club, local government, the PFLP, the Peasants' Union, and many others—to the point at which the wall meets the fence, joined by a military gate and a sniper tower. It was a beautiful site as activists flung paint balloons at the hated wall, and covered its surface (the lower half, at least) with messages of liberation. We were met by soldiers in jeeps who had their guns at the ready, but when they saw that the line of internationals facing them was neither advancing on them nor heeding their orders to disperse, they chose restraint. It's entirely possible that restraint was a policy insisted on from above, considering that the photo of soldiers tear-gassing activists in Annin on Monday went all over the world.

The giant banner flew only briefly before the balloons popped, but long enough for some good photos. It will now hang from Ash-Sharqa Girls' School next to the Wall, a school that has been tear gassed in the past by the Israeli army while the students were present.

There was a fair-sized crowd of Israeli activists from Gush Shalom and other groups outside the military gate. They got short notice from us about the demo, but filled a bus for their companion demo nonetheless. We ended with Noura, Palestinian-American from ISM, delivering a message of peace to them (which was permitted after a lot of wrangling with the soldiers).

August 4–9, 2004

Jayyous is lovely, despite the ugly scar that runs across its lands where the Apartheid Wall has been built. Lately, Border Guards have been coming in at night and shooting water tanks on people's roofs. My landlord here, a local activist I'll call Saleh, overheard them saying to each other, "shoot the white ones [the hot water tanks], they're more expensive to fix."

Jayyous, population 6,000, is not connected to the Israeli power grid. The illegal Israeli settlements that surround it of course are connected to the grid. Power here comes from a generator, is astoundingly expensive, and is switched off every evening from 5:00-7:30 and every morning from 2:00-8:00. Cell phone coverage is poor, it's hard to keep phones charged with daily power outages, and the Internet café is slow as molasses (when the power is on—no Internet of course when the power is off). It's hard to stay connected here.

Chapter 2

Joel Kovel

J oel Kovel is an author and Professor of Social Studies at Bard College since 1988. He has campaigned for the US Senate as a representative of the Green Party. He is a former psychiatrist. His last book *was The Enemy of Nature: The End of Capitalism or the End of the World.* He is currently writing a book on the Zionism and the oppression of the Palestinians.

SF: The main theme of Ellis's work is not just the horrors committed in Israel but the whole American Jewish reaction to it, and one of the more positive things, although it doesn't seem to be something that is having an immediate impact, is the resurgence of a kind of diaspora Jewry activism against Israeli policy. And Ellis points out that it's taking pretty much secular form, whereas originally, forty years ago the Jews that were—he cites them a lot, too: Martin Buber and Magnes and all, they were all speaking in religious terms.... Ellis writes about the idea of this Constantinian Judaism, —you might not use the term, but you write about the same thing, which is not only an immense advantage to a state which cloaks state-terrorism and its crimes against humanity with the symbols of the Jewish heritage and tradition, but also leads to a complete destruction of the Jewish tradition....

JK: But before I begin.... Well my name is Joel Kovel, and I'm 67 going on 68. I was born in Brooklyn of immigrant parents. I'm the first generation, so to speak. Both my parents came from the Ukraine, and they both had pogroms in their towns just shortly before they came here, so they knew it first-hand. I had a very complicated background in that my family was sharply divided on the question of Israel. My father was anti-Zionist, but from the Right. He was with the American Council on Judaism.

SF: That was the first anti-Zionist organization—

JK: Yes, oddly speaking, because he was very politically a strange man. He was an extreme right-winger, and his notion was that Zionism posed a question of divided loyalties to the United States and he wanted to be totally assimilated into American culture. My mother, on the other hand, was a fierce Zionist and went the whole route with Hadassah and planting trees in Israel and doing all that stuff. So I always remember it as a very contested area. It took me a while to develop my own ideas on the subject, and in large part because of that—it was a sort of a taboo—I did all kinds of left-wing things and always maintained a certain distance from Israel but became increasingly critical. But it really wasn't until the 80s that I started becoming openly critical. And it wasn't until the second Intifada that I decided that I could not tolerate it any more, and started speaking out and starting writing about it. And now I'm engaged in, you know, writing a book on the subject.

So that's the general introduction to where I am, but perhaps you can focus on question, areas that you want to develop.

SF: The conflict between Jewish moral or ethical religious ideals and Zionism? Mark Ellis sees the former as integral to the covenant.

JK: Well I think the covenant is the central theme, it's the central notion of Jewish history and identity, and it has many deep ramifications and leads to all kinds of contradictions. And it has to be seen as internally contradictory but with potentials for manifold possibilities. The strongest destructive potential in terms of actual history is the growth of Jewish exceptionalism, the notion that Jews are a chosen people, that Jews are special, especially smart and, even more dangerous, that Jews have a higher moral ethic and moral standard. And this is contained within the covenant. God says to Abraham, You should be a light unto the nations and lead the way. This notion however is extremely dangerous, because it contains an internal betrayal of its own ethical promise in the sense that the ground of any ethic is a universal recognition of humanity, and so that if you have a notion that you're exceptional or special, even if its morally special, you're on very shaky ground ethically, really.

SF: Mordecai Kaplan says that even the Orthodox Jews—I don't know how authoritative he is, he's the founder of the Reconstructionist movement—but he said that even the modern Orthodox movement gave up the idea that Jews had something special about them.... He said that rabbinic Judaism tended to stress the moral superiority, but after the Emancipation, even the—not the older Orthodox, but both Reform and the Orthodox—gave up the idea that Jews had anything special about them whatsoever, and affirmed that they had a special task but.... they gave up the idea that there was anything superior about them that made them suited for that task, which was the task of educating people to ethical ideals. There is another, different but similar telos in Reform Judaism in its origins (not anymore). In both reform Judaism originally and in modern Orthodoxy, Jews have special obligation to act in such a way as to hasten the coming of the Messiah, as the neo-Orthodox saw it. For Reform Jews originally they had to educate humanity in ethical monotheism in order to bring about a reign of justice on earth–the messianic age, as the first Reform Jews saw it. So although there was the special *role* that Jews played, it was no longer bound up with having been specially *qualified* for it–certainly not after the Enlightenment. They were given the covenant and they would observe it...

JK: But they never abandoned the notion that they are a separate people, a people apart, which is something that comes from deep in the Torah, and that they are unique among the nations, and that what applies to them doesn't have to apply to others. And if you look closely into the Orthodox and especially the ultra-Orthodox ideologies, you will see that very extreme statements occur, such as but there's not even the same species between Jews and the rest of humanity. Rabbi Abraham Kook, who was very influential in the founding of modern Zionism in its messianic and Orthodox wing, said that the distance between Jews and Gentiles is greater than the distance between humans and cattle.

SF: I was talking about the Jews who have vitiated the worst aspects of Jewish particularism... Because you can find that position of humility, like this is our task but all glory belongs to God.

JK: They may not be specially qualified...

SF: or not genetically superior...

JK: Right, although some think they are.... Well the Reform movement... I mean it's dead because all of that was an effort to mediate and synthesize Judaism with the Enlightenment and with the principles of universal human rights, whereas the Orthodox tradition never cared for that in the first place. That was a non-starter as far as they were concerned—

SF: The founder of the modern—I don't know what they called it at the time, neo-Orthodoxy—was Hirsch, Samson Hirsch. I found a remarkable passage from him in which he talks about Jews having to root out the cult of violence that exists within their nature to serve as an example to non-Jews.

JK: Well it's a very complex and intricate story we have here. But I think the point about the covenant is that it does have a possibility of a universal and transcendent ethic coming out of it, but only if you negate the negation, so to speak, I mean that if the original Jewish relationship to God, that our God is different from all other gods, and we can't exchange Him with any other god. So we are the people of this one God, and there's an inherent not just sense of superiority but a rejection of everybody else. And one of the interesting findings about the ancient Middle East is that all the peoples sort of exchange images of God and religious ideas with each other except for the Israelites, and they said, No, we're apart, we're very separate from you. And this I think is the notion that persists, but it does have a transcendent ethical potential in it, because it makes the bearer of this idea aware of a burden, so to speak, to realize justice in the world. And that can only be done, in my view, by abandoning Jewish particularism and abandoning the notion that you are the chosen people. So you negate the negation of the God that made you special, and then you become universal and God is everywhere. And the former position, which is the dominant position, has the Jews construct themselves as a tribal ethnicity within the modern state, and reinforced the modern state—and that of course is transferred into Israel. The transcendent possibility is to look beyond the state itself, to look towards a universal society. And I think the Judaism that I feel proud of belonging to is one that strives to realize that potential of a universal negation of the negation of their God, so that in effect, it's not that you become atheist, but rather that you develop a notion that sees God everywhere, that sees spirit everywhere, and that certainly regards all human beings and indeed all life forms as sacred. And there's ample evidence that Jews have been very active in the pursuit of that ideal, however short we have fallen, in terms of the Jewish sympathies for revolutionary causes and the brilliance of Jewish culture, which borrows their Emancipation, which is to me a cultural efflorescence that compares to Ancient Athens or Elizabethan England or Renaissance Italy. There are times in human history when people become great, and I think there is true greatness within the Jewish tradition insofar as it negated the negation of their tribal God and sought a universal humanity and sought justice for the universal humanity.

SF: Would you say, as Reform Jews first did, that the attitude of universalism came about in the scriptures, not in the early books but with the Jewish prophets...

JK: That's right, and there is a scriptural basis in the prophetic books. Certainly the Prophets. And there's a whole other story about the relationship about that Jesus which we probably shouldn't get into because it will take us too long. But I mean that, to me, those are the texts and the glory of the Jewish tradition. And I think there was a long night, through the Middle Ages, when this was all buried and suppressed, but I think the possibilities of Emancipation, the Enlightenment, brought about this extraordinary creativity in every field, every field from science to music, politics and what have you. And that's something that I've always been very proud of personally and tried to identify with.

SF: Do you think it **was** more pronounced in Jewish groups than in some other ethnic groups–the universalist ideal—the non-Jewish Jew, Isaac Deutscher called it.

JK: Well, the desire for universalism comes out of one's sense of contingency, one's sense that you don't really belong and that human beings have to create themselves because we don't have any kind of fixed boundary and we're not locked into anything, and I think that that's what made Karl Marx, that's what made Proust, who's actually Jewish, a Jewish writer. You know, the possibilities of Jewish creativity are just immense in this period. And I think then the Zionist idea came along as a vicissitude of that, as an alternative, although it was actually disguised as an emancipatory, Enlightenment idea.

SF: I like that—-before the Zionist perversion—the idea that the Jews could play this emancipatory role perhaps because they were stateless. Several Jewish theologians said this.

JK: Stateless...

SF: ...and they were not identified with the nationalists, it made them perhaps...

JK: Open...

SF: ...the subject/object of history, the elusive subject/object of history that leftists have always been searching for....

JK: The totality...

SF: In fact there were some Jewish thinkers—Hermann Cohen and others—who saw Jews after they were dispersed—I thought Franz Rosenzweig, too—that they were not gathered in any particular tribe, as the reason that they could play this catalytic role in bringing about a realization of a messianic society based on universalist ideals.

JK: Yeah, but of course messianism is a trap, obviously, because it involves the notion of final things, of an overturning of history. There's an implicit violence in messianism, and at every turn here there's a danger, you know, there's an opportunity and a danger. Certainly Jewish messianism is something that Marx acquires, there's no question about it, although it's also seen in terms of the radical Reformation—but that, too, is based on the Old Testament. And so the proletariat becomes the messiah for Marx, or what have you, but we know those are dangerous ideas. They can easily lead to totalizations, they can lead to all kinds of violence and suppression of otherness and alternatives. But the main point about it, which I've always adhered to, is that to be a true Jew in this respect is to be open and not to be contained in any nationalism or ethnicity, and my favorite in that respect would be, as you mentioned, Isaac Deutscher, *The Non-Jewish Jew*. And Deutscher, to me, is a very great man. And so what I'm trying to say is that there's definitely this potentially stemming from the prophetic books and re-awakened in the Enlightenment and the post-emancipatory period.

SF: I've been trying to find answers to this: John Howard Yoder—did you know if him? —he said...he's a Christian Anabaptist who was part of the radical Reformation, not part of the Establishment—they were persecuted by it...The Reformation was no great revolution, it was just, I think, fighting for the spoils.

JK: Oh no, the Reformation was. I mean the radical Reformation.

SF: I'm talking about the Lutheran and Protestant, the "real" Reformation. The radical Reformation was different; unfortunately it didn't have...

JK: It was the Reformation itself that was the prelude to capitalism....

SF: I'm saying that people have the idea that the Reformation—Lutheran and Calvin—was some kind of break, and I'm saying it was just a bunch of crooks fighting over the spoils.

JK: But it did create the possibility of a genuine emancipatory movement, and certainly there's no privilege about being Jewish that it gives you genes for radicalism or cultural achievement, but there is something in that sense of discontinuity, of not fully belonging, which is enormously liberating....

SF: Ellis talks about returning to exile as a positive step...

JK: Yeah, I think it's a positive thing as long as that exile is a condition of grounding yourself in the universal.

SF: In fact he takes a next step, he says that we've become so involved—Jews—in the history of Palestinians because of the crimes we've committed against them...Christians realize, many Christians, enlightened Christians after World War II, that they could not go forward without the Jews, so the Jews cannot go forward without the Palestinians, and they have to include the Palestinians in the covenant. Perhaps they've already been....

JK: Well, to speak to that, there's no question that the Jews cannot go forward without the Palestinians, because the Palestinians are the people whom the Jews have injured, and you can't just abandon them, they have to be incorporated into the Jewish social body. Which means, again, you have to annihilate your particularism, and you have to annihilate the Israeli state, and you have to annihilate or transcend Zionism. I see Zionism as a horrible mistake.

SF: I wanted to actually focus on the thing about Zionism being illegitimate. But first I want to make the point about Yoder that I hadn't made: he says that the closest thing to the ethic of Jesus existing for 2000 years during the time of Christendom (the merger of the Church and the state)—obviously he saw Christendom as nefarious—was the rabbinic Jews. Now some people say that's a romanticization. Israel Shahak says exactly the opposite, that Jews are no better.

JK: I think Israel Shahak is the person I will dedicate my book to.

SF: So that you feel that universalists and the best aspects of the Jewish moral tradition were dormant until the Emancipation, and that they existed during the time of the prophets?

JK: Yes. And that's what has to be recovered.

SF: And so as much as one doesn't like Reform Judaism today, I think we have to give it credit *at it origins* for revitalizing the idea at the time of the Jewish universalist mission.

JK: Oh there are so many ways of being Jewish. One of the great curses that Zionism has imposed on us is to make us think there's only one way to be Jewish. You know the extreme point of view, Webster's international dictionary now defines anti-Zionism as part of the definition of anti-Semitism, or any criticism of the state of Israel. And that's pretty astounding as an exercise in propaganda and ideology and so forth. But it tells us how stifling Zionism is to the notion of Judaism, that is to say, you must identify Israel with the Jewish people, with the fate of the Jews, rather than seeing it as a false step taken by the Jewish people, as one which if the Jews realized, they could recuperate it, they could start anew. But in any case, there is no particular, there's no necessary way of being Jewish.

SF: Ellis says the Palestinians want us to confess (he tends to talk about the Jews as a collective entity). He says, The Palestinians want us to confess to them. He says we haven't. It's a mockery on Yom Kippur, all these rituals go on and not a word is said about the Palestinians.

JK: They don't exist. It's well known how their existence has been erased by the Zionist movement. One thing I'm in the middle of doing—I haven't finished the research—is to go through a lot of these Zionist texts ...and Hertzberg's books, and just see whether any of these people had any serious understanding of the actual human beings whom they had to displace in order to build their utopian society. I think there's a fantastic lacuna there, there's a gap, a non-presence of the actual, real human beings, which of course the practical Zionists, the Ben Gurions and the people on the ground, knew very well they had to take care of. But I mean, the ideologues consistently ignored, minimized, dehumanized, erased these people.

SF: They were pretty blunt about it back in the 1930s—in private, not in public. I mean Ben-Gurion and the founders.

JK: Oh they said all kinds of things.

SF: Transfer was the main thing on their mind.

JK: The people who were actually engaged in putting together the Zionist project knew perfectly well that there was an irreconcilable task, and the clear-headed amongst them, like Ben Gurion, said, you knew, We have to face up to it, if we want to build our Jewish state, we're going to have to eliminate these other people, we're going to have to get rid of them, transfer them, kill them, do something to them, and we have to be very brutal about it. That word was hardly ever used, but it was pretty much implicit in what they were saying and sometimes explicit in what they were saying.

SF: Two of my favorite quotes by Ben Gurion are horrific. There's one right after the war when he sees all the Arabs...all the Palestinians leaving, and he says, "Ah, what a beautiful sight." Did you read that?

JK: No, but I've read many similar statements.

SF: And then another thing he said which I think sums up the history of Israeli diplomacy (U.S. also, but even to a lesser degree it seems to me—you might disagree), when his followers were worried that the Jews made too many concessions, he said, "Pay no attention to what the Gentiles say (meaning also what we say to the Gentiles). What matters is what the Jews do." Okay, the question of legitimacy.... I'd mentioned over the phone that there's not only legitimacy, that Lerner and Susannah Heschel and all say that Israel, Zionism was a great left-wing project, a national liberation movement, an international affirmative action program for poor Jews.

JK: Yeah, this is deeply self-deceptive in my view to say this, and it constitutes a serious difference I have with people like Lerner and Heschel who do many good things, I don't dispute that. But I think one has to be clear-headed, and I understand that there is an ineluctable contradiction embedded in the actual Zionist project, which destroys its legitimacy a priori and leads to endless crimes against humanity which we see over and over again, but we also see in it an unfolding dynamic, like an Aeschylean tragedy, how an original crime gets repeated and expands and so on and so forth, and it's embedded in the very fundamental principles of the Zionist project. Can we just talk about legitimacy for a little bit? First of all, the notion of legitimacy is one inherent in the modern state. You can't talk about Pharonic Egypt or Charlemagne in terms of legitimacy, because it's not a category in societies at that level. But the modern state is grounded in a universalizing principle which Hegel expands upon and embeds in his philosophy but is nonetheless present in political form and certainly derives from the notion of a universal human right that the state is supposed to realize. Now we know, and it's certainly the case, that any state from the beginning of humanity is grounded in class society and exists to enforce the will of the ruling class. And there's a certain level that one must realize that all states are abominations, shall we say, insofar as they enforce the class system. However, those states which for one reason or another try to claim membership within the community of modern nation states need to prove that they are legitimate within the terms of the modern nation state, and the only way you do this is by providing a foundation within the covenant, within the social contract, that opens the state to all people–to all its citizens.

SF: That's one of Finkelstein's main—

JK: Well, certainly.... He's very clear about that and so is Chomsky and a lot of people. It's a no-brainer if you think about it. Now we're not saying that such states fulfill that contract. We all know that the United States in particular, which is the most important example, is a disaster right and left from this perspective, and that our own society is built on extermination and genocide and slavery and the rest, which we have constantly to take into account. However, precisely because the 13 colonies were all founded by different groups of religious fanatics, they had to adopt a measure of negating the ethnicity or religious basis of the state which was founded; hence our government was founded on the principle of universal human right, which is and remains its finest achievement. So that even thought it has been violated in any number of ways and is far from being realized—and as we know, the current Bush administration would like very much to turn the clock back to theocracy and eliminate that foundation in human rights—we still know that that's an active struggle in this country. Now there are states, however, that although they pretend to be members of the community of modern nation states, they do not have that principle built in. And such states do not have legitimacy, because "legitimacy" simple means: Are you capable of joining the community of nation states that are grounded in universal human rights? Israel is not. Interestingly, they know it, and they spend prodigious amounts of effort to mystify this fact and to hide from it and to do all kinds of tricky and complex things, including vast manipulations of the Jewish diaspora, including all kinds of demonizations of the conquered peoples and displaced peoples and saying, Look it's forced upon us because they're devils and terrorists and so on and so forth. But the fact of the matter is, there is this profound contradiction, namely, that Zionism—Israel as a Zionist state—says, "We are going to have a democratic state for the Jewish people, and that is perforce a lie and leads to a dreadful chain of consequences." It's played out in two major thematics, according to whether the Zionist is an adherent to the Hellenistic liberal tradition or whether the Zionist is an out-and-out theocrat.

SF: Israel is anomolous among states that advocated race nationalism. At least in one respect, they do have a free press, and they have, within their own society, freedoms that you—I don't think you saw that in South Africa, did you?

JK: Oh well, no, in some ways you did. South Africa is of course the most interesting cognate. And in some ways worse, in some ways better, than Israel.

SF: Their oppression of the natives there was mild compared to what the Israelis have...

JK: Oh yeah, as a matter of fact, in many respects, the indigenous peoples are worse off now after Apartheid, when they're simply the victims of the capitalist market. But this does not deny that they had a horrible time of it under Apartheid, and they were systematically deprived of fundamental human rights, and therefore the Apartheid South African state was an illegitimate state. And it's extremely important to realize that the Israeli Zionist state is different in a number of complicated ways but nonetheless shares with Apartheid South Africa a fundamental lack of legitimacy. And I think it's extremely important for people to realize that, because that lack of legitimacy translated throughout the western world, amongst people of good will (and I think the concept of good will is an important concept) saying, This state should be gotten rid of, and that you can get rid of a state—which is a basically an abstract program of running society and the people who staff it—you can get rid of a state without destroying a society. And they got rid through a very difficult, protracted, horrible conflict, which I was involved in. (I have family there, I know a great deal about this, but we can set it aside for now.) They got rid of it, and the society is in anything but good shape, but it's in far better shape than it was 20 years ago, and anybody who knows about South Africa knows that they're vastly happier, it's a vibrant, living society now, whereas before it was in a death grip. Now in my view, Zionist Israel is playing out sort of towards an end game. They're not yet at the end-game, that same kind of death grip, because the effort to sustain the illusion that you're having a democratic state for the Jewish people involves such prodigies of mystification and self-deception and such projection of evil onto the others and such thin-skinnedness and so on and so forth, and it's so destructive. And you can follow that destructiveness over the course of Israeli society. You can see Israeli society just turning into this beast, as it were, and engaging in these unbelievable things like that Apartheid Wall which they're putting up which, just to look at a photograph of it is enough to make you weep, to tear your hair out in rage.

SF: It's like the Warsaw ghetto.

JK: Yeah, very much. I mean, it's an unbelievable horror, and this horror is constantly developing. And you know, no two societies are ever the same. At a certain level of abstraction, everything is the same, you know, all societies are composed of human beings. Great, so therefore, you know, Nazi Germany is the same as Periclean Athens, because both are composed of human beings. It's reductio ad absurdum. At another level, every society is different, so obviously Apartheid South Africa and Apartheid Zionist Israel are not the same, but their fundamental distinction is that both of them have abandoned the legitimacy that adheres to even vicious states like our own, and which of course Nazi Germany abandoned, too. It's important not to belabor that distinction, because there are many differences there, too

SF: You mention that Jews freak out.

JK: Yeah, Jews freak out, and you have to be very careful.

SF: It comes up in interviews with Jews who stayed with Palestinians...

JK: Well, how can you ignore it?

SF: To point that out is a way to just to try to wake Jews up

JK: To wake them up, and it's a notion that people in Israel arrive at all the time. People in Israel are in general much more alive to this problem than the people in...

SF: You mean the few dissidents in Israel?

JK: Well, the few dissidents but even, I forget who it was who said that—he was a bureaucrat in a town in southern Gaza that they just mutilated, the one that Rachel Corrie was working on—but you know, he went in there after they were massacring, bull-dozing, and he said, It just came to me, spontaneously, that this is what my grandmother must have felt like in the Warsaw Ghetto. And he was not a radical, not a leftist.

SF: This was someone who worked for the Israeli government?

JK: Yeah, an Israeli official, whose grandmother was in the Warsaw Ghetto, and he said, It just occurred to me that the way these Palestinian women are going around trying to survive...it just spontaneously brought that comparison to his mind. But this is by way of saying that that notion is alive even in people who are not dissident Israelis. And of course most Israelis are numb and...

SF: Racist?

JK: Well the racism is something that emerges organically out of a situation like this. It's like saying that America under slavery couldn't help but be racist, when one group of human beings were systematically deprived of the basic human right which is to self-determine their...

SF: In your response in Tikkun you talk about the absurdity of trying to eradicate racism without changing the nature of the Jewish state—

JK: You can't do it, right. What's Michael Lerner going to do, have a human relations group, touchy-feeling and confessions? You can't. You have to make a fundamental change in the institutional framework.

SF: So let's operationalize what you mean now when you say "no legitimacy... I don't think the U.N. had a right in 1948 to partition Palestine over the wishes of the native inhabitants, to dump the whose problem of Jewish refugees on them, but one of the rationales is, well, this was the only solution to the problem of Jewish survivors.... Now, if it were the only solution, wouldn't one have to think twice? You know, there's one writer, A.B. Yehoshua the novelist, and he's not that leftist, but he's a little bit leftist, but he says, There's a right to survival. He called his book *Between Right and Right*. But I mean, I don't think in reality it was an issue during the war or in 1948 of the Jewish right to survival. Clearly Ben Gurion didn't really care about Jewish refugees, he cared only about creating a Jewish state, and Boaz Evron, I don't know if you're familiar with his work?

JK: No.

SF: He's an Israeli, relatively moderate leftist, and he calls himself a post-Zionist right now rather than an anti-Zionist. But he documented, as Lenni Brenner did. They wanted to...the Zionists interfered with rescue efforts that would not lead Jews to Israel. So under what conditions would other people had to be forcibly removed to make way for Jews who were victims of the Nazis, you know? Going back then, what would you have advocated then?

JK: Well, let me comment in general on that. At every point in this story, it could have been different. In 1895, in 1905, whatever. There are certain points, or flash points, intensities, certainly the period 45-49, etc., was an extremely turbulent and crisis-ridden and so forth. But at every point, it could have been done differently. The main point and the only time we can change is the here and now. So at this point, what can be done differently is for people, Jewish people in particular, to wake up and start radically questioning the Zionist legacy, to rethink the Jewish identity, to recognize that this notion of Zionism has not at all made life safer for them—the most dangerous place in the world, the only dangerous place in the world to be a Jew is in Israel, which was supposed to be a haven for them and so on. What we can do now is to begin rethinking the question of Zionism, and whatever human beings make, they can unmake. I'm not saying they will, I'm not saying it will happen, but I can comment on what should have been done in 1945-46. All right. There's a very interesting meeting between Franklin Roosevelt and King Saud of Saudi Arabia—Ibn Saud—and the king says to Roosevelt, who was trying of course to curry favor with him because he wanted to establish a protectorate over the oil—he says, Listen, I have an idea about the Jewish question. You're wondering what to do about all these Jews and victims of this terrible Nazi plague. Well, Germany should pay for it; they created the problem, you have total power over Germany at this point. Who's to blame? They're to blame. We know about civilization and so on, imperialism and so on. But clearly, that blame focuses on the Nazis. There should be space in Germany set aside for the Jewish resettlement.

SF: A territory in Germany?

JK: Yeah, a territory in Germany. That's what the king said. And he said, why should you make innocent Arabs, who have been kicked around enough, pay all the more for this? Of course it was a non-starter, because it would have involved a breakdown of a fundamental identity between the U.S. and German interests that characterized the entire war. I mean, there's a really basic ambiguity about World War II in that the U.S., and all the ruling elites of Europe, were reluctant antagonists of Hitler.

SF: Because of the Bolsheviks?

JK: Because their fundamental aim was to contain Bolshevism and Communism, and they were hoping that Hitler would wipe them out, which was Hitler's number one paramount goal. There's a very interesting book by Arno Mayer, who's the best historian of this, *Why Did the Heavens Not Darken?* You know this book?

SF: I've come across it.

JK: Oh, it's a wonderful book. *Why Did the Heavens Not Darken?* It's a Pantheon book. Splendid book. He's the best historian of this period, and his view of the Holocaust is I think very cogently argued. Except that Germany was always riddled with anti-Semitism during the Hitler period, but the exterminationist impulse didn't arise until the war against Bolshevism and the Soviets started running into trouble. And that was what led to the so-called final solution. It was a way of displacing the crisis onto the backs of the Jews. So the fundamental goal was always to eliminate the "red menace," and that was a goal that all the ruling elites of Europe and certainly of the United States shared. There was a racial identity.

SF: Do you know that before the U.N. came up with this partition that would have given Jews all of this land that they hadn't managed to acquire through purchasing and evicting the Palestinians, the Arab states all got together and came up with another proposal for the U.N., in which Palestinians would retain sovereignty, and anyone could become a citizen after living there ten years. And Khalidi points out that the important thing is that citizenship was not based on being an Arab but being a Palestinian. Eventually Jews would be citizens and not only was there a provision for Jews becoming citizens, but also that there would have been protection over Jewish holy sites and their rights as a minority. At the time the Arabs had a majority, so how many Jews would have been let in would have disputed but the proposal could have been a basis for negotiation. Of course that was rejected.

JK: Also a non-starter, but that could have been done. At that time in history, the United States in particular just held all the cards. The U.S. could have done anything it wanted. Everybody else was in ruins.

SF: Well there are some that saw the creation of Israel as a regrettable necessity. I think Lerner makes it into a great victory, but let's start with the regrettable necessity, which you said something about, and then go to the great victory. What could have been done if everything else was rejected for the Jews during the war? Would they have been justified if that was the only option?

JK: I think the notion of regrettable necessity is correct, but only if necessity is interpreted rather broadly. Truman, who was candid, said very explicitly, and I think Roosevelt would have said the same—although Roosevelt was on the whole our best president of the 20th century—that, Listen, I think the Arabs have a tremendous case here, and what you're saying along these lines is very appealing. On the other hand, he says, I have hundreds of thousands of Jewish voters in strategic cities—he really said that—and I have to get re-elected, and I have hardly an Arab voters, and I'm sorry, I just have to go with the emerging power of the Jewish vote and the Jewish lobbies and so on, and he said, This is what it's about. So that necessity has to be seen in terms of domestic political calculation, not necessarily in terms of what's best for the world or indeed best for the peoples involved. I think that had this been a better world and done properly at that moment in history, given the extraordinary power that the United States possessed, it could have imposed using—and the U.N. certainly would have ratified—a solution that would have created a non-ethnic state, and that's what should have happened: a state where everybody who lived there in good faith would be protected and could worship and so on—and that's a valid notion. I mean, everyone should feel that their past is respected and that their heritage and traditions and their ancestors are taken into account. But, no, the Jews wanted an ethnocracy, they wanted...

SF: Not the Jews, the Zionists.

JK: I mean the Zionists. You're quite correct. The Zionists wanted an ethnocracy.

SF: But the ones in the concentration camps, they didn't want to go over to Palestine. They had no desire to go.... If they'd been given a choice, they'd have gone to the United States. The ones that were exterminated were not Zionists.

JK: Right. Most probably weren't. Zionism was always a minority movement, and it became a majority movement once the state got going. But it could have been nipped in the bud, and—I don't even like the word "binational" state—a multinational state, a state where anybody could go and try to make a living under a free and just and democratically governed society. I don't see that there's any necessary connection between having a society where Jewish people are safe and secure and where they rule as an ethnocracy. In fact it's quite the contrary. But that dominant urge to rule as an ethnocracy, which is really the western imperial attitude transmogrified through the Jewish identity had the upper hand. And it is a great tragedy that the guilt amongst the western intellectuals and politicos for abandoning the Jews during the Holocaust, which we know was a terrible turn of events—that could have been stopped...

SF: It could have been stopped?

JK: The Holocaust could have been stopped! At least they could have bombed the trains going to Auschwitz. I mean, at that point, Germany had no air force. You could fly over any part of Germany, you could have wiped out those camps. They knew where the camps were. No, there's a great deal of complicity between the western so-called democracies and the Nazis: there's no question about this. A deep, dark undercurrent here. And a profound guilt set in after the war.

SF: This was a motive—

JK: Roosevelt was... a great politician, but he still was a politician. Roosevelt's most important—well, one of his most important—bases of support were Catholics, urban Catholics. And it's not that the Catholics themselves wanted that to happen, but it was certainly the case that the pope, Pius XII, who was the patron of Frances Cardinal Spellman, who was sometimes called the American pope and who was the most important Catholic in the United States until John F. Kennedy emerged, that Pope Pius XII was an active collaborator with the Nazis, and he's a bag-man who gave money to Hitler in the 20s, and he was a monster, despite the odor of sanctity which accompanied him. And I just think that Roosevelt made a calculated decision, or he was told by Spellman: "Don't do anything to help these Jews because it might expose what Pius XII has done," and in any case, the pope doesn't want it. And Roosevelt was a politician. I don't think Roosevelt was an anti-Semite, but he had to play that game. It was the same reasoning that kept Roosevelt from defending the Spanish Republic. They certainly could have turned the tide in that war; there was no necessity for Franco...

SF: Moving on to...what about those people like Lerner—I don't think I'm misquoting him—I mean, I appreciate his contribution to building a movement to counter AIPAC, but the idea frankly always makes me sick...when I look at one of these anti-occupation groups or Jewish peace groups—not JATO, not more radical ones—and they start their literature with, "We love Israel."

JK: What's up with that?! I think it's very, very incorrect from a moral, intellectual, historical, political, philosophical notion: there is no reason to love Israel. You can have deep compassion for the Jewish people, you can say certain good things have happened in Israel—that they have a good press and so on and so forth—but that does not mean that you should love Israel. You have to look at that with a hard, cold eye as, is this state deserving of support and allegiance? Or, on the contrary, is it so internally constructed as to sew discord, racism, imperialism, to be subject to internal expansive forces, the motion toward "Greater Israel" or not? That's been present from the very beginning, and only a blind eye or one mystified by propaganda cannot see it. It's perfectly patent, and I think that people who soft-pedal that, they, like Lerner, as you said, may do it for what he thinks are noble motives, in other words to bring in people....

SF: You think he doesn't really believe in it?

JK: I don't know, he probably does believe it, that's immaterial, I can't say what he believes, but what he does do is he wants to reach out to liberal U.S. Jews who...and so he's fortunate that he believes that because he can then speak in such a way that he can get people to read his magazine, give it money and so on. But it's never a good idea to turn away from truth, and the truth is that it may be lonely in this country to hold onto that truth, but people like Finkelstein who do it and Chomsky—and there are others. One has to be faithful to that, and in the long run, it's only the truth that can make people free. You cannot free people until you free their minds, and you cannot free the mind when it's subject to a mystification like there's something fundamentally worthwhile about the state of Israel.

SF: Yes. Let's go back to that again, okay? They claim not only is it worthwhile, it's better. They act as if somehow the Jewish ethical tradition still exists in Israel! For people like Lerner: it has to be recovered, but it *can* be recovered. Whereas the right-wing Zionists, I mean American right-wing Zionists, the Jewish establishment, act as if it's still operative in Israel. So the difference between Lerner and the right-wing Zionists is they both see the Jewish ethical tradition or religious spiritual tradition as embedded in Israel but the right-wing think it's there today, and they deny what's happening, and people like Lerner believe it's dormant and can be reactivated.

JK: Yeah, well that's astounding. Because really, there's very little of it and less all the time. Not just the right wing, but the whole spectrum of Zionist apologists and ideologues to the right of Lerner. Somebody like Alan Dershowitz, for example, presents himself as a great "progressive," because he will talk vaguely of Israel making a few mistakes now and then. But whenever challenged on a serious issue he reverts to form and "proves," like the trial lawyer he is, that Israel never does wrong. For example, he recently rejected the International Court of Justice's verdict on the "apartheid wall" by claiming the court was illegitimate because it is stacked with enemies of Israel, which is to say, people who can't see how profoundly ethical the Zionist state is. Further to the Right, Martin Peretz frankly avows that anyone who criticizes the virtue of Israel is objectively in the camp of the terrorists. These people seem to not realize how ethically debased it is to smear one's adversaries this way. Secular Zionists, whether in the U.S.

or Israel, generally suffer from what I've called the "bad conscience." That is, they are caught up in the vicious circle resulting from the need to maintain the Jewish identity as a supremely ethical people in the face of expanding human rights violations by the State of Israel.

SF: Yes as I said they claim the Jewish ethical tradition is operative in Israel. Deshowitz is a good example because on so many others issues he was the quintessential liberal—a symbol. But his support for Israel tugs him to the right. Not to speak of liberals who championed civil rights for blacks (including Dershowitz) and are despicable racists when it comes to Arabs.... And liberal Jewish support of Israel has led many former radicals to support American imperialism. Paul Berman is one good example of that. Whereas in Congress you see this bizarre psychological split in the psyche where strongly anti-war liberals like Nadler or Pelosi will give carte blanche to any war crime Israel commits. And I don't think it's purely opportunism on the part of Nadler et al.

JK: This by the way is in contrast to another path of justification used by the religious Orthodox, again, whether in the U.S. or Israel. I recently received an interesting letter from an Orthodox rabbi—an American—who had been reading my stuff, and in certain respects agreed with my argument. But he held that what I had argued as the notion of a bad conscience applies only to the secular liberals who try to reclaim the ethical tradition and are constantly faced by its violation. He said, in effect, that we truly Orthodox, such as myself, who have studied philosophy and are very literate, don't worry about that, because we don't ground our claim to Israel in any kind of ethical ideal. We ground it because God says it's ours, and that's it! And so I don't have a bad conscience. That's the genius of fundamentalism at work.

SF: Yes religious Zionism is rabid, and as you say seemingly unencumbered by guilt at all.

JK: In my view, this dynamic accounts in good measure for the rise of the religious Right within Zionist circles. Originally, the predominantly secular founders of the Israeli state sought to marginalize the Orthodox rabbinate by just giving them control over marriages, which by the way is not trivial. But over the years, they have become bigger and bigger, because they have the painless way of legitimating Zionist aggression. And particularly with the settlements, they're the force that the state gets behind as the advance columns of the expansion into that part of Palestine the Zionists didn't take in 1948—the expropriation of that 22% of Palestine, the measly portion that was given over to the Palestinians. Only these ultra-Orthodox have the nerve, the will, and the lack of scruple to do this, because they feel the divine mandate, and they don't care what the rest of the world thinks.

SF: They always say the whole world is against them.

JK: And they like it! .... And it's a very, very grave turn of events, and it should be noted that, after 9/11, UJA (the Jewish philanthropies in the United States) started funding the settlements, which they hadn't done before 9/11/01.

SF: Okay, two questions. I just want to point out that there are the Neturei Karta, which is an Orthodox group that believes the opposite, that God doesn't want us to go back there until the messiah comes.

JK: With Jews there's always somebody to disagree.

SF: Why the romanticization of Israel among Jews, particularly in the west?

JK: Right, but those movements are all integrally tied to the development of nationalism.

SF: Lerner does it too with the...

JK: They all do that, yeah.

SF: Lerner's group is certainly not nationalistic in terms of the United States.

JK: No, but some people are. Many Jews are.

SF: No, I'm talking about the Zionist left in America...

JK: I'll just say this. When I was a boy, I remember being thrilled, before I had any understanding of what was going on, by the notion of the Sabras and of the Jews being pioneers and hewing a civilization out of the wilderness, and identifying with them. And I think it has to do with a sense of being freed from the ghettoes, of being freed from the stifled, closed-in life of the diaspora for so many centuries.

SF: You think Susannah Heschel or Lerner feels that way today?

JK: There's no reason why that should go away. The notion that you can build a society, that you can create a society that's yours is very appealing...

SF: OK. Next. Critics of Zionism are often criticized; why don't you pick on the Arab countries? —Which is of course that lawyer at Harvard, Alan Dershowitz—okay, that's his thing. And Lerner does it too: How can they criticize Israel? They tell you, "All these horrible Arab states, the United States has given them money, and the left only focuses, if not exclusively, primarily on Israel."

JK: This is an old saw, and you can reduce it to an absurdity and say, "Why not Genghis Khan, why not Atilla the Hun, why not the Emperor Caligula? I mean, there's always evil out there in the world. There's an immense amount of evil out there in the world. Clearly, the only coherent moral position is to give priority to those evils in the degree to which you are complicit and responsible. And I deplore the Arab states, but I have had almost nothing to do with them. But I've lived my life as a Jew in this country, I've seen my family rise up in support of Israel, I've seen institutions in which I've worked give support to Israel (I remember, I worked for many years at the Einstein Medical School of Yeshiva University), I see it at Bard College, where I teach. I mean, this is where the dynamism involves. The criticism should be as a function of the historical dynamic that's driving a society onward.

SF: You would say that exclusively, or primarily, the distortions that existed in the Arab states—for instance in Saudi Arabia, where women can't commit adultery without getting stoned, etc.—would you say that was created by imperialism? Obviously the dynamic was partially influenced by US imperialism.

JK: Well I think that there's no question. And it's not that I think the Arab states are neat in any which way. I think that largely, the issue of their legitimacy doesn't even arise because you take something like Saudi Arabia, it's a monarchy, and a monarchy is, prima facia, a bad thing, and it should be gotten rid of. As a matter of fact, I think Saudi Arabia is a dreadful state, and it's completely artificial, it was created first by the British and then by the Americans, and it's been under U.S. control and U.S. thumb for all these years, and it's a nightmarish place. But it doesn't fall under the same category as Israel. It's not a settler-colonial society, it's not a society that was made by the invasion of people from my country or people from Europe and my own ancestors.

SF: Is that the main difference? In Israel there is more US complicity.

JK: It's not even complicity... Israel is... Israel is *us*. It's really different from whether the U.S. has feathered the beds of these corrupt kings and potentates, and they execute people publicly and they're dreadful. They're hard, *but Israel is us.*

SF: It's proper to focus more on Israel.

JK: Absolutely proper. It's not even proper, it's necessary. It's us. I mean, it's our institutions, it's our people, it's my family.

SF: I would say Jews in particular have a responsibility.

JK: Absolutely, an obligation.

SF: Finkelstein as an atheist who doesn't even think of himself as a Jew...

JK: Well...

SF: ...he says, It doesn't matter, he just wanted to attack one imperialist project and because of his background as a child of survivors and credentials he thought he'd be most effective by choosing Israel—

JK: Well, everybody has their own take on it. I don't agree with that, because I think that we speak from our own history, and every politics is or should be an attempt to transcend one's personal history as well as one's collective history. But my personal history is a history of a people—hundreds of people I know have been actively involved in fomenting Zionism and building Israel along the lines it that it currently exists. They haven't been involved directly in the same way as in supporting Saudi Arabia, and again, you have them both—we haven't even begun talking about this, I know you didn't want to digress too much, but a quick one: the most unbelievable, the way in which the U.S. Congress passes these resolutions saying that anything Israel does is a good thing—what was the latest one, 450-10 or something like that, and last year it was 410-1 (I always want to hear the position of that one who wasn't behaving properly.). A resolution saying we give a blank check to anything that Israel does—. And the most recent one was a resolution that basically institutionalized the occupation of the territories and went against the United Nations, went against international law, against the spirit of the whole human race. Now this is serious! You have this massive lock step, totalitarian support being granted by the United States Congress. You can't tell me that that doesn't constitute an obligation to criticize not just Israel but to criticize the deep penetration of Zionist lobbies of both mainstream parties.

SF: People like Landes would say, "Why are you so much harsher on Israel, it's a young country, why does it not have legitimacy, whereas the United States was a place where Blacks were 3/5 of a person and had slavery and wiped out the Indians etc." And yet you wouldn't say that there is a difference?

JK: Well I think I've answered that, but I'll just say that the United States is a dreadful country but nonetheless has a constitution which provides the hope and provides certain pathways toward a democratic society.

SF: But would you say that was true in 1776 as well?

JK: No, it took that kind of struggle. And it took civil war, it took a lot of bloodshed, it took long years of struggle.

SF: If you were around back then you would have said the US had no legitimacy?

JK: Probably would have, but I would say now that Israel should learn from United States history and start building in those mechanisms which would allow for the democratization of its society, and if not, we should find a state structure that does so.

SF: Correct me if I'm wrong, I'm thinking that in the United States at the time, there was more of a tension than there is in Israel, because there was at least this commitment to egalitarianism, like on the part of Thomas Jefferson, which you frankly don't have...I mean, they don't even have a constitution in Israel.

JK: It's extremely important to bear in mind that they've never been able to put a constitution in Israel, because they know very well, if they put in a constitution, what they would have to do. They would have to nullify the Israeli state. That state cannot have a constitution, because it's not grounded in constitutional reasoning. Constitutional reasoning is prima facia the expression of a universal human right. The King of England didn't have a constitution until the monarchy was replaced by parliamentary democracy and so forth. And Israel's inability to maintain a constitution, it's reliance upon this common law of the supreme court and so forth for governance, is the best evidence we have that that society is fundamentally awry, that it does not possess legitimacy. It would have to cancel itself if it had a constitution.

SF: So in fact, in that way, it is worse than the US was?

JK: Oh, I don't even know about that, because you know, we had slavery for centuries and so on, and what we did to our indigenous people is really horrific.

SF: Comparable, actually.

JK: Comparable to the Nazi Holocaust. Not so much to what Israel does to Palestinians but to the Nazi Holocaust. Ward Churchill has a very good article on this in a recent issue of the journal, *Socialism and Democracy*, which is on the subject of racism—excellent article—point-by-point showing how the main difference between the U.S. relationship to indigenous peoples and the Nazi Holocaust is the timetable. The Holocaust was accelerated, it took place in a few years, whereas the U.S. did it over a few centuries. But that's an important difference but by no means a fundamental one.

SF: But it's similar to Israel with the settlers going out and shooting Palestinians.

JK: Yeah, but Israel is not at that level, because they are constrained by dependency on world opinion, by the fact that the Jews do have a conscience—it's a bad conscience, and a burdensome one—and they are tormented. I see Israel and Judaism in general as tormented by the contradiction between their own high moral ideals and the raw, sordid practices of Zionism.

SF: You can't say that about someone like Sharon.

JK: No, but I'm saying...I mean, there's obviously a hard, immoral, nihilistic element in him. But I'm talking about, even a Sharon has to make a political calculation based upon Jewish opinion which simply won't stand for that.

SF: But it has no impact in the US on Jewish opinion...

JK: No, virtually no impact...

Chapter 3

Norton Mezvinsky

N orton Mezvinsky is a Professor of History at Central State Connecticut University. He is the author of numerous articles on the Mideast and the co-author with Israel Shahak of Jewish Fundamentalism in Israel in 1999. (See Daniel Pipes warning about him at the end of this chapter.)

SF: We might as well start with some current events. I did notice that you're one of at least the potential victims of the Bush administration. Do you have any feelings about the Commission Bush appointed that has censured you? The one run by Richard Pipes. I noticed that in January 2003, they stated that Central State Connecticut University was added to the list of institutions that Pipes would monitor—it sounds like 1984. You were singled out as one of the troublemakers because you taught in summer school and referred to the "state terrorism" of Israel. They objected also to your promotion for "outstanding teaching and scholarly achievement" by CSU Board of Trustees. Pipes wrote about. "And rewarding Norton Mezvinsky for spewing anti-Semitic calumnies is a scandal. President Judd and the CCSU administration need to be watched carefully and critiqued when they make such mistakes."

NM: Yeah, it's terrible. I mean, Richard Pipes has among other things this thing called Campus Watch and also Media Watch and he simply labels people anti-Semitic who are critical of Israeli policies. Especially American Jews; hardly any Israeli Jews. But any Americans who are critical he labels self-hating, anti-Semitic Jews just because they're critical of certain Israeli policies, which is invalid, unwarranted, undue, and it's about as bad as it can be.

SF: It seems the project is to keep American Jews from talking critically about Israel.

NM: Well, that's correct, but that fits in with Anti-Defamation League approaches and other—not all but some other—American Jewish organizational leaders. That's just one part of Richard Pipes that's bad. I mean, his views about Islam are also just horrible.

SF: Yeah, and actually Huntington has gotten more mellow over the years, I think.

NM: Well, there's a huge difference between Richard Pipes and Huntington (Samuel Huntington). I mean, agree or not with his theory, Huntington is and has been for a long time a first-rate scholar. Pipes has written a few things on, as you probably know, on the Soviet Union and Russia that some people adhere to and swear by, but he is not really a very good scholar in any area.

SF: So is this one of the wages of being a Jew who is critical of Zionism. People who've taken an anti-Zionist stance like yourself presumably encounter a lot of opposition and hostility, even among families, a number of people have reported....

NM: Uh, well, it certainly happens, and it's happened with me for thirty-five years. Sometimes family members, but more often, right up to the present, as I've said, some leaders of American Jewish organizations, nationally and in the areas in which the person resides. I can just give you two quick examples. Nationally, a few weeks ago, I had an opposing op-ed piece in *USA Today*, as you may know...a daily newspaper, national and international, and they usually have an editorial, and then they have someone write an opposing view to their editorial, which is quite a good thing to do. And this was an editorial on Sharon and his saying that he would take out settlements in Gaza and so on, and they praised it. And so they asked me to do an opposing view that gave another view, which I did. The very next day, Abraham Foxman, the national director of the Anti-Defamation League of B'nai Brith, all over the internet and in a letter to USA Today, blasts me—didn't say anything about the substance about which I wrote, or very little—and simply blasted me as a self-hating Jew for a long time. He used...no, he didn't use "self-hating," but he used terminology that indicated that clearly, and said that I had been this condemner of Israeli policy for all of these years and so on and so forth. Now, that's a *national* example recently. There are plenty of local examples. Recently we had an institute on my campus for a week in the summer on the Middle East, and I was one of the people who participated, and lo and behold—although I put that in quotation marks, because it wasn't so surprising—the Anti-Defamation people in Connecticut, the main office being in New Haven, and then in Hartford, the head of the American Jewish Committee locally, and the head of the Jewish Federation all wrote pieces for the newspapers how anti-Semitic Norton Mezvinsky was and always had been. So I mean, I could go on and on, and that's just my own personal example.

SF: Sure, Henry Siegman, who is one of the pillars of the Jewish Establishment albeit critical of Israel...in an profile of him in the New York Times talked about all the opposition he encountered and said if we make criticisms of Israel, it's not your politics in question, it's your Jewishness itself. One becomes considered a heretic.

NM: Well, yeah, and I mean, to say that a person's a self-hating Jew, if the person's Jewish, is even I suppose worse than being called a heretic.... They'll say anything, they'll lie, they'll cheat, they'll say one thing behind closed doors and another thing when the doors are open. You've got to take them on publicly. You take them to the public forum, you say, "Come and discuss or debate this with me in an open meeting," and they are usually not prone to do that, because they know that if they are confronting someone that knows anything at all, they'll come off looking very badly. So they are the stereotype bully: they use bullying tactics.

They try to scare people, and they often have scared people from speaking out. They haven't scared others.

SF: Well, obviously they haven't scared you.

NM: No, they haven't scared me.

SF: It's all bluster and threats. No on has actually physically assaulted you or anything.

NM: No, no one has.

SF: But I suppose there have been threats to your life?

NM: Oh, yeah, there have been threats to my life.

SF: Every critic of Israel I spoke to experienced—

NM: There have been threats, sure, there have been threats to my life.

SF: Going back to current events in Israel. I read the recent piece by Chomsky, interviewed by Stephen Shalom… Did you see the piece?

NM: Well I didn't see it.

SF: Chomsky took a position that, I don't know if one would have predicted… I guess you know that a lot of Jews critical of Israel have been skeptical about, *now,* the viability of the two-state solution which for many years was the fall-back position even for Jews who claimed to be anti-Zionist, at least we can get this two-state…Chomsky still seems to hold out hopes…. Chomsky said that with enough pressure on the part of the United States by the organized progressive community it's possible to get the president—I assume he's talking about someone other than Bush—to pressure Israel to withdraw from the territories and to make an agreement like the Geneva Accords. And I might contrast to that one thing that Tony Judt said in his article—did you read that one?

NM: No…yeah, I did, I did.

SF: I looked it over last night, that's why I'm— He said it's inconceivable to him a U.S. president telling Israel anything, so even though there is some support within Israel for a withdrawal, he doesn't see that as a viable option any more, whereas Chomsky seems to imagine a scenario where progressive Jews could put pressure on the U.S. government….

NM: You want me to comment on that?

SF: Yeah.

NM: I don't think a real two-state solution has been and/or is now, or will be in the near future any more realistic than to argue for a binational state. And I'll tell you why. We have to go to what the definition is. The Israeli government…all Israeli governments as you may know up until the early 1990s would not officially even talk about a Palestinian state. *Then,* actually, Rabin and Peres were smart enough to understand—sufficiently sophisticated to understand—that well, that was a term that they needed to use. So they used the term "state." But they defined it clearly in the same terms as it had been defined when the term wasn't used–not a real state. In other words, they said, that well, not certainly from all areas of the West Bank, but from some areas of the West Bank—very limited—but from some areas of the West Bank, additional areas, the Israeli army might well pull back, and then Palestinians could have "autonomous rule." That's the term: autonomous rule. Autonomous rule means you can have your own police, you can have your own courts, you can take care of your own services so we don't have to do it any more, you can do all of that until and unless we, the Israeli government, think that whatever you're doing is a threat to us, and then we have the right to come in and do what we need to do to stop you. Which simply means that Israel retains sovereignty. Now when Palestinians have talked about a Palestinian state, understandably, they have talked about an independent, sovereign Palestinian state. So I'm saying we have one definition on the one side that is autonomous rule. We have a definition on the other side that is sovereignty. Menachem Begin in 1978 and 1979 offered Palestinians more autonomous rule in Gaza and the West Bank than Yitzhak Rabin offered them in the Oslo agreement or than Barak really offered them at the end of the 1990s. But that's autonomous rule, and Palestinians rejected it in the late 70s, and they continued to reject it because they want an independent sovereign state. The United States government to date has always without exception backed the Israeli definition fully and totally. So I'm saying that a two-state solution that is a real two-state solution simply has not been in the cards, is not in the cards, is not realistic. Look, over forty percent of the water for all of Israel comes from aquifers the Israelis have built in the West Bank. Now what knowledgeable person could believe that any Israeli government to date is going to say, Okay Palestinians, you can have your state, and your state will be territory in which our aquafers exists? Or who could also believe, given what has been consistently the case, that the Israeli government will indeed do away with Jewish settlements in the West Bank? They simply won't do it; they haven't done it; they've only expanded those Jewish settlements. The whole argument that Barak said he would give ninety-five percent of the West Bank back to the Palestinians is nonsense, because the Jewish settlements and Jewish settlers control...they have...the Israeli government has confiscated the land, given it to the settlers. Forty-three percent of the land in the West Bank. If you have forty-three percent, and the Israeli government has given no indication of giving it back, how can you give Palestinians ninety-five percent? I could go on and on. Now, so I'm saying that is...I'm not saying it could never happen. I'm saying that if people say that a binational state is utopian because it's not realistic for now or the near future, you can say that just as much, indeed just as much, for a real two-state solution. Therefore, I would say two things. I would say 1) by far the better solution, the more democratic solution, the better solution for both parties in terms of a peaceful arrangement would be a binational state—not necessariiy a secular democratic state (one person, one rule; one person, one vote), but you have two communities. We have those kinds of federal states around the world. We have different patterns of binational states. You could build in guarantees for both communities. We have had—we still don't have very many, only a very small number—of Israeli Jews and Palestinians who are now ("now" being the last six to twelve months) talking in favor of that. But if you just look at the small number, that small number is an increase over what we had before. So I'm not saying there's very much hope in that, but I'm saying it's a far, far better idea, and therefore, if one idea is no more realistic than the other, then why not be in favor of—I say you should be in favor of—the better approach. The better approach morally and democratically is a binational state.

SF: When you talk about the Israelis won't grant sovereignty are you talking about an army and control of borders.

NM: No, no. An army is one factor, but that's not the whole factor. They say, we—for our security—we have the right to determine when and if Palestinians would do anything that threatens us. We define it. And if they do, we're the stronger force, we want to maintain ourselves as the stronger force, we can go in and stop it. Moreover, there's a lot of reason to believe that the Israelis would still limit economic development of Palestinians. Then there are some other factors. I'll just mention one more. If we ever did have a Palestinian state in part of the West Bank and Gaza, the likelihood, I think, is it would be an exclusivist Palestinian state. It would grant rights and privileges to Palestinians not granted to Jews. Then what...

SF: An Islamic state?

NM: Well, it may or may not be an Islamic state. It may be the kind of state Israel is as a Jewish state. It's not a theocratic state. But, as you know, by law, it grants certain rights and privileges to Jews not granted to non-Jews, even for those 1.2 million Palestinian citizens who are non-Jews, Palestinians who are citizens. Well, that's a Jewish exclusivist state. If the Palestinians had a state that was a Palestinian exclusivist state, then I'm saying we'd have two states that I think should be opposed morally as exclusivist states; and secondly, those two exclusivist states side by side, made up of people who have been at one another's throat for all of these years, well over fifty-four years; that might even increase, that might even intensify the conflict even more than now.

SF: Are the fundamentalists actually a major reason Israel won't negotiate a real settlement?

NM: The fundamentalists? Well, it's one of the reasons, but I don't think that...it's certainly not the only reason, certainly not the only major reason, because secular Israeli Jews are just as opposed as are religious Jews. We have growing numbers of Israeli Jews who oppose, as you know, certain parts of Israeli policy towards the Palestinians, including certain parts of the Occupation policies. But you have to look very hard in Israel to find Israeli Jews who are willing to say there should be any Palestinian return to Israel itself. —You'll find a few, very few, you'll find a few *anti-Zionist* ones…but you'll be very hard to find any of the Peace Now, for example. . They don't want *one* Palestinian back whose land has been confiscated. The argument is, if you open the door an inch, it may be pushed wider. Well, if you have a state that has a law of return, as it's called in law for Jews, so that any Jew from anywhere, even one who converts as far away as Japan or somewhere, and converts through an Orthodox conversion can come to Israel under the law of return and be a citizen automatically simply by opting to be one, of course we're going to have Palestinians who either were ousted from their land, or their parents were ousted from their land, or their grandparents were ousted from their land, who say, Well, we should *also* have a right of return. You simply are hard-pressed to find Israeli Jews who will accept any iota of that.

SF: The Geneva Agreement does not even pay lip service to the right of return for Palestinian refugees.

NM: No, that's right. That's one of the great problems.

SF: What would you say—this is a related issue—about the myth of Barak's so-called generous offer... That Arafat refused.

NM: He didn't make an offer as it's been described. He didn't make an offer that Palestinians could have a state as they defined a state—independent sovereign state—with ninety-seven, ninety-five, ninety percent, eighty percent, even seventy percent or sixty percent of the West Bank. Not an independent sovereign state. They might have some limited amount of autonomous rule. That's not an independent sovereign state.

SF: The Israelis and the Americans said it was all Arafat's fault.

NM: That's always the case, that's always the case.

SF: Has it always been that way?

NM: It's always been that whenever anything goes wrong, or whenever there's isn't something that's been put forward that the Israelis have agreed to, it's always the Palestinians' fault. Really, it's always the Palestinians' fault.

SF: They talk as if Arafat has all the power…

NM: Well, it's not only…. Whether he has the power or not, it's always his fault. If the Israeli's don't get what they want, that's the fault of Arafat.

SF: Sharon doesn't seem too concerned about the security of the Israelis…

NM: Well he says he is. But he's not the only one. Don't forget that the general approach of…the way to handle Palestinians is to hit them and to beat them like dogs. Quote unquote. That comes from Labor as well as Likud. When the first Intifada broke out in 1987, in December of 1987, Yitzhak Rabin, who was Defense Minister (this was picked up even in the New York Times), he said, "That's right: the only way to handle Palestinians is to beat them like dogs." Well, the point is, when you beat them like dogs and you attack them, when you assassinate them, then you provoke more violence from them. So I'm saying that hasn't worked, that's a snowball going down the hill negatively. The Palestinians have their negative snowball going down the hill, too. They believe—they have come to believe—that by having (not all of them; some number, a minority) that by having suicide attacks and so on, that can scare the Israelis, and that will somehow drive their case home. Well that hasn't worked; that's made it all the worse for them. And they're in a worse condition now than they've been in since this conflict began.

SF: Do you have any thoughts on what Sharon is up to by pledging to withdraw from Gaza?

NM: Well, there are certain indications of this. He's already said that he wants to expand, in some way, settlements in the West Bank. He has said, and he is going to say to the president of the United States, that he wants the United States to pay a huge amount of money to take down the settlements in Gaza. And there's a lot of commentary within Israel that he wants to do that because he wants to expand the settlements in the West Bank. Well, the Gaza settlements first of all have been extremely costly to the Israeli government. They haven't really done any good. The Israelis say there are seventy-five hundred Jews in those settlements. There aren't five thousand. At any one time there may have been two or three thousand. Because some go there for two weeks and then leave and come back three months later for two more weeks. They go back to where they live. We have only a few Israeli Jews in Gaza in the settlements. We have two hundred and sixty-five thousand or two hundred and seventy or seventy-five thousand Jewish settlers in the West Bank. And it's in the West Bank that the population is divided by the settlements and so on. The settlements that are important are in the West Bank, not in Gaza, for the Israeli government.

SF: Do you see anything positive happening in the next five years in Israel?

NM: Five years is a little too long for me to look at or to consider. If I would say the next year, it's hard to think that it's going to get better in the next year. The hope is that *increasing* numbers of people on both sides, the two major parties...

SF: Not American Jews?

NM: No, forget Americans. Israeli Jews and Palestinians. Increasing numbers will decide and think. And we have had some increases. We've had some increases the other way, too. We've had some increases. People are saying, look, we don't want to fight and kill anymore. We don't want our children to be put in danger. So let's settle this....But I think that this conflict will be settled simply because the human condition, if it gets worse and worse, and more and more people are killed, I think that's going to convince, as I've said, increasing numbers of people that we'd better settle this. And in order to settle it, it's going to mean there will have to be, by definition, compromise on both sides.

SF: There won't be two states?

NM: I doubt it. I doubt it, although a great many other people think that it will be, I doubt it. I think that by far, the best way to approach, giving the greatest number of positive options, is a binational state.

SF: Do you think that neoconservative Jews in the Bush Administration as well as the Christian Zionists who are Bush's mass base wanted to invade Iraq to strengthen Israel in the Mideast region.

NM: In terms of Israel/Palestine, we really do not have any indications, except maybe in one respect, otherwise we don't have any indications that a Democratic Party administration would have been or would be better than a Republican Party administration. I mean, after all, we have had almost blind support of the state of Israel, of the positions of the government of the state of Israel. We've had blind support from the time that Israel was created, even just before, especially since 1967. This includes political support, military support, making Israel one of the great powers of the world militarily, and economic support. We got that consistently and increasingly in every administration, Democratic and Republican. The Democratic candidates for the presidency have been every much as pro-Israel to the extreme and blindly as have the Republican candidates, so you can't really say that there's a basis for that. On the other hand, it is true that Bush is probably influenced more by, as you said, Christian Zionists (I'm doing a book on that now; that's a little complicated), but they're very important, and he may very well be influenced more by them, which is a dangerous influence on him, than some others might be and maybe than a Democratic candidate would be. But that really is something that piles on, that you add on.

SF: So you don't anticipate the US at any point in next ten years pushing for negotiations.

NM: The only way that the United States can do what I think it has the potential to do as the superpower of the world and the backer of Israel—the only way the United States government can do anything is if the United States government says to Israel, "Look, you've got to do this, you've got to do that, we're not going to call the shots for you in terms of exactly how you negotiate, but you've got to really start negotiating or we're going to start withdrawing some of our support. That would probably have an effect. And we have one good example of that when we had the Madrid conference before Oslo. Far more important than Oslo, it was the former Bush, the father, who really said to the Israelis, Listen, you're going to sit down and negotiate realistically with the Palestinians, which means recognizing them, and Yitzhak Shamir, the prime minister, told his Likud party people, Look, I don't want to do it, I'm going there strictly screaming and yelling, but if the president of the United States tells me to do it, then I have to do it. Now you know, we could find out later that Bush and Shamir sat down and had a talk, and Shamir said, Look, the only way I can get this going is to be able to tell my people that you really forced me and I don't want to, and Bush may have said, Yeah, do it that way. I mean, maybe it was that, maybe it wasn't. But the point is, that opened the door to a possible process leading to resolution. If you open the door, people don't have to walk through. Unfortunately, no one walked through. Then we got Oslo, which was a terrible agreement because…

SF: Bush opened the door to Oslo?

NM: Well, Oslo itself set things back, because the Israelis then dictated something that was clearly a dictation by the oppressor upon the oppressed, and what made it worse was that the acting government of the oppressed, the Palestinian National Authority, accepted it, and Yassir Arafat became a partner for a while with Yitzhak Rabin and Shimon Peres. By the way, they weren't equal partners, even when they said…even when Rabin and Peres said, you're our partner, they clearly meant our junior partner, and you're our partner as long as you do what we want you to do. But if you don't do want we want you to do, and you don't accept what we want you to accept, you're not a partner anymore. So that partnership simply broke up by the time we come close to the end of the 90s.

SF: But you said Madrid opened up—-…

NM: Madrid opened…. Listen, before that, even though we had unofficially the Israeli government recognizing Palestinians politically, the Palestinian National Authority recognizing the Israeli government, we had them—we still, officially—we had this ridiculous situation of neither recognizing the other side politically, which was stupid. After all, here are the Palestinians, yelling about Israel oppressing them (and of course Israel did), saying, we don't recognize Israel as a state. What do you mean you don't recognize Israel as a state? They're not only a state, but it's a state that's oppressing you, and you say so. You don't have to say it's legitimate, but… Now, as they were saying that, the Israelis were saying, we don't recognize you politically. Golda Meir said in the early 70s that there's no such thing as Palestinians. Then we had people say, Well, yeah, there are Palestinians, but the PLO doesn't represent them. Well, as soon as we had the Madrid conference, and we had Israeli governmental representatives sitting down and beginning to negotiate (whether they got somewhere or not is another story) with political representatives of the Palestinians, no one had to say anything. There was recognition, and no one could ever go back on it. Because now, if you're negotiating with the other side, you're by definition politically recognizing them. So I'm saying, that was a step forward. It was amazing that it took us all the way from 67 to 92-93 for this…91-92, but the point is, I'm saying, that opened the door. They sat down and began to negotiate. Oslo almost shut the door again.

SF: Is there a greater danger of Bush invading Iran if he got in again?

NM: Well, I don't know that he will. He might. In my estimation, George

W. Bush is the worst president we've ever had in the whole history of the United States, and for people who know something about the history of the United States, that's really saying something.

SF: You have the neo-cons saying we want to topple the Arab governments and win World War IV—that's what Podoretz calls it, WWIV, the war against Islamicists...

NM: Well, I think that sometimes there may be exaggeration. See, I'm not even very happy just using terminology like conservatives or neoconservatives. That terminology is sometimes ambiguous and vague. If you name the people, then we know who we're talking about, if you name the people, you specify what...

SF: Perle, Wolfowitz—

NM: Yeah, I know that. But I mean, but they all are not quite the same, and I think they're all negative. I think these are about the worst advisors one could have. So I don't need to give terminology to them. As I've said, I think George W. is the worst president we've ever had, and potentially the most dangerous.

SF: When fid you first meet Israel Shahak?

NM: 72.

SF: When did you first become a supporter of Palestinian rights?

NM: 66-67.

SF: Was that a change?

NM: Well, yeah, I came out of a Zionist family. When I started college, I intended to... We lived in Iowa, but we have lots of relatives in Israel and some were key people in the government. And when I started college at the University of Iowa, my university, I intended to graduate, get my B.A., and do aliyah (go to Israel to live). And one day when I was a junior (in my third year), after I'd taken a couple of history courses, I asked myself a basic question: Could it be that in a conflict this big, this significant, that one side, mainly the Israeli Jews, are one hundred percent correct as I'd always been led to believe, and all the Arabs are one hundred percent wrong? If my father were alive and with us today, he would probably say that from his point of view, it was all downhill for me after I asked that basic question. And then I asked myself, how many Arabs—

SF: Did he get mad at you?

NM: Yeah, he did, after I started to write. But I asked myself, how many Arabs I knew in Ames, Iowa? We didn't have any Arabs in Ames, Iowa. I knew five Arabs, and they'd been introduced to me in Israel by my relatives whom I knew were the most chauvinistic Israeli Jews you could find, and I knew something about what an Uncle Tom meant in the United States, so I figured for sure those five were Uncle Toms, and then I thought, I'd better go out and meet some Arabs on my own who are not introduced to me by my relatives. So that's how I started. And I must say that at first I became antagonized by the situation and by the oppression of the

Palestinians, because it seemed to me that what were the true values of Judaism as I understood them, those true values of Judaism were…they held exactly opposite from what was being done by Jews to Palestinians. So then I moved from that, and I just moved right down the path and became…

SF: You grew up in a Reform—

NM: No, I grew up in an Orthodox Jewish family.

SF: But you were close to the anti-Zionist Reform Rabbi Elmer Berger

NM: Oh, yeah, Norton Mezvinsky was known by many people as the protégé of Elmer Berger. But we came out of totally different Jewish backgrounds.

SF: But Shahak was very down on Judaism altogether? So you disagreed?

NM: No, I know that. No, I don't disagree with him. I mean, he didn't think much about traditional Judaism. But that's how traditional Judaism became defined, especially as it was early laid down by the Talmudic rabbis. And Israel Shahak was a great follower of the prophets of prophetic Judaism. For him, the real…he was certainly someone who was influenced a great deal by the prophets. Now, I would say that in terms of a belief in God per se, he was an agnostic. I mean, I remember that we were in Prague together, and we were with a friend, and the friend asked him one at dinner, do you believe that God exists? And he thought for a moment and he gave a profound answer. He said that if God does exist, then I'm going to oppose God because of all the terrible things that have happened in this world, such as small babies dying of starvation, such as all the oppression. And if a god is an all-powerful and so on and allows that to happen or dictates it to happen, then I'm an opponent.

SF: He did not consider the possibility of a god who was not all powerful—because that's a very classical idea, that God is omnipotent—-

NM: Well, no, he never said that he did not, but that's the kind of answer he'd give. So Israel Shahak was a person with a philosophic mind, and he was a genius. The reason why Shahak and Chomsky … were the best of friends. One reason was that both of them…Chomsky's still alive, Shahak was…both of them were, and Chomsky still is in the genius category. By my definition, we don't have very many geniuses. If we had a lot of them, the term wouldn't mean anything. They were both in that category.

SF: Have you read Marc Ellis?

NM: I know Marc Ellis.

SF: He says that Chomsky and Shahak both were exemplifying the ancient Jewish tradition of refusing idolatry–the idolatry of the state of Israel.

NM: Well there's something to that.

SF: I guess Rabbi Berger on the other hand saw the Torah as based on a primitive understanding compared to the later prophets—

NM: Well, his answer also was…I mean there's a…he was a classical

Reformed Jew, and Reform Judaism does not accept what we can in Hebrew call Torah Minashimaim meaning every word of the Bible is the word of God. So the idea is that there are a lot of things written there that are probably not from God, and the idea is in Reform Judaism that it's the moral principles that are important. Of course, you have to go even further and say, well, it's what they consider to be the positive moral principles. There's a moral principle here too: go out and kill all of the men and children, but save some of the young women for yourself. That's right out of the Bible. Now we can say that's a moral principle, or we can say that's an immoral principle. The problem with Reformed Judaism, I think, it has a theology, but if you accept that theology, there's a basic question that then can be asked: Why remain a Jew? They say this is a universal religion with universal values. If it's universal values, then Jews should give them to the rest of the world. Well they've been given to the rest of the world. That's why we have over on the West Side, as you know, I think not far from where you live, we have the Ethical Cultural grouping. Well, they're mostly Jews who were Reformed Jews, and they somehow have gone right along the rational path and said, We don't have to remain Jews anymore to be ethical human beings. So I'm saying, that seems to me the theological problem for reformed Judaism. Why remain Jewish? I'm not saying that you should or shouldn't. I'm just saying that's a problem if you are still going to maintain being Jewish and having Judaism.

SF: Do you believe in God?

NM: Yeah, I believe in God, but it's…but I…it's a major…that's something that would take a lot of discussion. It's a major philosophical problem. We don't know anything more about God today than human being knew one thousand, two thousand, five thousand, or seven thousand years ago.

SF: Do you think God is the creator?

NM: I don't really know. And I'm…

SF: Either life is accidental or it's a product of will?

NM: No, there's another alternative. The other alternative is, we don't really know what happened. If we don't know what happened or will happen, and if we don't know ("we": the collective We) any more today, with all the advances of knowledge, if we don't know any more today about what happened, what is happening, and what will happen, then that's an answer. We don't know.

SF: Then you're an agnostic?

NM: I said that I believe there probably is, there may be some other power. I don't know for sure.

SF: Let me ask you a question about Reform Judaism. When was the original platform?

NM: Well, let's see, Bertrand Russell was 36 …. It was the Baltimore Platform in 1886.

SF: They rejected the idea of a messiah but they affirmed the idea of a messianic era?

NM: No, there was a mix in reformed Judaism about the messiah's coming. There was a growing feeling in Reform but that there was not really a coming of the messiah but of the messianic age.

SF: I read Petuchowski who believed in a messianic age. But he did not accept the Zionist idea that the foundation of the state of Israel put an end to the exile–in any genuine spiritual sense.

NM: Petuchowski... Yeah, that's right, but there are others. I mean, Petuchowski was one of the, I'd say, major Reform theologians in the United States in the 20th Century ... they are plenty. Well, in terms of what you're doing here, I think there's a good deal to study in terms of what the classical Reform position was in regard to Zionism and Jewish nationalism, and then the fact that it changed. It started to change in the 36... and then it changed in the forties. The question is, why did it change? Yeah, obviously the Holocaust had a great deal to do with it. I think that's an important consideration, and how logical was the change? If you just follow the logic of reformed Judaism, it's totally illogical and irrational.

SF: Once Reform Judaism repudiated the messianic ideal, did it not lose its raison d'etre?

NM: No, not necessarily, no. ... There are more ethical principles coming from God. No, you don't have to project a messianic outcome?

SF: Primarily, for a non-Orthodox it would be universalism of the prophets–the ideal of justice

NM: Yeah, well, we've got modern people, also. Certainly prophets were universalists.

SF: You admire them?

NM: Yeah, I do.

SF: Prophets like Isaiah, Jeremiah?

NM: Yeah, they talked about universal principles. I admire them.

SF: Unusual today among Jewish theologians?

NM: Well, I admire some modern theologians who say the same thing. I admired Elmer Berger, for example. He said that. I admired Israel Shahak. We have a lot of Israeli Jewish...and let me say something else about the prophets. You know all these people who say, if you're critical of Israel or if you're ever critical of Jews, you're an anti-Semite or a self-hating Jew, then from their point of view, it's only logical to conclude that all the prophets were self-hating Jews.

SF: Yeah, Yeshiyahu Liebowitz said that today they'd all be considered traitors.

NM: But of course, he was a great advocate of them, and he was one of the great thinkers of traditional Judaism.... I mean, then they would—what do you say about them? Then they would all be self-hating, anti-Semitic Jews.

SF: What do you think is the philosophical basis of Reform Judaism?

NM: Well, I'm saying that the logic of Reform Judaic theology... what's classic reformed Judaic theology: that logic could lead you to... say, Listen, these principles are known around the world—it doesn't mean everyone's following them, if they're known around the world—so, why be Jews anymore if it's just to propagate that. Why not be Univeralists? So the Ethical Cultural people say, we're Universalists, and why should we be parochial or limit ourselves to Jews and Judaism? Well, they had a pretty good argument.

SF: They still have a raison d'etre, considering the state of the world, but not a raison d'etre to remain Jewish?

NM: That's right, and in fact, that may dictate against it. That the exclusivity is a bad thing. That is, that you could argue that if you preach universalism, you're really preaching the opposite of exclusivity.

SF: Do you agree?

NM: Yes, I agree with that. Well, I agree with that to a certain extent. But I also agree that if you come...I also agree with Mordecai Kaplan, who I think is one of the—if not the—greatest American Jewish thinker of the twentieth century, who said, Listen, there are such things as religious civilization, and if you're born and raised in a certain grouping, that then, the universal values as you perceive them, not fully and totally but to some extent, are going to be within that context. Therefore, there's a Jewish religious civilization, there's a Christian religious civilization, there's an Islamic one. I'm not convinced of that necessarily, but I'm saying, he was also very logical. And in his classical work—he had a lot work —but in his classic work, Judaism as a Civilization, published in the early 1930s, he has a chapter there on reformed Judaism, on Orthodox Judaism, and another chapter on conservative Judaism, and to this day, seventy years later, those three chapters I think constitute the best three critiques of Orthodox, conservative, and reformed Judaism that we have.

SF: So there is a basis for Jewish culture?

NM: Yeah sure, just as there is for... Christian. But then, there's...complicated. The complexity is his view of God, which is very different from—But it's difficult, but he was a...And even on a practical basis, we have Jewish community centers in this country because of the theology of Mordecai Kaplan

SF: But he was a Zionist?

NM: Yeah he was a Zionist, but he was a Zionist of a certain kind. He came out of the Ahad Ha'am... but then he wrote some things that were more exclusivist than that.

SF: But the Reform movement originally said Jews were not a nation but purely a religious community?

NM: The Reformed movement said that Jews are not a nation, the Jews are not a people, there's no such thing as Jewish nationalism, that it's a false doctrine. Then they adopted Jewish nationalism—-they adopted Zionism. That's why I wrote that by the late 30s they had rejected their own philosophical basis! I mean, you can't have it both ways.

SF: Most Jews are fairly secular.

NM: That's right. It's also very rational and so on. And I can say from my point of view that there are a lot of attractive things in Reform Judaism. The problem, however, is those attractive things do not logically lead, it seems to me, to remaining a Jew. And that's why Israel and Zionism have become so important, I think, in Reform Judaism, because that somehow becomes a reason. And so if you say we need Israel because of the Holocaust and we adopt this absolute theory of anti-Semitism, then you have a reason for being a Jew. It's a negative reason. I think it's unwarranted, I don't think it really holds. So they've adopted that, which I don't agree with.

SF: So if Reform Judaism is faithful to the original principles then the main thing left to do is oppose Jewish people who are not holding to those principles, not setting an example–just supporting a Jewish state?

NM: That is correct, and that is why you have very few who are that way. That was actually…that was the raison d'etre of Elmer Berger, who I think was, in this way, the most profound Reform Jewish thinker that we've had in the twentieth century. In the United States.

SF: I think Marc Ellis has a similar perspective: The only way to fulfill the covenant in this era of Jewish empowerment is to remember the victims of Jewish power and to support the Palestinian people.

NM: Well, I don't disagree with that, but that's not all of it. Marc Ellis is a liberation theologian—that's part of liberation theology. I think that there is a good deal to that. But there's a good deal more to it.

SF: More in terms of?

NM: Well, there's a good deal more in terms of…it's not the only liberation theology. No, it's important to do that, and certainly in terms of the oppression. That definitely should cease. I mean, you don't oppress other people; that's not fulfilling the covenant. But of course, then, you know you have these other problems about people who say, Listen, the covenant—and if you believe Torah Minashemaim, every word of the Bible is the word of God…the Five Books of Moses is the word of God, and then you have these things about slaying men, women and children— if that's the word of God, if that's part of the covenant, should you be embracing that? Now Marc Ellis would say that it's not really part of the covenant. And you see, then you get the different definitions of what…. A covenant's a contract. So then there are the differing definitions of what are the terms of the contract.

SF: Do you consider yourself Jewish?

NM: Oh, yeah, I certainly consider myself Jewish. No question.

SF: But you're not sure about God?

NM: Well, no. I, well…there are some religious elements for me. I mean I would say that maybe you would say they might even be mystical. I mean I, for example, sometimes like to go to the synagogue. But I don't like a Reformed synagogue because it doesn't do anything for me. I grew up in very small, Orthodox synagogue where there wasn't much unity in the service, where people were doing things but, you know, everybody sort of had an individual relationship with God or the power…. That's the kind of synagogue I like. I like the synagogue where they sing with a niggun, where the tunes are as they are in the most Orthodox…. I grew up with that. That creates the atmosphere that I like. That atmosphere is sometimes important for me. So, now granted, I think it's because that's how I was raised. If I'd been raised in some other religion, there would probably be some things in the other religion that created the right atmosphere for me. So I don't rule religion out of it totally, it's just what we mean by religion. If we come to the serious questions, such as God, existence of God, belief in God, those are serious…. I don't expect that in the Orthodox synagogue I go to, unless I go to a synagogue where there are some great thinkers, that I'm going to get into a discussion that's going to do me much good in terms of coming to some theological resolution, but that's not why I would ever go to a synagogue.

SF: You keep the Sabbath?

NM: Once in a while, yes, sometimes I do. And for example, my mother and father are both dead, and it's important for me to go to an Orthodox synagogue when it comes time for the Yahrzeit or the mourning to say the mourning prayer for my parents. That's important to emotionally. I don't know…I can't say rationally what it means. I'm just saying that's important for me. And I'm not going to walk into a Reformed temple to do it. I'm going into the kind of synagogue that my father always went to. That only makes sense, right?... You know, the Carlebach schule on 79th Street? That's a place I love. I like to go there. Well I like to go there. I've gone there since, too. I like to go there. I like…. Now, do I believe in everything that a lot of those people believe in? The answer is no. But I also know that I don't have to. I know that the greatest of the Jewish philosophers, Maimonides said that a person who is a Jew…you can believe in Judaism and question anything. You can even question the existence of God and still be a person who believes in Judaism. If you *deny* the existence of God, then you're out of the realm, because…. So, I can go to any synagogue or anywhere else, and I can question anything. So that's the kind of a synagogue I like to go to.

SF: I liked Shlomo's music, Rabbi Shlomo Carlebach's songs—they were spiritually uplifting, moving. At best a mystical experience.

NM: That's right, he was terrific. Yeah, well, and they kept a lot of that, so I...that's the kind of synagogue I like to go to. I don't like the idea that the men and women are divided from one another, and you draw a curtain in the between them—but, you know....

SF: Why did you get involved opposing Israeli policies?

NM: As soon as I started to look more closely at the situation, and I saw that Jews who had been oppressed were now oppressing other people, that got me into it, and then, people sometimes ask me, why are you so much more concerned? I'm concerned about oppression anyway. They say, why are you so much *more* concerned about Israel than about other countries? My answer to that is simple. My answer is, there are only two governments in this world, two countries who presume to speak for me. One is the United States. Because I'm an American, it can speak for me in a sense, or it can presume to speak for me. The other is the state of Israel. It says it speaks for all the Jews in the world. I don't agree with that, but it says so. Therefore, if those two governments and countries say they speak for me, and they do things I don't like, then I feel more of an obligation to stand up in opposition, because if I don't, then it could be presumed that I'm in favor of it. Listen, Israel says we represent the Jews of the world, and we're doing this for and on behalf of the Jews of the world. I consider myself a Jew, and if I don't agree with that, I'd better speak up. At least I can say, when the Union of South Africa existed as oppressive to Blacks, the Union of South Africa didn't stand up and say, "We're the government speaking for Norton Mezvinsky." They didn't do that. The government of Israel says, If Norton Mezvinsky says he's a Jew, we're speaking for him. Or if the government of the United States says, we're speaking for Americans, it's speaking for me, so I have more of an obligation and responsibility to speak up against that.

SF: In what ways?

NM: Through my writing, and I've done a lot of human rights work, especially in regard to Israel. I was a U.S. representative for the Israeli League for Human and Civil Rights for twenty years. I've done a lot of political work as well.

SF: You've said that Zionism is inherently racist.

NM: Yeah, I said that... I'm opposed to the idea of a state that is an exclusivist state that by law and its public policy grants rights and privileges to one people not granted to anyone else. And Israel does that. There's no constitution. There's nothing above the law. Israel is an exclusivist state that grants rights and privileges to Jews not granted to non-Jews. I oppose that just as I oppose Saudi Arabia, which in its laws gives Muslims rights and privileges that non-Muslims don't have. I oppose that just as I opposed the Union of South Africa that gave whites rights and privileges that non-whites didn't have. I oppose that morally, I oppose that from any reasonable democratic perspective.

Chapter 4

Ora Wise, The Rabbi's Daughter

Ora Wise is a 23-year-old activist in Jews Against the Occupation.

SF: Anyway, so this is introduction: you're Ora and you're in Jews Against the Occupation. How long have you been in it?

OW: I've been involved with Jews Against the Occupation for the past year since I moved to New York. Before that, I was a founding member of the Ohio State Committee for Justice in Palestine.

SF: Yeah.

OW: And my process of political awakening about the Israel-Palestine conflict began when I was working with Rabbis for Human Rights in the West Bank.

SF: I heard you say some of the things you said in the JATO meeting and also on BAI, on BAI [WBAI, radio station in New York] that time. I think you said that your parents were very pro-Israel. Can you say that?

OW: Yeah, my father is a Conservative rabbi...

SF: They're very liberal on other issues.

OW: Yeah, my father is a Conservative rabbi and my mother is a Hebrew school teacher and they are both definitely very Zionist and they brought me up to feel... they brought me up to feel a stronger allegiance to the State of Israel than to the United States—even though we're American—and they brought me up to be very critical of US policy about the process of colonialism as it took place here in the Americas, but... unfortunately, like many other liberal or progressive American Jews, they did not extend their concept of social justice to include Palestinians.

SF: When you say they were critical of American colonialism, do you have anything specific in mind?

OW: Well, that they brought me up to be specifically very sensitive to and aware of the devastation that the white colonizers here in the Americas caused to the American Indians here. We... I was raised to be very educated about the history of the creation of the United States and that history, of course, is a history of land appropriation, of massacres of the indigenous population, and continues to be a story of marginalization of indigenous people who have survived this onslaught, and inequality in terms of their access to political representation, health care, education, housing. So...

SF: You're talking about American...

OW: I'm talking about American Indians...

SF: And blacks?

OW: ...and my parents raised me to be also very aware... very in touch with and educated by the Civil Rights Movement here in the US, the history of resistance to slavery here in the US. So my heroes were people from... you know, were American Indian, were African American freedom fighters. However...

SF: Like?

OW: Like Crazy Horse, or Chief Sitting Bull, or Ella Baker, Martin Luther King: all of the... you know... the more well-known, you know, peace activists from these different groups from...

SF: I never heard of Crazy Horse, but anyway go on.

OW: From within the US. However, when it came to Israel, I was only taught the very skewed Zionist version of the history of the creation of the State of Israel. When I first saw the conditions that Palestinians were living in under military occupation in the West Bank, I was shocked to discover that *my* state, the State of Israel, was similar to the United States, in that it is enacting injustices on, you know, the indigenous population. It is... I mean, as far as I could tell by the way that I was encouraged to feel and towards and think about Israel, it was shocking to find out that it had environmental problems.

SF: Uh-huh. How old were you...? I mean, when were you born...? When did you...?

OW: I was born in Jerusalem in 1981.

SF: Oh. So, I was gonna say...

OW: I'm very young.

SF: Yeah, you...

OW: Twenty-two.

SF: You're only twenty-two! I thought you were like mid-Twenties or something.

OW: No.

SF: Not that you look so old, but you seem pretty sophisticated. Oh. [Laughs] So... okay, I was wondering why you didn't mention Vietnam, but that was long past.

OW: Right, I mean...

SF: You mentioned colonialism, you mentioned American Indians, you didn't mention Vietnam.... How old is your father?

OW: My father is as old as the State of Israel. Which is fifty-four? Fifty-five.

SF: Oh, so he's only a few years older than me. So he went through... was he in American during the Vietnam War?

OW: Yeah, and he was very much opposed to it!

SF: Well, that's another... that's a not uncommon contradiction.

OW: Right, that's what *I'm* saying, that's it's very common for liberal or progressive or sometimes even radical American Jews to have a selective social justice conscience, where they... there is a tremendous disconnect between their critique of the rest of the world and their critique of Israel. And for my father, it definitely comes... and my mother it comes from this place of feeling vulnerable as Jews...which to me is really frustrating, because it's a... I feel like it's a perceived vulnerability that's based on, kind of like... tribal memory and is not reflective of the reality of most American Jews today, that their survival does *not* depend on the state of Israel, their survival, you know, is pretty much guaranteed in terms of most American Jews having gained a relative amount of power and privilege within this country.

SF: Yeah. Some critics of Israel have even said that Jews in the Diaspora are *endangered* by the actions of Israel, more than made safe by it.

OW: I would agree that the... that the actions of the State of Israel and the unconditional support that the Diaspora—the *organized* Diaspora Jewish community lends to Israel and its policies is *definitely* endangering Jewish communities throughout the world. One, it's endangering us in a number of ways. One is, that this insistence on unconditional tribal loyalty, this insistence on unconditional support of the State of Israel claiming to act in the name of all Jews, claiming to be the state of the Jewish people, not a state of its citizens...

SF: Yeah.

OW: ...this insistence by the organized Jewish community is basically insisting on a fascistic definition of Jewish identity and Jewish community, it's insisting that Zionism is the only way to be Jewish, that it's the only history, that it's the only narrative, which is simply not true. So basically we're endangering the Jewish community because we are destroying diversity and the continuity of Jewish critical thought and cultural development. And it also is *physically* endangering obviously, especially, *Israeli* Jews.

SF: Yeah.

OW: Contrary to Jewish popular belief, Israelis that are killed by terrorist attacks in the State of Israel are not being killed *just* because they're Jewish. They're being killed as a product of a brutal, vicious, controlling, oppressive military occupation that is destroying the lives of millions of Palestinians and is *deliberately* destroying Palestinians' ability to organize in *non-violent* ways, and democratic ways. As we know, Israel has a policy of targeted assassinations of Palestinian leaders and activists. As we know, Israel enacts... Israel declares twenty-four hour house arrest, curfew on towns and villages and refugee camps for days on end, which of course is designed to break the spirit of Palestinians and to prevent them from organizing themselves. So it is no surprise that then there are certain not very democratic, not very liberatory forms of resistance manifesting, and taking the lives of... civilians.

SF: You are talking about obviously, among other things, the suicide bombings...

OW: Right.

SF: I guess I should ask you questions about that, 'cause.

OW: Well, before we go on to that, I want to finish my thought, which is that one more way that unconditional support of Israel is endangering the Jewish communities throughout the world—not that that should be our main or our only motivation for supporting Palestinian struggling for liberation—is that it is increasing and *encouraging* anti-Semitism in the world. It is the Jewish... the organized Jewish community and the State of Israel that insists that there is *no* difference between the State of Israel and Jews.

SF: Yeah.

OW: And it is our responsibility as critical thinking people of conscience to insist on making that distinction that Israel or the State of Israel and the organized Jewish population refuses to make. Israel... we have to insist on making that distinction between a state and between Jews who are religiously or ethnically or culturally Jewish throughout the world.

SF: I was thinking... shortly after, about eight months afterwards September 11 there was this article in New York magazine that said Jews all over were afraid that the State of Israel would be destroyed and that *they* would be destroyed, that there would be another holocaust. Even among intellectually sophisticated—probably not sophisticated on the issue of Israel, since most people who read The New York Times don't know anything about Israel other than the bias of The Times—some of them were afraid, claimed to be afraid that there would be another Holocaust. That was when Edward Said said that American Jews were living in a delusional state. He's pointed out the way in America in which—probably in contrast to Israel where most intellectuals at least know that Palestinians exist, and in horrific conditions—but in America, as Said said, there's no understanding, even among quite sophisticated people—if the Palestinians exist *at all* in their minds, it's only as terrorists.

OW: Right and... So there's a number of things. One is that: we have to insist on identifying Zionism as one specific political ideology and project. At the time that Zionism started gaining momentum in Eastern Europe—and as we know, Zionism was born out of Romantic European nationalism, which gave birth to the concept of a pure nation for a pure land and, of course, the impurity was the Jews who were aliens, at that point in Europe, so Zionism has definitely taken its cue from anti-Semitic European nationalism. The difference now is that the Palestinians are the ones who are aliens, instead of the Jews. But at the time that... the Zionist Movement was gaining momentum in Europe, there were thousands and thousands... there were plenty of Jews suffering from the same oppression that Zionists were suffering from and looking to find answers in terms of how to resist, how to survive, how to be safe and self-determining—and these people came to radically different conclusions. Zionism was and is and always will be only one narrative available to Jews, just unfortunately way too many of us have chosen it. And... I would like to call people's attention to the Jewish Labor Bundists who opposed Zionism, because they opposed... they said that nationalism of this kind will... can *never* be the answer and that if we're truly concerned about... ending anti-Semitism, then we have to concern ourselves with fighting fascism and white supremacy. American Jews and Jews throughout the world need to stop treating anti-Semitism as a unique form of racial oppression, a unique phenomenon that only Jews experience. And if we're truly interested in fighting anti-Semitism, then we must align ourselves with other people struggling against fascism and white supremacy throughout the world. We have to stop seeing anti-Semitism as something separate from those things. And we also have to stop seeing ourselves as having only one option in terms of how to be self-determining or how to be safe. Zionists—the early Zionists whether willingly or... sometimes willingly, sometimes unwillingly—collaborated with the anti-Semitic European powers, by agreeing that Jews can never be safe, self-determining communities within the places that they lived. And of course as we know, that was not always the situation for Jews in other parts of the world, that... Particularly, I've read memoirs of *Indian* Jews, who said they didn't have that experience of anti-Semitism—

SF: I didn't know there *were* Indian Jews.

OW: Yes, there's plenty of Jews from India...

SF: Oh.

OW: Many of them have, you know, now ended up in Israel. There's still smaller communities in Bombay and Kochin... But that, you know I... that they *didn't* have that kind of experience, that Jews living in the West under Christian rule had a particularly harsh and isolating experience, and now within Israel and within the rest of the world, that experience, that European Jewish experience has been projected onto Jews throughout the world. And now in Israel, Iraqi Jews, Moroccan Jews, Yemenite Jews, Tunisian Jews are taught the Holocaust—the history of the Holocaust—as if that were *their* history. And in a way, oppression of anyone and tragedies like the Holocaust are *all* of our history. Just as the, you know, the brutal disappearances of people in Argentina or in Chile during the dictatorships, or just like slavery here in the United States, that *all* of those tragedies are part of *all* of our history. But... but at the same time, when Arab Jews in Israel are taught that the Holocaust is *their history*...?

SF: Wow.

OW: It's inaccurate. And so it's completely projecting European Jewish history onto them as if we have one homogenous population, which of course is what nationalism does. All nationalism, including Zionism... Zionism is based on the false premises that there is a homogenous population and one unified experience.

SF: Let's me just go back and clarify a couple of things—first of all, what you're saying, in the first part of the 20th Century, probably up until the *Nazi* Holocaust—Finkelstein always refers to it as the *Nazi* Holocaust.

OW: Right.... Which even the survivors of the Holocaust don't refer to it as "The Holocaust."...I'm under the impression that the word "Holocaust" comes from *Christian* terminology...

SF: Oh.

OW: ...meaning to burn up, and that even the Hebrew word "Hasholah."

SF: I didn't know that...

OW: the Hebrew word "Hasholah" was a Zionist invention... and that survivors of the Holocaust refer to it as the Yiddish word for "the catastrophe." Which is interesting, because that is the very word that Palestinians refer to the process of the creation of the State of Israel. They refer to it as "Al Naqba," which is "the catastrophe."

SF: Yeah. Uh, I didn't know that. Of course, the idea that the Holocaust was unique, that Holocaust ideology, as Norman Finkelstein says, was a post-1967 phenomenon after that war. I think that what you meant to say is that we have to stop thinking racial oppression is unique to Jews.

OW: What I was saying is that Jews when they talk about how awful anti-Semitism is, and how dangerous it is, they have all these separate organizations and of course they support the State of Israel, because they say we're still so vulnerable to anti-Semitism and we need a safe place... what I'm saying is whatever you call it—anti-Jewish sentiment or anti-Semitism, however you define it—it is *not* a unique phenomenon, it is yet one more form of racism and white supremacy... And that it's... if we're truly committed to that, we need to be fighting racism and white supremacy and fascism in *all* their forms.

SF: But to go back to the first part of your story, your father was a conservative Rabbi. You said he had a social justice orientation...

OW: Right. And he still does. I mean, he gives...

SF: Was he influenced by Abraham Heschel? Heschel was a prominent Jewish Conservative theologian who had a strong social justice orientation, and who marched with Martin Luther King in the civil rights movement.

OW: Yeah, *definitely* he references Heschel.

SF: Uh...

OW: He's not as critical as Heschel publicly, because I think my father has this feeling that he needs to be... you know, you have to present a united front.

SF: Critical? What do you mean?

OW: Well, Heschel made a number of statements critical of, Zionism...

SF: I haven't read one where he made any critical comments

OW: Really?

SF: You may know more than I do... He died in the early 70s, but he never criticized Israel publicly. Although if he was alive now I think—Buber was very critical of Israel.

OW: Well, Buber definitely. Maybe I'm mistaken. Well, Susannah Heschel definitely. [Heschel's daughter], a professor of Jewish studies, is critical.

SF: Yeah, she accepts the Tikkun position. She strongly opposes the Occupation but accepts the basic premises of Zionism.

OW: Right, right.

SF: Heschel died in the early '70s not long after the occupation began... I guess there were a lot of Jews who didn't become critical of Israel until after the occupation, or—

OW: The invasion? Well, until the invasion of Lebanon...

SF: Yes.

OW: It was really.... The invasion of Lebanon was really what started a solid, mass... more massive peace movement in Israel.

SF: I'm thinking of American Jewish leftists, someone like Michael Lerner, for example...

OW: Uh-hmm.

SF: Reading him you would think everything was fine...well the Palestinians didn't have it so good... but basically everything was fine up until 1967...

OW: Right.

SF: That is not uncommon in Israel among the Left either, isn't it?

OW: No, unfortunately, there are way too few people who will actually look at the roots of the problem and look at the process of colonialism and the process of colonization of Palestine... and look at the... and even beyond that look at, like, the ideological roots of Zionism...

SF: Uh-huh.

OW: And really if you look at the ideological roots of Zionism, the way that it's played out has been incredibly self-hating!

SF: Yeah. So you are twenty-two. When did you go to the West Bank and see the oppression of the Palestinians?

OW: When I was eighteen. I went to live in Jerusalem...

SF: Up until then... were you... did you...?

OW: I was Zionist by default. Like, I... I never learned anything different. I didn't go around identifying as Zionist...

SF: So you lived your entire eighteen years in Israel?

OW: No. I was born there, but I was just a baby when we came back to the US. And then I lived there when I was in third grade, and then I spent a summer there, and then went back when I graduated high school.

SF: Your father spent most of his life in America?

OW: Right. Both my parents are American, they were just living in Israel at different points. My father's family, though, actually were Ashkenazi Jews who lived in Palestine for generations and...

SF: Yeah.

OW: ...and came to the United States in the early 1900s.

SF: Hmm.

OW: There's actually a street named after my great-great-great grandfather in downtown Jerusalem. But what... I mean, I didn't identify as Zionist as I was growing up, because Zionism has been deliberately de-politicized for Jews. That you... you're not taught as growing up to know, learn about or identify Zionism as a political ideology, but it's just *the way you are*. Zionism and Jews...

SF: You mean, in Israel, not in America...

OW: In America... In America more so!

SF: Oh.

OW: Because you don't learn the history as much, and you... you don't learn about even the divisiveness within the Zionist Movement, in terms of Ahad Ha'am versus Hertzl—you just learn everybody was happy and, like, everybody agreed and, of course, the entire Jewish people and all of Jewish history has always been on this trajectory leading towards the Jewish state, the State of Israel, which is, of course, like, one very narrow, very biased interpretation of history. And so... but you're not politicized about it. You're not taught... being Zionist means you are subscribing to a certain political ideology. It's just being... there's no difference between Israel and Jews, no matter if you're an American Jew or an Australian Jew or an Iraqi Jew...

SF: Yeah.

OW: ...and that Zionism is inherent in Judaism, which is obviously false. That, you know, we're talking about a modern, political, *nationalist* movement that started in the late 1800s. And we're not... that's not make clear to us. So when I moved back to Jerusalem...

SF: How old were you then?

OW: I was eighteen...I graduated high school. I moved back to Jerusalem to... for half a year.

SF: By yourself? Not with your family?

OW: I moved by myself, but I moved in with a cousin.

SF: Oh.

OW: And I just wanted to... you know, I had been involved in kind of, Amnesty International and the Gay-Straight Alliance at my high school and things like that, and, you know...

SF: A high school in New York or...?

OW: No, in Ohio. Cincinnati.

SF: Oh.

OW: And so, I went... you know, so I was generally involved in... in social justice issues, as my parents raised me to be—they raised me to push the boundaries, of course they didn't push the boundaries far enough—but they raised me to realize that was a priority...

SF: Did you never talk about the Palestinians, or what?

OW: No, we just talked about Yulizika Aron ceremonies, then we talked about all the Israeli soldiers who had been killed, and we talked about...

SF: About the Israelis soldiers, but not a word mentioned about Palestinians?

OW: Right, except for just that they were... you know, like really, probably not even that they were Palestinians, we would talk about Arabs...

SF: Yeah, the Arabs... Let's see. This was in the 'Eighties then... 'Eighties and 'Nineties... they were still...So they were still referring to Palestinians generically as Arabs?

OW: Right.

SF: Uh-hmm.

OW: Well, I think it's still very painful for most American Jews to acknowledge Palestinians.

SF: Yeah, you know that famous quote of Golda Meir: "There are no Palestinians."

OW: Right. Jordan is Palestine...

SF: When I tell most Jews... first of all, there are some Jews I wouldn't even tell that I'm writing on this topic because they get too angry...

OW: Right.

SF: Some that seem a little more to the Left... even them, unless they're radicals...the first thing they say is, "The Arabs are pretty nasty people," or something like that...

OW: Absolutely! Racist!

SF: They don't mention Palestinians.

OW: Right.

SF: Yeah.

OW: Right, they obscure the origins of this conflict. And I think a lot of liberal Jews, still... a lot of liberal Jews really still have a lot of racist notions about Arabs in general and Palestinians specifically.... We say things like, you know... I mean, Israel's whole line is "shoot and cry," right? [A criticism of Zionist idea that Israeli soldiers are pained by the acts they "have" to commit to safeguard the occupation.] As well as.... This notion that these Palestinians are *forcing* us to kill them. These barbaric Palestinian families... or parents, are throwing their kids in front of our guns and they're sacrificing their lives, and you've heard the whole, you know, racist... not saying... if the Palestinians finally learn to love their kids...

SF: Golda Meir again...

OW: Right. She said if they... learn to love their kids as much as they hate us the problem would be solved... which is ridiculous! And so what we *should* be saying is, "What, you know, what is wrong with these barbaric Israeli parents who are sending their kids out...in uniforms at age seventeen with guns in their hands into stolen land, in the middle of hostile territory, to protect wingnuts who are living with swimming pools and palm trees and...?.... About one fifth of whom are members of Jewish fundamentalists groups who advocate ethnic cleansing of Eretz Israel, as defined in the Hebrew Testament. I mean, that's *barbaric*! Why not say it's—what we say about suicide bombings, it's so barbaric and uncivilized? So what? It's more civilized to be dropping bombs from an F-16 and not having to ever, like, be involved?

SF: Golda Meir... part of the myth of the "purity of arms"... do you know that saying? Golda Meir also said, "We can forgive them for killing our sons, but we can't forgive them for making us kill *their* sons."

OW: Right, it's...

SF: So there is this idea that the Israeli army... and you hear it repeated, even a Refusnik I heard speak who refused to serve in the Army anymore because he opposed the Occupation, said that he thinks that the Israeli Army is the best army...

OW: Right, because Jews are inherently moral.

SF: Because Jews are somehow more conscious.

OW: Because what they're saying is Jews are inherently more moral and noble than any other people on earth. It's another form of the Chosen People mentality. It's very disturbing.

SF: And that's common in Israel and among Jews, that the Israeli army has not committed any war crimes in the last...

OW: Right. We're a *moral army*.

SF: Let's see... What does your father think about your activities now?

OW: My father is deeply disturbed by the position that I take... He becomes more and more reactionary...

SF: Yeah.

OW: Feels more and more threatened. He refuses to have mutually respectful dialogue about these issues; he tells me that as long as I am not a Zionist, I have a problem with my Jewish identity; and does the classic Jewish anti-Palestinian thing of... whenever I'm... he reads about me in an article where I'm part of organizing efforts with Palestinians, he says I'm being *used*. So what's happening is... and other people within my Jewish community have said that about me as well. So here are people—my teachers, my parents, people that I went to camp—Jewish summer camp——with, all these people who know me very well—throughout my life they encouraged me to be and acknowledged me as an independent, strong-willed, intelligent, critical-thinking woman. And then when it comes to the position I take on Palestine, they all of a sudden are saying I'm being used and brainwashed. So all of a sudden they cease to see me as that intelligent, independent woman that they've recognized me as all my life.

SF: Is your mother like that, too?

OW: My mother is... slightly less reactionary, but still definitely the only information that she has ever exposed herself to or accepted about the history of the conflict has been complete, skewed Zionist propaganda.

SF: You can talk to them, you just can't discuss this issue?

OW: Right, and sometimes, things get pretty rough, like, they almost... I was involved in an action at the end of March after Rachel Corrie had been murdered by an Israeli soldier using a bulldozer. We did an action where we... I think, six... how many of us were there? Over sixteen of us locked ourselves together across Fifth Avenue in front of Bank Leumi, in order to call attention to the murder of Rachel Corrie and all Palestinians on such a regular basis. And I got arrested and when my father found out, he said that as long as I... My parents told me that they were going to withdraw all moral, psychological, financial, emotional support.

SF: Did they?

OW: No.

SF: My parents—Jewish parents—they make threats...

OW: Exactly. Right.

SF: On other issues...They made a lot of threats like that...But they never follow through on them. I didn't *know* whether they were going to on certain occasions but they didn't.

OW: Right, that was one of the situations where I didn't know what was gonna happen next.

SF: Yeah.

OW: My father said— It's so ironic, Passover is supposed to be the story of liberation and struggling against slavery and oppression...

SF: Yeah.

OW:...and he said that—the action happened right before Passover—and he said as long as I'm not a Zionist, I can't sit at his seder table.

SF: And what did he mean by Zionist... you know, specifically?

OW: That I believe that...

SF: I mean what did *he* mean by it?

OW:...a Jewish State must and should exist.

SF: And what about if you said to him: "I *am* a Zionist, but I oppose the occupation," as some people say?

OW: Then we'd probably have more civil discussions... But he would probably still call me misguided.

SF: So your position is... just briefly, when you say you're not a Zionist, you mean you're in favor of a secular state in Israel in which all people have equal rights. Is that what you mean by that?

OW: Right. I support Palestinian right to self-determination—and I support everybody's right to self-determination, including Jews—so there must be one single entity there that is democratic and truly representative.

SF: You support the two-state position as a transitional—it looks like *anything* slightly better looks like pie-in-the-sky now under Bush—do you support that, because of the international consensus?

OW: I think that... I support... I will follow the lead of my fellow Palestinian activists and intellectuals and the Palestinians living under occupation. I know right now, they are simply calling—so many Palestinians living under occupation are so miserable and just need to get the boot of the Israeli military off their neck—that they're simply calling for an end to the Occupation. And so I will follow the lead of Palestinians and their communities and... however, I believe that a two-state solution will never lead to true justice or equality.

SF: I've got to ask you some questions and we don't have a lot of time... you said that you were in the West Bank and what you saw there was horrifying—you saw Israel was emulating the same kind of things that America had done to the Indians, which you thought was a horrendous thing—that what you saw in the West Bank opened your eyes; I don't think you said what specifically what you saw in the West Bank, and after that I wanted to ask you what it means to be Jewish.

OW: Well, here's something very specific. That—when I was working with Rabbis for Human Rights, I... went to the West Bank and worked with... er, it's, actually it was in East Jerusalem...

SF: Uh-hmm.

OW: ... I was working with the Jahalin Bedouin, who, when the State of Israel created... was created had been living in the Negev, and then when the State of Israel was created, they fled to Jordan, and then in 1967, they came back under Israeli control when the occupation began.

SF: Uh-hmm.

OW: Then... ever since then they had been living in this valley peacefully to the east of Jerusalem, and right before I got there, they were being displaced with bulldozers and army trucks, in order to build yet another security road to Maale Adumim, which is the largest Jewish settlement in the West Bank. So they had been forcibly removed, their tents bulldozed, they... the people themselves forced onto buses, and they had now been forced to settle on a barren hill not 500 meters from Jerusalem's largest dump in Mezzherea...

SF: Uh-huh.

OW:...where this barren hill, they cannot graze their goats, which is their main source of livelihood and they actually just won... you know, before I had gotten there... an unprecedented court case in Israel winning some kind of building rights to build homes. But as you may know, the Bedouin are a semi-nomadic people...

SF: Uh-huh.

OW:...and being forced to become sedentary has created a lot of issues for them. So... this is what I see is walking down... one day walking down... so they have no schools... you know, they have no school system of their own, many of them were illiterate, because they had oral... they had *oral* education. But now they're being forced to attend Palestinian schools...

SF: How many people was this? Did you say?

OW: A couple of hundred? This is the Jahalin... is this tribe. And... and one day I was walking along this dusty path, they're living in... The Israeli government gave them shipping crates to live in as housing...

SF: Wow!

OW:...that fell apart in the winter and were boiling hot in the summer, and, as I said, they had nowhere to graze their goats, they had *nothing*, it was right next to Jerusalem's garbage dump. And I said: *this is a reservation*! And it was at that moment that it clicked for me—this was the indigenous population uprooted, physically and forcibly displaced and forced to live on the most barren, environmentally destroyed land with no kind of self-determination.

SF: Yeah.

OW: And so that's when I realized that this was the same process as what had happened in the Americas and what happened in Europe with the Gypsies and that this was something that I never knew my beloved country Israel, that I had been given such a glorified perception of... I never knew they were doing that.

SF: When you say "beloved," now, you're not being sarcastic...?

OW: I *am* being sarcastic!

SF: Did you grow up having that roseate a view of Israel?

OW: Yeah, that's what I've been saying to you! I grew up thinking Israelis' shit didn't stink.

SF: Uh-huh.

OW: I grew up encouraged to feel a stronger allegiance to Israel than to anything else in my life.

SF: Oh!

OW: I cried when the El-Al plane landed on the ground in Tel Aviv every time.

SF: Okay.... Let me just ask you this: do you believe in God? There are people who say they're Jewish that don't believe in God.

OW: Right. I believe that... I can't give a definite answer to whether I believe in God or not, but I will say that God is in my house and in my life; at all points, God is a part of my culture; it's a part of the language that I speak. There's a very thin line between... a not such a clear distinction between religion and culture in my life.

SF: Hmm. I'm just going to read you a quote from one of Ellis's book. I guess you would call him a Reform Jew, but he seems to be unusual. But he says that, "What the Nazis have not succeeded in accomplishing, undermining at a very fundamental level of what it means to be Jewish, we as Jews have embarked upon. I witnessed this in 1988 in the hospitals and the street of Israel-Palestine where Palestinians struggling to assert their own dignity were being systematically beaten, expelled and murdered by those who had suffered this indignity themselves less than fifty years earlier."

OW: Right... I would say that... not only... The Zionist project and the State of Israel has not only been self-hating in that it's been enacting, like Marc Ellis was saying, the same horrific, dehumanizing behavior against Palestinians that we experienced in different points in *our* history. But also that Arab Jews have been coerced into changing their names and dropping their native tongues, that Yiddish-speaking Jews were encouraged to get the ghetto out of themselves and become these new... you know, the Sabra, the hard, brave, like...

SF: The negation of the Diaspora? [This is a Zionist concept originating with early pre-World War II settlers: it meant that Jews living in "exile" had developed an abnormal psychology that had to be "negated" by Zionist experience.]

OW: Right, the negation of the Diaspora! And that is an incredibly destructive and self-hating process.

SF: Ellis believes that there is something essential about the Jewish tradition that is betrayed by the activities the Zionists took in Israel. You're saying the same thing, but I'm not sure what you think is being betrayed. Presumably, you think there is something about the heritage...

OW: I don't... I... I think it's ironic, but not surprising that here... communities that had been oppressed and marginalized and displaced and exiled and massacred throughout their history are now enacting those same things on another people. It certainly seems to be the pattern of the world in how it's organized. But I wouldn't say that... I don't think that Judaism or Jews are inherently moral or holy or that "Jews should know better than that," because Jews are not any more moral or noble than any other people on earth. But what I would say is that given what— what *is* being violated is the *diversity* of Jewish heritage. That there *isn't* one Jewish heritage; there *isn't* one Jewish history. That communities within Poland thrived or suffered in unique ways that produced unique cultural, religious, ethnic, familial *products,* rituals, histories, stories, languages. And so did the Jews in Portugal, so did the Jews in Mexico, so did the Jews in Iraq, in Iran, in Tunisia. That... and then of course... so that's one kind of Jewish diversity. Then, of course, intellectual and theological Jewish diversity... *political* Jewish diversity: communist, socialist, capitalist, anarchist! All of these different Jewish heritages are being negated and denied and systematically erased by having this one Zionist, hegemonic story.

SF: So in what sense do you consider yourself Jewish?

OW: In that my... I have... I am Jewish in that my community is Jewish, that—Many of my communities are Jewish—my Jews Against the Occupation community, the community that my family is a part of, which is my synagogue...

SF: Yeah.

OW:...and my extended Jewish family. And I'm Jewish culturally, and my religious upbringing is part of that.

SF: In what sense, culturally?

OW: Well, that... we act as if this is... that there is some very easy... easily distinguished place where religion begins and culture ends, or culture begins and religion ends. And like so many of Jewish religious rituals are part of my *cultural* heritage...

SF: For example?

OW: For example, having Shabbat dinner. So I might...

SF: You do that every week?

OW: Not every week, but I do it frequently, and I *always* do it when I go home to be with my family, that's a *cultural* ritual for me. So whether I believe in God or not, it's a part of the way that my world has been shaped. Or saying even, like, "Thank God" or "God willing"—that, you know, saying those in Yiddish and Hebrew which I've grown up doing. So part of the things that I... the way that I've been taught to express "thanks" has to do with religion, but it doesn't really when I'm saying it, that's just the language that I've been taught...

SF: Why is it important to retain all that?

OW: Because I think it's important to retain as much diversity, whether it be ecologically or culturally or racially, as possible.

SF: But you could be diverse in another way... you don't necessarily have to be Jewish.

OW: But I *am* Jewish, so I don't want another way...

SF: But what if you had kids and they converted to Christianity, for example? I'm just probing this question.

OW: I probably would feel very alienated from them!

SF: (Laughs.) So you would want to see Judaism continue in some form?

OW: When you're saying "Judaism," I would say Judaism, Jewishness, different Jewish...

SF: Oh!

OW:...political thought, or community... What I'm interested in... but, real quick, what I'm interested in is queering Jewish identity.

SF: Is what?

OW: Queering Jewish identity. Queer theory...

SF: Uh-huh.

OW: Queer theory articulates the concept that gender is performed, that sexuality is fluid, that... that this world is not as full of binaries and is not as polarized as we try to force it to be. And so I like to apply queer theory to everything else in my life and including Jewish identity stuff. That... I'm interested in queering Jewish identity. That's why I'm interested in Misrahi culture, Sephardic culture, these... or Ladino, the hybrid language of Spanish and Hebrew, and these... these different places in the world where everything is in-between, where it is not... it is not Arab versus Jew, it is not Jew for... versus Christian, it's not Israeli versus American, that these... that these are false binaries. And it's not *religion versus culture*.

SF: Uh-hmm.

OW: It's not politics versus religion, or politics versus culture. That those are false binaries, and that, like, being Jewish is something that is much more fluid and *performed* and chosen, in a way, than just whether you are religious or not religious, whether you're ethnic or...

SF: Okay, so converting to Christianity was one way in which one wasn't Jewish...and then you mentioned queering Jewish.

OW: I really have to go, Seth. I'm sorry. I have a conference call starting in a few minutes.

Chapter 5

Norman Finkelstein

Norman G. Finkelstein received his doctorate from the Department of Politics, Princeton University, for a thesis on the theory of Zionism. He is the author of four books: *Image and Reality of the Israel-Palestine Conflict* (Verso, 1995), *The Rise and Fall of Palestine* (University of Minnesota, 1996), with Ruth Bettina Birn, *A Nation on Trial: The Goldhagen Thesis and Historical Truth* (Henry Holt, 1998) and *The Holocaust Industry: Reflections on the Exploitation of Jewish Suffering* (Verso, 2000). His writings have appeared in journals such as the *London Review of Books*, *Index on Censorship*, *Journal of Palestine Studies*, *New Left Review*, *Middle East Report*, *Christian Science Monitor* and *Al Ahram Weekly*. Currently he teaches political science at DePaul University in Chicago.

Norman Finkelstein was born in Brooklyn, N.Y., in 1953. He is the son of Maryla Husyt Finkelstein, survivor of the Warsaw Ghetto, Maidanek concentration camp, and Zacharias Finkelstein, survivor of the Warsaw Ghetto, Auschwitz concentration camp. He dedicated his first book to his parents in which he wrote: *"May I never forgive or forget what was done to them."* His brothers Richard and Henry Finkelstein would like all visitors to his web site to know that the surviving family fully supports Norman's efforts to maintain the integrity of the history of the Nazi holocaust. May we never forgive or forget what was done. (This information is at Norman Finkelstein website at www. normanfinkelstein.com.)

NF: Well, first of all, I don't think the pre-'48 history of Israel is all that complicated and all that unknown. People understood it who were watching Israel, the Zionist movement, carve out a state in Palestine. They freely compared it to what the Americans settlers did in the United States and what they did in the West. The difference is that when they were compared it, for example, pre-World War II, they saw what the United States did as being a good thing, a positive thing.

SF: Well, who was saying that now?

NF: Well, you look at even people on the Left like Henry Wallace and others, they supported the Zionist enterprise, because they identified with what quote-unquote the Founding Fathers did in the United States. So it's not as if people didn't know that Israel was conquering a territory from the indigenous population, was dispossessing it and so forth, they were fully privy to it, but they thought that this was the march of progress and, you know, these... those who get in the way regrettably have to be cut down. Even if you look at, for example, the diaries of Victor Klemperer from World War II, he makes several allusions to what the Jews are doing in Palestine and he describes it as, quote, "a red Indian fate." He was very anti-Zionist...

SF: Who was he?

NF: Yeah, he was a German liberal, a German Jewish liberal... and he described it as the "red Indian fate." So whether looking at it from one direction, namely, the Indians deserved their fate, or their fate was an inexorable concomitant of the march of progress, or you thought the Indians *didn't* deserve their fate—people like Victor Klemperer in his diaries—people had a pretty clear idea of what was going on. During the 1950's, American Jews didn't really care very much about what was going on in Israel. I don't know the extent to which they completely identified with it. The first major work which introduced Israel to American Jews was Leon Uris' *Exodus.* ...I just re-read it just last week, and you know, what he has to say is pretty much what mainstream American Jewry still believes. Palestine was a wilderness, Arabs were backward, the Jews wanted to bring progress, the reactionary effendis and feudal landlords were afraid of the progress the Jews were bringing, so they stirred up the fanatical, ignorant, emotional masses—Arab masses—to resist Zionism... and that's basically the story, which is pretty much the same story today.

SF: So in that story the Arabs were not depicted as a kind of Hitler, Nazi-like...?

NF: Oh no, they were.

SF: I mean the Arab masses.

NF: No, the masses were depicted as duped, stupid... yeah, the masses are depicted as duped, ignorant, emotional, given to religious fanaticism, backward, and as he keeps saying, they're smelly and stinky and smelly and stinky, over and over again, he tells you that.

SF: Was there also a Biblical claim, that God gave the land to the Jews?

NF: No, I don't think that there is a strong sense of that...The Jews want to return to their homeland, of course, but when you have to deal with their claim, versus the rights of the indigenous population, he basically says: one, the place is empty; two, the place is backward; three, the indigenous population has done nothing to improve the place; four, they could go elsewhere—you know, just every standard argument you hear nowadays... not much different.

SF: In the Sternhell book I read he says that Jews were bringing technological progress to the Arab world, from which they would have profited.

NF: Well, there are a number of aspects to that. Number one, even if they were backward and they... even if they *were* backward, people have a right to be backward.

SF: Yeah.

NF: Number two: since the Zionist movement, as he acknowledges, never had any intention of living *with* the Arabs, rather intended to live at their expense,

I don't see how technological progress would have benefited them. And number three: you know, there's the argument that, okay, it wouldn't have benefited the indigenous population of Palestine, but it would have benefited the Arab world generally. That's a very specious argument, because the Zionist movement, from the very beginning, its biggest fear was a modernizing Arab world. So, whenever there were intimations that the Arab world might modernize—like, for example, under Nasser—they mobilized all of their force to crush any modernizing movement. So, whether they ever envisaged that the technological know-how was going to help the whole modern Arab world modernize, I very much doubt it.

SF: Now we're on the topic, Michael Lerner who is the editor of Tikkun— You've probably read Tikkun?

NF: No, I don't read it at all. I've no interest.

SF: Well he has a lot of influence among Jewish leftists who are at all critical of Israel, and of the Occupation. Well, one thing he says which I found particularly offensive, was that the Jews, the Jews who went over there, had a right to the land—He says that if we're socialists, we can criticize the Zionist movement before World War II from a socialist perspective. But anyone who buys private property can't blame the Jews pre-1948—they were buying the land and they had a right to buy the land and to do what they want with it, and it's anti-Semitic for anybody who buys private property themselves to criticize the Zionists for buying private property from the rich Arab landlords and then evicting the poor Arab tenants from the land, or the poor Arab laborers.

NF: Uh-hmm. Well, of course, you have the right to... you know, so long as everybody else has the right to purchase land, you have the right to purchase land, but of course, that's not the issue at all. The issue is: first of all, let's be clear about how much was purchased—about 6% of Palestine was purchased by the Zionist movement in 1948. A very small portion Most of the land was taken by the Zionists during the war. They ended up... the figures are, they purchased about one million dunams of land by the eve of the war; by the end of the war, they controlled 20 million dunams of land. So the percentage of land they controlled... of the total amount of land they controlled, they had only purchased the tiniest percentage. But, leaving that aside for a moment, the issue is *not* whether or not you have the right to purchase *land*, the issue is the purchase of the land with the intention of doing *what*? The purchase of the land was to establish a foothold from which... which would serve as a springboard for the conquest of all Palestine and the expulsion of the indigenous population. You can't separate the purchases of land from the purpose to which those purchases were supposed to be put. Secondly, on the land that they purchased, they enforced what back then was clearly referred to by many people as the apartheid principle of Hebrew-only labor.

SF: Yeah, that was my point.

NF: So it wasn't just purchasing land, it was purchasing land with the proviso of expelling all non-Jewish labor and employing exclusively Jewish labor, so it was purchase of land with a purpose... with a straight-out racist purpose. Both the means and the ends were objectionable. They purchased land and established the apartheid principle of Hebrew labor—a racially exclusivist principle—with the end of establishing a racially exclusivist state, and the purchase of the land was to serve as a springboard for creating a Jewish state.

SF: And you think that less than the immediate economic effects was... the inevitability of the clash between nationalisms.

NF: I don't think it's a clash between nationalisms. It *became* a clash between nationalisms *after* Israel established itself as a state. But originally it wasn't a clash between nationalisms at all, it was a displacement of the indigenous population by foreign settlers. That's not a clash between nationalisms.

SF: So it was then the actual material deprivation that the Arab settlers there were suffering?

NF: No. There's mixed... the balance sheet on whether the Arab population of Palestine suffered or benefited from the Zionist colonizers is... the balance sheet is unclear. There were large numbers who were thrown off the land, probably in the thousands, who lost their plots of land, but then there were also new opportunities that were opened up in the cities where they went to work, so it's a mixed picture.

SF: If the policy was Jewish-only labor how could the indigenous Arabs benefit from opportunities in the cities? Was it that the Jewish-only policy would take awhile before it became prevalent? Thus the benefits would be predictably ephemeral? I'm speculating here.

NF: The Jewish-only policy applied to "Jewish capital." But then there were the effects of the modernizing and expanding Jewish sector in Palestine, as well as job possibilities in the British-owned public sector, also growing, that was not Jewish-only. The issue was that the Arab population understood from the beginning what the goal of Zionism was—to establish a predominantly if not exclusively Jewish state—and by the 1930s, they were seeing the handwriting on the wall with the massive immigration of Jews and the purchases of land, not just from foreign, absentee landlords, but from Arabs in Palestine itself. And so they saw where things were headed, and it didn't take too much imagination to realize where they would end up.

SF: Lerner criticizes the indigenous Arabs for not distinguishing between the Zionists and the Orthodox Jews who were just there. You said they did in the beginning.

NF: Well, they did at the very beginning, but as Yehoshua Porath writes, it became inevitable at a certain point that if the Zionists claimed to speak for all Jews, if there are no articulate Jews dissenting from what the Zionists are doing, if the non-Zionist Jews become a more and more trivial minority within Palestine, it's inevitable, as Porath says, that they're going to assimilate all Jews to the Zionist Jews...

SF: Lerner also argues that the Palestinians should have sought a path of mutual cooperation with the Zionists,

NF: Anyhow, this is a kind of blaming the victim... The Zionist movement was clear about what it intended to do. And I don't think the burden should be on the Palestinians. The moral burden is on the Zionist movement to justify the creation of an overwhelmingly Jewish state in an area which is overwhelmingly non-Jewish.

SF: Let me go back to some personal background. Are you a tenured profession now?

NF: No, I just was offered a tenure track job at DePaul University in Chicago, but that will be several years down the pike.

SF: Obviously, you must have faced obstacles in academia that wouldn't have been there, if you had the same intellectual output with a different perspective.

NF: I think that's a fair inference. I'm not going to... I see no reason to engage in self-abnegation. I think I would have been successful. Reasonably successful.

SF: Here's a more personal question. You make frequent, if fleeting references to your parents in your book, I think, your scholarly books? To what degree did their experiences color their lives when you were growing up?

NF: Both my parents, they didn't trust anybody—except each other.

SF: And their children, too?

NF: I'm not so sure. I'm not so sure.

SF: Was that a difficult situation?

NF: Everybody has difficulties with their parents.

SF: Yeah, oh yeah.

NF: I see no reason why to... put myself in a second... separate category. My parents were not happy people, for sure.

SF: Apparently, I presume, you didn't, at least not totally, assimilate their pessimistic attitude?

NF: No. No, I didn't have their experience.

SF: But your mother gave lectures?

NF: Not too much. Once in a while, I took her to speak, and once in a while, she would attend a gathering and she would speak. She was a person of very strong opinions, and not easily repressed.

SF: When you speak of her... you speak of your her honorifically, not everybody speaks of their parents...

NF: I think it's... it's the... let's see... the honorable thing is to preserve what's best in your parents and to simply accept what's worst in them. In the case of my parents, what was good was damn good; what was bad was bad... like, with myself... but what was good was pretty impressive.

SF: What was that?

NF: First of all, they could never be bought.

SF: Yeah.

NF: My parents liked money, *very* much, but not *so much* that they would ever sell even so much as a period or a comma of their beliefs for money.

SF: To the Holocaust industry?

NF: To the Holocaust industry, to the United States, anything. They were deeply respectful of the sacrifices that the Soviet Union endured during World War II—they would never say anything against the Soviet Union publicly [during the Cold War]—and they would not go along with the exploitation of the Nazi holocaust to justify what Israel was doing and certainly not the crimes it was inflicting on the Palestinians. You could disagree with my parents, but they were certainly not—they were not to be bought.

SF: Were they in the Communist Party?

NF: Absolutely not. They had no interest in things like that. They saw the world strictly through the prism of the Nazi holocaust.

SF: Really?

NF: The Soviet Union defeated Nazism: the Soviet Union was a friend. The Western powers in their view were... built up Hitler, and then he turned on them, but they were pretty conventional in their views. They saw the Soviet Union as— what, in fact, was the case—the main... not the main but the overwhelming force defeating the Nazis. And for that reason, they were staunch defenders of the Soviet Union.

SF: Were they intellectuals... or professionals?

NF: My mother was very smart. She attended Warsaw University before the war. She studied mathematics; she had a classical education. She knew Latin; she knew languages; she knew music—she didn't know art—she knew music... she was very well educated. My dad was a... went to a technical school, he was good at what he did.

SF: What did he do?

NF: He was an engineer.

SF: So he wasn't so cultural, then?

NF: No... he wasn't.

SF: But your mother was?

NF: Very!

SF: Were they Jewish liberals?

NF: (Pause) They were Jewish survivors of the Nazi concentration camps. That was their identity. And everything they did was seen through that prism, and everything they thought.

SF: Yeah.

NF: I don't know if you could call them a liberal. They hated... basically, they didn't trust anybody. They hated the United States. They hated the capitalist system. They liked the Soviet Union. They were profoundly anti-racist, antiwar. But none of that had much to do with any ideology. It had to do with what they endured.

SF: I never had a conversation with Holocaust survivors...

NF: Uh-hmm.

SF: You think they contributed in some way to your activism. Most of your activism is on behalf of Palestinians?

NF: Now it is.

SF: What was it?

NF: I only got involved with Palestinians in 1982, after the Israeli invasion of Lebanon. Before that, I was mostly involved in antiwar and issues relating to race in the United States.

SF: Yeah. So you must have had, as an activist, some sense that humanity is at least not incorrigible, is perfectible?

NF: No, I don't think—most of humanity doesn't need to be perfected. Most of humanity is just fine as it is. Certainly, with greater opportunities, I suspect more would be developing—I can't say for certain and I don't want to pass any value judgments—but I suspect more would be developing the intellectual and cultural sides of their human capacities. But most of humanity I don't find particularly... I don't see any reason to *want* to perfect; morally, they seem to be pretty decent. There are people who have power, and the more power you have, the more corrupt you become.

SF: Yeah.

NF: And I don't think they're perfectible.

SF: When you became an activist what did or do you see as the recipe for changing that?

NF: I don't think in big... I don't think in cosmic terms, anymore. You fight the little struggles and if you can make a small contribution to making a few people suffer a little less each day, then you're satisfied.

SF: On the other hand it seems like you don't adopt a *tragic* view of history.

NF: No, I think tragic views are mostly a product of age.

SF: (Laughs)

NF: I do! The older you get, the more you become... you know, you become sensitive to your mortality and wonder about the pointless—the point or pointlessness—of everything you've done. But, no, I don't... see any grounds. There are certainly grounds for despair, but tragic, no.

SF: You don't see yourself as a postmodernist...?

NF: I don't know what any of those terms mean. .... I just think that whole trend is a pointless, meaningless fad.

SF: Okay, I was just wondering how much your own sensibility has been formed by that, but apparently it hasn't?

NF: I would say... I can give you an exact calculation. This is one of the few places where a mathematical precision is possible—zero.

SF: I wanted to read a quote from Marc Ellis the Jewish theologian and see if you identify with it at all and I'm sure you'd want to qualify it... Anyway, he says: "Those who carry the memory of Jewish suffering and act in solidarity with the Palestinian people, may ultimately decide the future of the covenant"—which of course you wouldn't be interested in—"and the Jewish people."

NF: I have no interest in covenants; I don't know who the Jewish people are. These are all metaphysical, extraneous terms for me.

SF: What about carrying the memory of Jewish suffering?

NF: I *don't* carry the memory of Jewish suffering! I carry the memory of my late parents' suffering. They happen to have been Jewish. I don't carry *any* memory of Jewish suffering. I care about the suffering of all of humanity, but I *am* the son of my parents, and so of course I was very sensitive to their particular suffering. But beyond being the son of my parents, the suffering of everybody touches me equally. Period.

SF: How do you explain then the passage in The Rise and Fall of Palestine when you express indignation and regret that as a result of the Zionist atrocities, "Jewish people's name will now be inextricably linked not just with Marx and Menuhin, but also with Sharon and Shamir?" Does that not imply a sense that you felt that there had something positive about the Jewish tradition that was worth preserving and was betrayed by Israel?

NF: Tough question for me to answer, because I'm not always consistent on this. Let's just say that it's nice to know there were decent Jews in history to balance out the nasty bunch that has now taken center stage.

SF: You said that you didn't want—by the way, I may refer to—I noticed when I read your book that you never refer to "the Holocaust," but always to the *Nazi* holocaust.

NF: Correct.

SF:I may slip and refer to it just as the Holocaust.

NF: (Laughs) I'll let you go. I'll give you a pass on that.

SF: I guess... how many were killed in the Armenian holocaust?

NF: I think the estimate's about a million.

SF: And there were... what did you say? A half a million Gypsies.

NF: Nobody knows. Nobody knows, because first of all, demographics even nowadays are very tough. Nobody even knows if New York City has seven or nine million people

SF: I think you said somewhere that the numbers that were killed...as a percentage were equivalent to that of the Jews

NF: I would change that now. . First of all, nobody knows what the *total* figure was. . Probably about hundred or three hundred thousand Gypsies were killed. But we really don't know.

SF: Gypsies, they were the invisible victims, obviously...

NF: Oh, I think nowadays, there are a lot of invisible victims. I mean, twenty to thirty million Russians were killed, that's no picnic! Those are invisible victims. Three million non-Jewish Poles were killed...

SF: They were mostly soldiers...

NF: Yeah, but, you know, a lot of them... they estimate about three and a half million were starved to death in the concentration camps. That's not a small number.

SF: Do you think this eclipse of the non-Jewish victims is a product of the Holocaust industry?

NF: Yes, it's a mixed bag. Part of the eclipse was because during the Cold War they didn't want to acknowledge who defeated the Nazis. Number two, they wanted to put forth this Hollywood version that it was the United States that won World War II. And then part of it, of course, was the Holocaust industry.

SF: The Holocaust industry wanted to create the impression, as you wrote in your book, that only Jews were exterminated, that the Holocaust belonged to the Jews. That's why the Russians... the Gypsies were invisible Holocaust victims.

NF: Oh, the Gypsies... nobody cared about the Gypsies. And still, nobody cares about them.

SF: And the mental patients?

NF: They were the first victims of the Nazis.

SF: Actually German psychologists killed them on their own initiative at first without even seeking authorization from Hitler. ...You said just now that you don't carry the memory of Jewish suffering, but you did say that you cared about preserving the memory of your parents?

NF: Of course. I do.

SF: And you wrote that catchy phrase that you didn't want their martyrdom to be reduced to a stature of a Monte Carlo casino

NF: Right now, the Nazi Holocaust is an extortion racket. Or it had been during the Clinton years. That's pretty much over now. But roughly you could say from the early 1990s through 2000, it was simply a bludgeon to extort money from Europe. It was a... there was a blackmail racket. I think that's pretty disgusting.

SF: Yeah.

NF: For sure. And before that basically from the 1980's, or mid-'Seventies, it's basically as a blackmail weapon to bludgeon the critics of Israel into silence. So it had very... so it had very little to do with the actual suffering of the Jews themselves.

SF: So to ask a kind of a metaphysical question, what do you think is the potential function of memory...?

NF: I don't think anybody has the right to define what's the right lesson of the Nazi Holocaust. You know, some people walked out saying, "Nobody gave a darn about us, so we won't give a darn about anybody"—that's the lesson they learned—that now Jews have to look after each other. Other people walked out saying precisely because nobody gave a darn about us, we have to care about others. We have to... because it was wrong that nobody cared about us, then we have an obligation to care about others. So that's the lesson my parents imparted.... I have my own view of what remembrance should be, based on lessons they imparted to me, but I'm not going to claim it's the only lesson.

SF: What would it be then?

NF: The lesson they taught me was: Let nobody else suffer the way we did.

SF: And that's the importance of remembrance?

NF: Oh, I think independently of the lesson you learn from it, those who died... those who suffered such an atrocious experience deserves to be remembered. It's a... it's another milestone in the annals of man's inhumanity to man which ought to be remembered.

SF: Yeah. It's unusual that your parents had sympathy for the Palestinians, isn't it?

NF: No, I remember the first Palestinian I met in graduate school—his name was Muhsin Yusef and he said, "I can't believe after what your parents went through, that you feel sympathy for me." And I said to him, "That's funny, because I saw it always just the reverse, I can't believe after everything they went through, that I *wouldn't* feel sympathy for Palestinians." That's how my parents thought... there was nothing unusual about it.

SF: Don't you think that's... obviously that sensitivity you don't find among American—

NF: Most American Jews are out of touch.

SF: Don't you think they've been corrupted over the past thirty or forty years? I mean the elites and Jewish leaders

NF: American Jewish leaders, political and religious, are not corrupted, they're *intoxicated* by all their power, all their wealth and all their success. The power, the wealth and success has gone to their heads. They've put on this mantle of the Nazi Holocaust to immunize themselves from any criticism—the moment any criticism is ever voiced, they immediately smack down the charge of anti-

Semitism—and so it's a very lethal brew, and the result is a very ugly perception of American Jewry in other parts of the world.

SF: At least in the 'Thirties, and probably the 'Fifties, too, I read that half the people in the Communist Party were Jews? Two thirds of the whites who were Freedom Fighters in the South during the civil rights era were Jewish. You criticize many Jewish liberals for copping out on liberalism when it comes to Israel, of adopting a double standard—of justifying the merger of religion and state when it comes to Israel. .

NF: It's not possible to reconcile classical liberal values with the Zionist idea: the former starts from the concept of citizenship, the latter starts from the concept of a "people," outright rejecting the concept of citizenship—that's a pretty stark difference. Or take, for example, that liberal Jewish organizations like the ADL are always fighting against the introduction of any Christian symbols, every a Santa or Rudolph the Red-Nosed, in the classroom. Yet, when it comes to Israel, they uphold a state legally defined as Jewish and replete with Jewish symbols as well as discriminatory laws privileging Jews

SF: You said your mother wasn't all that unusual about the Palestinians...

NF: I said, for *them*—my mother and my father—it was *unthinkable* to feel otherwise.

SF: But they weren't typical of Holocaust survivors, were they?

NF: I don't know what Holocaust... ah look, when I was growing up, my parents' circle of friends consisted of those who they knew before the war, or those who they met in the DP camps. Of that whole circle—which probably was around, we can estimate, twenty to thirty people—the only ones who were actual survivors of the camps were my parents. The others either had lived with Christian families underground, or had overwhelmingly lived in the Soviet Union during the war. I don't know where all these Holocaust survivors came from. Raul Hilburg estimates it was under 100,000 in May, 1945, so you can guess that, by the 1950s and 'Sixties, where I'm becoming fairly conscious as a young man, there's probably down to about 50,000 worldwide. Of those 50,000, about half are in the United States; half are in Israel. So you're talking about 25,000 in the whole of the United States. And I didn't know many. I knew my parents. I knew a few others.

SF: How do you explain your nemesis took the attitude that he took?

NF: Which nemesis?

SF: Elie Wiesel.

Finkelstein on Elie Wiesel, The Holocaust Industry

"By conferring total blamelessness on Jews, the Holocaust industry immunizes Israel and American Jewry from legitimate censure. Arab hostility,

African-American hostility: they are 'fundamentally not a response to any objective evaluation of Jewish action.' (Goldhagen)."

(Finkelstein, 2000, p.53).

"Wiesel's prominence is a function of his ideological utility. Uniqueness of Jewish suffering/uniqueness of the Jews, ever-guilty Gentiles/ever innocent Jews, unconditional defense of Israel/unconditional defense of Jewish interests: Elie Wiesel *is* The Holocaust"

(Finkelstein, 2000, pp. 54-5).

* * *

NF: Look, Wiesel comes from an obscure Rumanian shetl and he preserves the mentality of an obscure Rumanian shtetl (Jewish small village). And he sort of like... he sort of created this "Fiddler on the Roof" image of the shtetl, which Jews love to listen to, so he goes to the 92nd Street Y and he tells his stories about the shtetl. But his mentality is the shtetl... he has a shtetl mentality.

SF: Even among young, middle-class Jews, maybe liberal on other issues, they're more likely to act like Wiesel in terms of *any* criticism of Israel...

NF: Right. Because there's a repellent chauvinism among many Jews. It's the view that we do no wrong, and if anyone criticizes us, it's not because of anything we've done, but because they're anti-Semites. And they're anti-Semites, fundamentally, because they envy all of our successes, and envy the fact that we're better. And that's how they reason.

SF: Everything that happened up through the 1948 so-called war of independence seemed to follow inexorably from the premises of race nationalism, of Zionism. Zionism, political zionism, requires the expulsion—

NF: Ah look, nothing follows inexorably, because in history, you don't always get what you want, as Mick Jagger would say. The Zionist Movement was very good at mobilizing its material and human resources at crucial junctures and making things *happen*, in accordance with their aspirations and goals. So you can't say anything inexorably happens in history. There are crucial junctures in the history of Zionism—the Balfour Declaration, the 1947 partition resolution—those junctures, they did not inexorably happen. The Zionist Movement made them happen.

SF: Yeah, uh-hmm. But...

NF: But apart from that, I think it's true to say that, as many historians now freely acknowledge, a conflict was built into the premise of Zionism. A conflict with the indigenous population was built into the premises of Zionism, *and* that the only way to resolve that conflict was, as Benny Morris puts it, between expulsion and apartheid. Those were the only options available to the Zionists given their premises, either expel the Palestinians or subject them to apartheid.

SF: A mythology was created around people like Ben-Gurion as if he was a great humanitarian which was far from the truth. But despite his racism and his ruthlessness and that of his fellow Zionists—was there anything that could have happened differently if there had been a large Palestinian movement that sought some kind of compromise—

NF: Yeah, there were... Look, there were the Hashomer Hatza'ir which was the mainstay of the kibbutz movement, was for binationalism. There were minorities—you know, they weren't significant—but there were minorities who recognized the injustice of Zion—of political Zionism. Whether they had any chance to carry the day... probably not. I don't think so.

> (I interviewed Norman Finkelstein several months before I interviewed Noam Chomsky (see above). In the meantime I had read Aharon Cohen's book on bi-nationalism and letters by Judah Magnes and concluded, as I remarked to Chomsky, that the bi-nationalist movement probably would have succeeded in gaining the allegiance of the Palestinians had the efforts of the movement not been sabotaged by Ben-Gurion and his circle. Chomsky takes a more agnostic position).

* * *

SF: When people say that if the Palestinians, if the indigenous people had been more compromising, more willing, than people like Ben-Gurion would have taken a softer line.

NF: No. I don't think... I think it's silly to try to shift the burden of responsibility to Palestinians. The Zionist Movement came with an aim, and the aim was plainly in conflict with the rights of the indigenous population. There were *some* dissenters within the Zionist Movement. Even the dissenters never believed that the real responsibility rested on the indigenous population to be more flexible. I mean, I never read that. I've read the dissenters. Some of them I like. I thought Judah Magnus was a decent guy.

SF: Yeah.

NF: But, you know, there were decent people dissenting, and Hashomer Hatza'ir seemed okay. You have to remember that this is the 1930s. Everybody was... carrying the racist baggage at that time. Even the best, you know. They come, what do they see? They see primitive Arabs. And even those who wanted to live with them, didn't think of them as much more than... you know, the way we picture noble savages.

SF: The old story about the '48 war is that the Arabs wanted to drive Israel into the sea. They say that the Palestinians, in compliance with the calls of their leaders, left their homeland. And that's one of the myths I think you demolish.

NF: There's a huge body of scholarly literature now, which debunks, demolishes that myth. Though the older historians say that never was even a myth! They claim it was already well known that the Arab armies weren't really... didn't really numerically overwhelm the Zionist armies. Actually, I can give you... do I have? Where did I put that article?... I have the article somewhere here I can give you by an older historian who claims most of the myths weren't even myths. That it was well known from early on that the Zionist armies were numerically, basically, on par with the invading Arab armies. The whole talk about the expulsion... it was already known in the early Sixties that there were no Arab radio broadcasts [calling on the Palestinians to leave their villages]. Erskine Childers and Walid Khalid demonstrated that definitely. But plainly, the so-called "new historians" have pretty much demolished those ideas.

SF: But the contention that the Palestinians left their villages during the war because Arab leaders told them to was the myth that was accepted by...it was the main part of Israeli propaganda.

NF: Yeah... and still is, it still is.

SF: And American Jewish propaganda for Israel—they still say it?

NF: Yeah. Well, American Jewish academics live on Mars... you know.

SF: The updated version is that there was a security threat to Israel. Its existence was endangered but of course what really happened in '48, there was a determination on the part of Israel *not* to abide by the United Nations partition which they had formally acceded to—at least in part... So as you and Masalha show Ben-Gurion and all the Labor Zionists who founded Israel had long privately been in favor of ethnic cleansing as a means of creating a pure Jewish-state and when the war came around they saw it not as a misfortune but as an opportunity. There's a good quote—I probably found it in one of your books from Ben-Gurion—"The war will give us the land. The concept of "ours" and "not ours" are only concepts for peacetime, and during war they lose all meaning."

NF: Uh-hmm.

SF: And then somewhere else it describes Ben-Gurion standing on the battlefield watching all these Arab villagers fleeing from the Israeli Army in terror, and abandoning their homes, and Ben-Gurion says, "What a beautiful sight!" Could you say something brief about the war?... You quote the head of the Israeli Army archives who said "Not a single village did they go where they didn't rape women and murder them afterwards."

NF: Well, first of all, the 1948 war was an opportunity to execute plans which had long been in the... not so much plans that had been long in the making, but concepts which had long sustained the movement. The concept of transfer and the

Zionist... the 1948 war opened up the opportunity, created the opportunity to execute the transfer. So in that respect what happened in 1948 wasn't serendipitous. It was part of a long-term, enduring concept in Zionist thinking. The murder, killing, and so forth... that's what it takes to expel a population. And the Palestinians were an overwhelmingly rural population and they were deeply rooted in the land, and to get them to leave, that's what you had to do, especially in the second half of the war, when Palestinians realized that those who left weren't coming back. And so in the last months of the war, especially, like, October and November, it became a very ugly, bloody and brutal affair.

SF: There a account from a soldier who was at one of the massacres by the Israelis and he talks about normal people—that is one of the themes in your book on Goldhagen—ordinary people being turned into "base murderers." He says that was pretty much the norm during the 1948 war

NF: I don't know if it was the norm, but it certainly was pervasive. As I say, it's revolting, but it's not shocking.

The Conduct of the Israeli Army and the Dueima Massacre

Former Director of the Israel army archives, 1992:

> "[I]n almost every Arab village occupied by us during the War of Independence, acts were committed which are defined as war crimes, such as murders, massacres and rapes" (cited in Finkelstein, 1995, p110).

Aharon Zizling, Minister of Agriculture in Prime Minister David Ben-Gurion's Cabinet, November 1948:

> "I couldn't sleep at night. Jews too have committed Nazi acts" (cited in Ibid, p.77).

Yosef Nahmani, land-purchasing agent for the Jewish National Fund (land acquisition arm of World Zionist Organization):

> "Where did they come by such a measure of cruelty, like Nazis? They [i.e. the Jewish troops] had learnt from them [i.e. the Nazis]" (cited in Ibid, p77),

Meir Ya'ari, Mapam [Socialist] Party—co-leader:

> "[T]he youth we nurtured in the Palmah [elite strike force], including kibbutz members, have [occasionally] turned Arabs into slaves; they shoot defenseless Arab men and children, not in battle.... Is it permissible to kill prisoners of war? I hoped there would be some who would rebel and disobey

[orders] to kill and would stand trial—and not one appeared...What did we labor for?" (Ibid, p. 193).

Yosef Lamm. Member of Knesset (Israeli parliament):

> None of us behaved during the war in a way we might have expected the Jewish people to behave, either with regard to property or human life, and we should all be ashamed" (cited in Ellis, 1999, p.32).

A soldier who was an eyewitness to the massacre of the villagers of Dueima by the official Israeli army, the Haganah, in October, 1948:

> "[T]hey killed between 80 to 10 Arab men, women and children. To kill the children the soldiers fractured their heads with sticks. There was not one home without corpses. The men and women of the villages were pushed into houses without food or water. Then the saboteurs came to dynamite them.
>
> " One commander ordered a soldier to put two old women in a certain house...and to blow up the house with them. The soldier refused.... The commander then ordered his men to put in the old woman and the evil deed was done. Another soldier boasted that he had raped a woman and then shot her. Another Arab woman with her newborn baby was made to clean the place for a couple of days, and then they shot her and the baby. Educated and well-mannered commanders who were considered good guys...became base murderers, and this not in the storm of battle, but as a method of expulsion and extermination. The fewer the Arabs, the better...This principle is the political motor for the expulsions and the atrocities." (This account is cited with slightly different translations in both Finkelstein, 1995 and Schoenman, 1988. Originally published in Israeli newspaper, Davar, June 9, 1979.)

* * *

SF: The conduct of the Israeli military, and the soldiers who were following orders, doesn't that, as you argue, among other things, debunk the Israeli idea of a purity of arms...

NF: Yeah, the Israelis always claim they hold themselves to a higher moral standard. There was a period where they did engage in what was called "purity of arms" but that was basically for tactical reasons, because they didn't want the British to leave Palestine—they didn't want the mandate to end—and they knew that if they started using weaponry as well, the British would use it as a pretext to say, "well, they're all firing on each other, then we're just leaving." So, for some years—like 1936, '37—there was some application of this purity of arms. By 1938 and '39, they themselves were... I don't mean what were called the Zionist revisionists who were engaging in terrorism throughout the period '36 to '39, but even as mainstream Zionists were going on with this guy named Ord Wingate; they formed these special commando units, went to Palestinian villages and were killing them with certain indiscriminateness. And by '48, it was ugly, and after '48, if you read books like Benny Morris' *Border Wars*, they were absolutely ruthless and murderous.

SF: Of course, the most well known was Deir Yassin.

NF: Deir Yassin was psychologically significant, because it was widely broadcast and filled the hearts of Palestinians with fear. But overall, it was not among the largest massacres during the war. That's a kind of a... it's a partisan history. Basically, the Zionist labor movement wrote the history. Deir Yassin was basically a Zionist revisionist atrocity, so that was the one atrocity that was played up, and the atrocities of the labor Zionist Movement were left out.

SF: Arab historians point out that actually the Haganah played a role in Deir Yassin

NF: That's why I said "basically." I mean, the Irgun. The Haganah played some role, yeah.

SF: One of the things that were striking about Deir Yassin is that the Arab inhabitants had negotiated a peace agreement with the Jews.

NF: There were several examples of Palestinian villages which had either been neutral, or even favorable to the Zionist Movement where the inhabitants were expelled.

SF: I read somewhere that Jewish villagers tried to stop the massacre in Deir Yassin by the soldiers.

NF: Maybe. I wouldn't doubt it.

SF: The soldiers stopped for a few minutes...

NF: Plausible. I didn't hear that story. I wouldn't doubt it.

The Deir Yassin Massacre—April 9, 1948

Note—The Irgun and the Lehi were Zionist paramilitary organizations formed by Menachim Begin and Yitzhak Shamir, respectively. (Begin and Shamir became Prime Ministers of Israel decades later.) Deir Yassin had a peaceful reputation among its neighboring Jewish settlements, and had strictly observed a non-aggression pact with the Haganah.

Eye-witness account by Meir Pa'il, a Haganah officer who had helped coordinate the attack:

> "It was noon when the battle ended and the shooting stopped.... The Irgun and Lehi left the places in which they had been hiding and started carrying out clean-up operations in the houses. They fired with all the arms they had, and threw explosives into the buildings. They also shot everyone they saw in

the houses, including women and children—indeed the commanders made no attempt to check the disgraceful acts of slaughter. I myself and a number of [Jewish] inhabitants [from a neighboring village] begged the commanders to give orders to their men to stop shooting, but our efforts were unsuccessful." [Twenty-five villagers were taken to Jerusalem and led in a victory parade] "Like a Roman triumph.... At the end of the parade they were taken to a stone quarry...and shot in cold blood" (Hirst, 1977, pp.126-7).

Director of International Red Cross, Jacques de Reynier:

"I reached the village with my convoy, and the firing stopped. The gang (Irgun) was wearing uniforms with helmets. All of them were young, some even adolescents, men and women, armed to the teeth: revolvers, machine-guns, hand grenades, and also cutlasses in their hands, most of them still blood-stained. . [He went into a house.] The first room was dark, everything was in disorder, but there was no one....[A]SF I was about to leave, I heard something like a sigh.... I looked everywhere, turned over all the bodies, and eventually found a little foot, still warm. It was a little girl of ten, mutilated by a hand grenade, but still alive...everywhere it was the same horrible sight... There had been 400 people in this village; about 50 of them had escaped and were still alive. All the rest had been deliberately massacred in cold blood for, as I observed for myself, this gang was admirably disciplined and only acted under orders" (Hirst, 1977, pp.126-7.)

After the massacre Menachem Begin sent a message to the commanders of the Deir Yasin operation: "Accept congratulations on this splendid act of conquest. Tell the soldiers you have made history in Israel" (Palumbo, 1987, *The Palestinian Catastrophe: The 1848 Expulsion of a People from their Homeland*, London: Faber and Faber, p.55).

The message that Deir Yasin conveyed to Palestinian Arabs was they must flee or face dire consequences. Menachem Begin noted in his memoirs, "A legend of terror spread amongst Arabs....Arabs throughout the country... were seized with limitless panic... It was worth half a dozen battalions to the forces of Israel" (cited in Schoenman, 1988, p.34).

A year later as plans for re-settling the abandoned village by Israelis were being formulated, Martin Buber and three other Jewish scholars—Ernst Simon, Werner Senator, and Cecil Roth—wrote a letter to Prime Minister David Ben-Gurion. The letter noted that Deir Yasin had become "infamous throughout... the whole world.... The Deir Yasin affair is a black stain on the honor of the Jewish nation." Thus the authors implored, "Let the village of Deir Yassin remain uninhabited for the time being. And let its desolation be a terrible and tragic symbol of war, and a warning to our people that no practical or military needs may ever justify such acts of murder and that the nation does not wish to profit from them" (cited in Segev, 1986, pp.88-9) Ben-Gurion did not respond to the letter, despite the fact that it was sent several times. Finally

Ben-Gurion's secretary responded that the Prime Minister was too busy to read their letter (Ibid).

Shortly thereafter the press reported the re-settlement of the village, with the new name of Givat Shaul Bet. Historian Tom Segev wrote: "Several hundred guests came to the opening ceremony, including Cabinet Ministers Kaplan and Shapira, as well as the Chief Rabbis and the Mayor of Jerusalem. President Haim Weitzman sent written congratulations. The band of the blind played and refreshments were served" (Segev, 1986, pp.89-90).

* * *

SF: Those massacres in '48, you've compared it to the extermination of Native Americans.

NF: I think the same thing happened here in Americas.

The Cherokee Trail of Tears and The Lydda Death March

Norman Finkelstein:

"With nearly all the Cherokee standing fast, the U.S. army interceded in 1838 to finish the job. The tragedy that unfolded has come to be known as the Trail of Tears, an uprooting that historian Charles Royce says 'may well exceed in weight of grief and pathos any other passage in American history.' 10 'I fought through the civil war and have seen men shot to pieces and slaughtered by thousands,' a Georgia volunteer who later served with the Confederacy recalled, "but the Cherokee removal was the cruelest work I ever knew.' A century later, the former vice chairman of the Swedish Red Cross, Count Folke Bernadotte, said of the Palestinian survivors of the Lydda Death March, an expulsion ordered by Prime Minister David Ben-Gurion and executed by Commanding Officer Yitzhak Rabin, that 'I have made the acquaintance of a great many refugee camps, but never have I seen a more ghastly sight than that which met my eyes here.'

" Of the roughly 15,000 Cherokee forced into exile, perhaps as many as half perished. As seen through the eyes of the U.SF. Secretary of War, however, the Trail of Tears was a 'generous and enlightened policy...ably and judiciously carried into effect...with promptness and praiseworthy humanity.' In 1838 President Martin Van Buren apprised Congress with 'sincere pleasure' of 'the entire removal of the Cherokee Nation.... They have emigrated without any apparent reluctance.' Addressing the People's Council in 1948, Ben-Gurion plainly broke no new ground when he said of the Arabs brutally expelled from Palestine that they had abandoned 'cities...with great ease... even though no danger of destruction or massacre confronted them'" (Finkelstein, December 1999, The Background of the Visits, The Link, Volume 32, Issue 5, p.6).

Simha Flapan, Israeli journalist and historian in "The Birth of Israel," 1987, p. 100:

"The most significant elimination of these "Arab islands" took place two months after the Declaration of Independence. In one of the gravest episodes of this tragic story, as many as 50,000 Arabs were driven out of their homes in Lydda and Ramleh on July 12-13, 1948...In Lydda, the exodus took place on foot...With the population gone, the Israeli soldiers proceeded to loot the two towns in an outbreak of mass pillaging that the officers could neither prevent nor control."

Kenneth Bilby, correspondent for the New York Herald Tribune, who entered Lydda the second day it was occupied, writing in "New Star in the New East," New York, 1950, p. 43:

"Moshe Dayan led a jeep commando column into the town of Lydda with rifles, Stens, and sub-machine guns blazing. It coursed through the main streets, blasting at everything that moved...the corpses of Arab men, women, and even children were strewn about the streets in the wake of this ruthlessly brilliant charge. "

British General John Glubb, Commander of Jordan's Arab Legion, in "A Soldier with the Arabs," Harper, 1957, p. 162:

" No sooner were the enemy in the towns [Lydda and Ramle] than the Israeli Amy set about an intensive house-to-house search, all men of military age being arrested and removed to concentration camps. Then Israeli vans fitted with loudspeakers drove through the streets, ordering all the remaining inhabitants to leave within half an hour...Perhaps thirty thousand people or more, almost entirely women and children, snatched up what they could and fled from their homes across the open fields... It was a blazing day in July in the coastal plains—the temperature about a hundred degrees in the shade. It was ten miles across open hilly country, much of it ploughed, part of it stony fallow covered with thorn bushes, to the nearest Arab village at Beit Sira. Nobody will ever know how many children died... "

* * *

SF: Now among liberal circles, the slaughters of native Americans is considered one of the dark stains on—

NF: Right, 'cause they're all dead. So it's easy... It's remorse without consequence.

SF: It's what?

NF: It's *inconsequential* remorse.

SF: So, what...?

NF: Israel has the problem that each act of remorse has... any act of remorse has political consequences.

* * *

SF: The Zionists argue that the Israelis had to get rid of the Arabs for security reasons. They couldn't let the refugees back in which of course they had told the UN they would do, because if they let them back, the state of Israel would have been destroyed.

NF: And you know, if you let Jews back into Nazi Germany, they wouldn't have acquiesced either. It's a kind of crazy argument. Of course, you're going to... you're not going to acquiesce in a society which denies you your basic rights. But then the burden is on who, is it on you or is it on the society? Yes, if Palestinians were allowed back into Israel, and Israel insisted on calling itself a Jewish state, and Israel insisted on denying its non-Jewish population rights of equality, yeah, of course there's going to be resistance. So... that's surprising?

SF: What about after the war, what if the Israeli government had given the Right of Return to Arabs, to the indigenous population, and not treated them as second-class citizens?

NF: It wouldn't be a Zionist state.

SF: Yeah.

NF: I mean, the whole point... the main proof of all the falsity of the Zionist arguments is their *own*. What do they argue now? They say the Palestinians can't be allowed to return, because *if* they did return, it would undermine the Jews *demographically*... it would undermine the Jewish character of the state. That's what they state, right? They don't say it's a practical question: we have no room. No, they don't say that. They say it's a *political* question. *If* the Palestinian refugees were allowed to return, *then* demographically, it would no longer be a Jewish state. But what does that argument prove? What that argument proves is: they themselves admit, they have to expel the Palestinians! Because they say, had we now undone the expulsion, it wouldn't be a Jewish state. So that's an implicit acknowledgment, or a backhanded acknowledgment, that had they *not* expelled the Palestinians, they *couldn't* have had a Jewish state! So it has nothing to do with security, it has to do with the basic fact, as Morris at any rate freely admits, there's no way you can create a Jewish state without expelling part of the population. Period.

On Returning Palestinian Refugees After the 1948 War

United Nations General Assembly Resolution 194, December, 1948:

> "Resolved that the refugees wishing to return to their homes and live

in peace with their neighbors should be permitted to do so at the earliest practicable date and that compensation should be paid for the property of those choosing not to return...."

Israel pledged to enforce this resolution as a condition for admission to UN membership—but it reneged on its agreement and renounced any responsibility for the plight of the refugees.

Prime Minister Ben-Gurion, June 16, 1948:

"Their return must be prevented...at all costs." (Cited in Flapan, 1987)

Chief of Staff of Israeli Army, General Moshe Dayan, 1950:

"Are we justified in opening fire on the Arabs who cross the border to reap the crops they planted in our territory; they, their women and their children? Will this stand up to moral scrutiny...? We shoot at those from among the 200,000 hungry Arabs who cross the line [to graze their flocks]—will this stand up to moral review? Arabs cross to collect the grain that they left in the abandoned villages and we set mines for them and they go back without an arm or a leg...[It may be that this] cannot pass review, but I know no other method of guarding the borders. If the Arab shepherds and harvesters are allowed to cross the borders, then tomorrow the State of Israel will have no borders." (Morris, *Righteous Victims*, p.175)

Moshe Dayan, May 1, 1956

"How can we complain about their deep hatred for us? For eight years they have been sitting in the Gaza refugee camps, and before their very eyes we are possessing the land and the villages where they, and their ancestors, have lived.... We are the generation of colonizers, and without the steel helmet and the gun barrel we cannot plant a tree and build a home" (cited in Beit-Hallahmi, 1993, p.13).

Moshe Dayan, 1969

"We came to this country which was already populated by Arabs, and we are establishing a Hebrew, that is a Jewish state here.... Jewish villages were built in the place of Arab villages.... There is not a single community in the country that did not have a former Arab population" (cited in Beit-Hallahmi, 1993, p.114).

A member of Kibbutz Sasa, 1949

"Why are we celebrating our holiday in an Arab village? Once there was an Arab village here. The clouds of Sasa floated high over other people one year ago...The fields we tend today were tended by others—one year ago. The men worked their plots and tended their flocks while women busied themselves at baking bread. The cries and tears of children of others were heard in Sasa one year ago. And when we came the desolation of their lives cried to us through the ruins they left behind. Cried to us and reached our hearts, colored our everyday lives.... So we search for justification for the right to be here.... It isn't difficult to imagine how life must have been. Here a slipper, there a mirror, here a sack of grain, there a family portrait, a child's toy.... What gives us the right to reap the fruits of trees we have not planted, to take shelter in houses we have not built.... On what moral grounds shall we stand when we take ourselves to court?" (Cited in Beit-Hallahmi, 1993, p. 167).

* * *

SF: You spoke of some of the dissidents who were for a bi-national state...I think you said even most of them were also in favor of creating a Jewish majority in Palestine.

NF: Yeah.

SF: But you could conceivably have had a Jewish majority, in which Arabs would not have been treated like—

NF: Yeah, it's possible.

SF: To skip ahead, since we're on this topic now, what do you think would be the solution now?

NF: I think the two-state settlement has to be given a chance. I don't know if it can work, but it should be given a chance.

SF: You think at this point it's the only practical...

NF: Yeah. I'm not sure if it's practical. It has to be given a chance. It may not be practical.

SF: It's not practical because you've got Bush and Sharon?

NF: In that respect... no, there are different ways to... I meant "practical" whether, if Israel actually withdrew, you can actually create two sovereign states which respected each other, where there was mutual respect and mutual cooperation. I don't know if that's possible. That's what I meant by "practical."

SF: What would be the impediment to that?

NF: One impediment is the one that Benvenisti raises, that the two states are so inextricably intertwined at every level—geographically, population, water, everything—they share everything, that it's impossible to separate out one population from the other. That they're so intermixed at this point that you can't separate them out.

SF: But what about a democratic, secular state?

NF: I don't think it's possible. Now.

SF: You mean because of the enmity?

NF: Yeah. There's no *intrinsic* reason.

SF: What would be the features of a two-state solution—distinguishing it from a bandustan for example.

NF: Basically, I understand a two-state settlement to mean pre-June 1967 Israel, with all its Zionist trappings, alongside a Palestinian Arab state, which will probably be just as discriminatory. Not a very pretty picture, but the best that can be hoped for, if it can any longer be hoped for. Any Palestinian state short of a full Israeli withdrawal, except if there are one to one land swaps between Israel and whatever land Israel incorporates from the West Bank, would pretty much resemble a Bantustan.

SF: You picked up advocacy on behalf of Palestinians rather than some other group primarily because it was something that was being done in the name of Jewry...?

NF: No, I didn't pick it up because—I felt I was most valuable there.

SF: Uh-huh.

NF: And I don't... It was more useful for me to be there than in another struggle, that's how I felt. My voice counted for more, so... if I count for twice who I am in this struggle and once for who I am in another struggle, it's better to count for twice than for once.

SF: It counted for more because...?

NF: I was Jewish and I was a survivor—I was the son of survivors of the Nazi Holocaust.

SF: Yeah. You said you got involved in college... was your first political awakening the genocide of the Vietnamese people?

NF: Uh-hmm. Well Vietnam and the Civil Rights Movement, both. Both.

SF: One of the great myths of 1967 was that it was preemptive war. As you showed, the people who were running it, knew it wasn't—

NF: They knew two basic facts: one, Nasser wasn't going to attack, and two, if he did attack, he was going to be demolished in short order. Those two... there was a consensus within the Israeli ruling elite in those two points.

The 1967 War

Israeli Foreign Minister Abba Eban, United Nations General Assembly 1967:

"So on that fateful morning on June 5, when Egyptian forces moved by air and land against Israel's western coast and southern territory, our country's choice was to live or perish, to defend the national existence or to forfeit it for all time" (Finkelstein, 1995, p.123).

Israeli Foreign Minister Abba Eban, 1977:

1)"Nasser did not want war. He wanted victory without war" (cited in Thomas, 1999, p.172)

2) "Ben-Gurion later admitted that he never thought Nasser wanted war" (cited in Thomas, p.172).

Chief of Staff of Army, General Yitzhak Rabin, future Prime Minister:

"[I] do not believe that Nasser wanted war.... The two divisions he sent into Sinai on May 14 would not have been enough to unleash an offensive. He knew it and we knew it" (cited in Finkelstein, 1995, p134).

Menachem Begin, founder of Irgun, and future Prime Minister:

"The Egyptian Army concentrations in the Sinai...do not prove that Nasser was ready to attack us. We must be honest with ourselves. We decided to attack him" (cited in Finkelstein, pp134-5).

Chief of Mossad Meir Amit, June 1967:

"Egypt was not ready for a war; and Nasser did not want a war" (cited in Finkelstein, 1995, p.134).

President Lyndon Johnson, 1967:

"[A]ll our intelligence people are unanimous that if Egypt attacks, you will whip the hell out of them" (cited in Ibid, p.135).

Norman Finkelstein, *Image and Reality of the Israel-Palestine Conflict*, 1995

On the eve of the June 1967 war, the CIA appraised Israel's objectives as, first and foremost, 'destruction of the center of power of the radical Arab Socialist movement, i.e. the Nasser regime', second, 'destruction of the arms of the radical Arabs', and last, 'destruction of both Syria and Jordan as modern states.' In a word, Israel's overarching aim was to extirpate any and all manifestations of Arab 'radicalism'—i.e. independence and modernization. To do so, the Egyptian upstart [Nasser} had to be put in his proper place, cut down to size" (p.143).

* * *

SF: What drives these people? What seems to be unfolding before us now is not just Zionism, but a desire as Aruri put it to become the regional hegemon in the Middle East. You don't talk about that as much.

NF: I don't. I don't, because it would require integrating it into the whole US strategy in the Middle East, and I've never gone into that. But I think it's a combination of ideology and lust for power. It's a mixture.

SF: Chomsky has been criticized by a number of people who says Chomsky overlooks the power of the Israeli Lobby and that he underestimates the autonomy of Israel vis-à-vis the US... You don't think those criticisms...?

NF: I change my mind every hour on that.

SF: Yeah.

NF: I'll tell you the truth. I change my mind every hour on that. I don't know the answer to that question and I don't think it can be... I don't think any side can be proven.... The basic picture is like this: if you look at the... the documentary record up until, say, the late 1960s, it was very easy to identify—here was the Jewish lobby or the Israel lobby; here was the US national interest. And you see people like Kennedy, Johnson, Eisenhower, they complain... Truman, they complain about the Jewish Lobby, this entity that exists apart from them. But by the 1980s, what was called the Jewish Lobby and the national interest as defined by the bureaucracy, they had so completely merged that you no longer know: Is Wolfowitz speaking for the US government, or is he speaking for Israel? Is Perle speaking for the US government, or is he speaking for Israel? You don't know! So I don't know how you prove any of these theses: I just think they're unprovable anymore. They were provable when you had two clearly identified entities and then you could see how the power struggle plays itself out. But you can't prove it, when you have... when they're one and the same now. They've merged! I don't know who Wolfowitz is... I don't know if Wolfowitz knows who he's working for!

SF: Yeah. So the final question: what's going to happen to the Palestinians? In your Rise and Fall, you titled the last chapter, The End of Palestine.

NF: I don't know. I think a lot of it's going to depend on Iraq. If a resistance sufficient... if a sufficient resistant develops in Iraq, it will improve the morale of Palestinians. If Iraq is crushed, then the Palestinians will be crushed.

SF: And if they're not crushed, what do you think will happen?

NF: As my very dear friend, Moussa Abu Hashash has been saying for the last fifteen years: quote, "more of the same, but worse."

SF: But you keep writing and fighting. What's the motive then?

NF: Aye, look, if I were writing during World War II about the Jews, I wouldn't be optimistic either, but I wouldn't give up.

SF: Yeah. And you are going to continue writing and whatever... advocacy for the Palestinians?

NF: Correct. Until I die.

Part 2—Finkelstein on Zionism and Israel

Finkelstein's critique of Israel and Zionism is at the same time a defense of the liberal democratic tradition ond its values—and an attempt to redeem their promise. According to Finkelstein the Nazi holocaust does not (and did not) warrant the Zionist repudiation of secular democracy. (He argues that even had a Jewish state existed before the Nazis came to power it would not have prevented or mitigated the Nazi holocaust—but that issue cannot be discussed here). A reading of Finkelstein's first unpublished book (his doctoral thesis, *From the Jewish Question to the Jewish State: An essay on the Theory of Zionism*) along with his other books indicates that ultimately he views the ideals of liberal universalism— which is antithetical to Zionism—as the only firm foundation upon which to base the project for overcoming racism, including anti-Semitism (which he believes is virtually extinct as a social force within the United States) and creating a just social order. He argues that contrary to common belief the decline of anti-Semitism in America and Europe is not a result of the creation of a Jewish state—Israel—but is due to other factors (Finkelstein, 2001).

Finkelstein's work demonstrates that "the premises of Zionism and of liberalism are in fundamental conflict" (1988, p.28). In fact, ironically both Nazi (modern) anti-Semitism and Zionism are rooted in the same reactionary tradition of integral race-nationalism. Race-nationalism is antithetical to liberal nationalism, to the liberal-democratic tradition. In liberal nationalism, as defined by the theorists of the French Republic, the nation is viewed as subordinate to the state. Once the state is formed the nation emerges spontaneously as its extension. The unit of liberalism is the individual citizen. The individual chooses to become a citizen of a nation by indicating his agreement with the social compact upon which the state (and government) is based; thus "national belonging derives and follows as a matter of course from citizenship" (p. 116), from "incorporation in the body-politic" (Ibid p.48). In the liberal view membership in a nation is determined by a purely political criterion, independent of one race, religion or country of origin— the individual's voluntary acceptance of its democratic covenant. As Elie Kedourie puts it, "any body of people associating and deciding on a scheme for their own government, form a nation" (Finkelstein, p. 13). Thus "if all the people of the world decided on a common government, they would form one nation" (Ibid). Or as the President of the Jacobin Club asked rhetorically, "is it not true that all Frenchmen are born and are citizens before being Protestants, before being Jews?" In accord with this perspective, in the early 1790s Jews and all other minorities were granted full rights as citizens of France. (pp. 15-6)

This is entirely different from the integral race-nationalism, of which *political* zionism (i.e. the idea that Jews ought to have their own state) is one species. (Cultural or spiritual Zionism is a benign form of nationalism that demands only a territorial space for the revival of Judaism; it does not require a state for a Jewish nation). In integral race-nationalism the state is subordinate to the nation, it *belongs to the nation*. National belonging does *not* derive—as it does in liberalism—from citizenship per se. Rather authentic citizenship is a function of national belonging. Of course genuine national belonging and citizenship requires that the nation possess its own proper state. But the bonds uniting individuals of a particular nation are "organic" and innate—they are not voluntarily assumed by the individual, as they are in liberal nationalism.

It should be noted that for Zionism the Jewish nation in not necissarily comprised of those who accept Judaism, who are religious Jews. The first Zionists, including Israel's founders, were not religious, most were atheists—yet they did not think they were therefor less Jewish. As they saw it, they belonged to the Jewish nation, they were born into it. As to the few non-Jews who converted to Judaism, Zionists were not able to cogently explain—they still cannot—how religious conversion could make one a member of the Jewish race—or in other words part of a racially constituted nation. The ideal towards which race-nationalism points is a world comprised of numerous nations, each nation internally homogeneous, each belonging to one different race-nationality. As the German romantic philosopher and race-nationalist Fichte saw it, each nation "if it wished to absorb and mingle with itself any other people of different descent and language, cannot do so without becoming confused...and violently disturbing the even progress of its culture" (Ibid, p.33)

As a form of race-nationalism Zionism held that all Jews, wherever they lived, were united by deep organic bonds, however dissimilar Jews from different cultures might appear to be; thus they constituted a nation. At the same time they were an alien element within the European states where they frequently resided; *these states did not belong to them, but to the preponderant Christian race(s).* The anti-Semites, Zionists concluded, were right about this: Jews did not belong in Europe. Anti-Semitism was not a deplorable moral failing but rather a result of—to quote Jabotinsky, the founder of Zionist Revisionism—"the instinctive discrimination which every normal person makes between his or her 'own kind' and all outsider" (p. 70). Chaim Weizmann, who became the first president of Israel, wrote that European nations can only accomodate alien elements up to a particular threshold. In short, as Finkelstein sums it up, for Zionism "anti-Semitism is the rational (natural) impulse of a nation state 'infected' by a 'foreign' body or too-obstrusive a foreign body" (p. 70). It is not surprising that the Zionists did not condemn anti-Semitism but frequently sought out anti-Semites as potential allies (eg. financial backers) for their own project of creating a Jewish state.

Since Zionism accepted the logic of race-nationalism it had no basis upon

which to oppose the methods of anti-Semitism, as they existed at the time—
denationalization, denaturalization, deportation. For race nationalism minorities
are "an excrescence on the body politic.... Since the majority-race-nation holds
title to the state, minorities...exercise their rights of citizenship only on sufferance.
These rights may be granted but also—and with perfect justice and consistency—
rescinded. Indeed the revocation of these rights is proper and well-nigh inevitable,
for nation-states ought and properly do tend to (racial) homogeneity" (Finkelstein,
p. 70).

The Zionist solution to the 'Jewish' Problem

The remedy for the Jewish predicament followed from its diagnosis:
the creation of a Jewish state for the stateless Jews scattered in the Diaspora.
(Finkelstein, p. 73). Ben-Gurion expressed the essence of the Zionist idea quite
clearly in the 1950s: "*[T]he State [Israel] was made not for its citizenry, but for
all the nation of Israel, for those [Jews], too, who do not propose to dwell in it.*"
(Finkelstein, p. 92). In other words Israel was made for all Jews even those who did
not intend to live there, and it was not made for its own citizenry which includes
a minority of Arabs who were not expelled during the 1948 war. Of course the
corollary to this idea is that Jews in America (and elsewhere), regardless of their
American citizenship, remain alien elements within the American body-politic,
"exiles" from their true homeland in the Jewish state of Israel.

Ben-Gurion stressed that Jews needed a state in order to survive—existentially,
politically, literally. There is "a bond of life and death" between Israel and the
Jewish people. "Between [the Jewish state and the Jewish people] there exists
a natural bond, necessary and welcome, a historic nexus. That one should exist
without the other is fantastic..." (Finkelstein, p. 93). From this perspective Judaism
itself (the religion) has only parantheticl importance, as one manifestation of the
Jews' national identity. The Zionist perspective was incorporated into Israeli law
when 2 years after the creation of the state of Israel, the Law of Return was enacted,
granting every Jew who emigrates to Israel the automatic right of citizenship.
As Ben-Gurion put it, "this law lays down not that the State accords the right of
settlement to Jews abroad but that this right is inherent in every Jew by virtue of
his being a Jew." (Finkelstein, p. 95).

The Zionist political discourse was paralleled and reinforced by a territorial
discourse: Palestine/ Eretz Israel (which includes what today are the occupied
territories of the West Bank and Gaza—as well as other Mideastern countries by
some accounts) is the organic homeland of the Jews, and every other space is alien
to them. Although Zionism is a secular theory, it accepted the religious dogma
that Israel was the "Promised Land" given by God to the Jews, from which they
had been exiled for centuries. (Orthodox Jews originally repudiated the Zionist

program, as they believed that the land would be given back to the Jews only by the Messiah in the final days). In the Zionist perspective Jews could not realize their innate potentialities until they returned to the land which belonged to them; this position was also embraced by apiritual Zionists like Martin Buber. Jews in the Diaspora Jews were merely "rootless cosmopolitan," as Ben-Gurion put it. Conversely, Israel could be developed only by Jews. Ben-Gurion wrote: "[N]o one but a sovereign Jew can...bring forth the full benediction of our Land." (Finkelstein, 1988, pp. 108-9). On the other hand, the indigenous (Arab) inhabitants of the land of Israel were not intrinsically *of* it—they did not *belong* there.

The Arab Problem in the Jewish State

The founders of Zionism realizaed that the creation of a Jewish state required the existence of a Jewish majority in Palestine; achieving this goal ultimately entailed "transferring" the native inhabitants of Palestine out of and off the land that belonged by right to the Jews—according to Zionism. Most Zionists realized that the natives would not leave voluntarily. Thus how to most effectively bring about the involuntary "transfer" (i.e. the expulsion or, as we call it today, the ethnic cleansing) of the indigenous Arabs of Palestine became a persistent pre-occupation (and subject of private debates) of Zionist leaders—until the actions of the Israeli Army in the 1948 war solved the problem by effecting the flight of 750,000 Palestinians. (The commitment to the ethnic cleansing of Israel before the 1948 war, and again after 1967, is documented by Nur Masalha in tow books he wrote based upon his examination of recently unclassified Israeli archives, 1992, 2000). Ben-Gurion wrote in 1937 in a letter to his 16-year-old-son, "we must expel the Arabs and take their places...and...if we have to use force—not to dispossess the Arabs...but to guarantee our own right to settle in those places—then we have force at our disposal." (Mashala, 1992, p. 66). By February 1948 Ben-Gurion was looking forward to war with the Arab states as a means of solving the problem of transfer: "The war will give us the land.... The concept of 'ours' and 'not ours' are peace concepts only, and in war they lose their whole meaning." (cited in Masalha, 1992, p. 180)

The evidence suggests that few Jews within the Zionist movement questioned the morality of the proposed acts of ethnic cleansing. (Those who did were primarily spiritual Zionists, like Martin Buber, who favored a bi-national state). As a leader of Mapai (Ben-Gurion's party) and the kibbutz movement put it in 1948, "[T]he transfer of Arabs out of the country in my eyes is one of the most just, moral and correct things that can ever be done." (Masalha, 1992, p. 180). But this is not surprising—after all, the Zionists had accepted the anti-Semitic proposals to rid Europe of Jews, until of course it transmogrified under Hitler into genocide. (Even here there is evidence that the Zionists manifested a "horrifying apathy," as Boas

Evron put it, to the fate of the Jews that led them to boycott, if not sabotage, efforts to save European Jews from the Nazi genocide; see Evron, 1995.)

The transfer of Arabs was a moral good, or at worst a lesser evil, within the context of the Zionist paradigm. As Zionists saw it, despite the indigenous Arabs' emotional attachment to their homes they did not *belong* within the Jewish territory or the Jewish state—despite their wishes they belonged in an Arab country. As a non-Jewish minority they were at best "an excrescence on the body politic" of the Jewish state (Finkelstein, p. 88). A Jewish state may grant minorities citizenship but, as Finkelstein writes, "properly, they belong in/to the state(s) of their nations. Their presence in a Jewish state is fundamentally gratuitous and aberrant. National minorities may be tolerated, but they exercise their rights of citizenship only on sufferance. Jews are the only authentic members of the body-politic in [Israel]; the others are an inorganic graft on it."

Finkelstein continues, "such a discourse evidently legitimizes the 'transfer'—i.e. expulsion—of national minorities: cruel and harsh as such a measure may appear, it would, after all, 'normalize' an already abnormal situation." (p. 88) This discourse also legitimizes granting minorities (Arabs) "citizenship" but withholding from them the political and social rights that are granted to Jewish citizens—or that are generally entailed by citizenship in liberal democracies. One of the most egregious of many examples of the inferior status of Arab citizenship is Israeli land policy. 90% of Israel's lasnd it state owned but all of it is exclusively for Jewish use, in perpetuity. This makes sense from the Zionist perspective: The land belongs to the state and the state belongs to the Jews.

An understanding of the Zionist ideology and project clarifies why the indigenous Palestinians were so hostile to the Zionists in Palestine, and would have been so even had they been financially compensated—their rejection of the Zionist project had nothing to do with anti-Semitism, despite frequent assertions to the contrary by Israeli and American Jews. (This is not to deny that anti-Semitism may have been an incidental, albeit unfortunate, by-product of Zionist policies). As Finkelstein puts it, "[I]t is difficult to imagine any circumstances under which [the Palestinians] would have acquiesced to an enterprise that, in spirit and letter, sought to render them strangers in their own land." (Finkelstein, p. 111). As the spiritual Zionist Judith Magnes aptly wrote, "the slogan Jewish state...is equivalent, in effect, to a declaration of war by the Jews on the Arabs." (Finkelstein, p. 113).

The willingness of liberals to accomodate their principles to raison d'etat is exemplified to this day by the double standard of many Jewish liberals when the policies of Israel are at issue. For example, to cite liberal philosopher Michael Walzer in 1972, "[N]ation-building in new states is sure to be rough on groups marginal to the nation.... For them, the roughness can only be smoothed a litte; it cannot be avoided.... And sometimes it can only be smoothed over by helping people to leave who have to leave..." (cited in Finkelstein, p. 89). This is a crude attempt to justify ethnic cleansing. Walzer's position is not uncommon among Jewish (and non-Jewish) American liberals. Not the pariah status ("marginal") to which Walzer consigns Arab minorities in their original homeland—now transformed into the territorial basis of the "Jewish state." When such policies are practiced in other states, e.g. official enemies of the US government, liberals are quick to execrate these governments and to call for US intervention to put an end to "ethnic cleansing." (Yugoslavia is a salient recent example). But where Israel is concerned, many if not most Jewish liberals are prepared to embrace race-nationalism, and even to rationalize practices that the western world has publically condemned. Of course these methods are typically veiled with euphemisms and construed as humanitarian acts like "helping people to leave who *have* to leave." Evidently it does not occur to Walzer to ask himself: Why do they *have* to leave? Why *should* they leave?

As alien elements living on the land that "belonged" to the Jews, to the Jewish state, the indigenous Arabs were and are in the way, an inconvenience to the Zionists, an impediment to the realization of the Zionist dream. This situation was bound to engender racism and conflict. As Maxine Rodinson put it, "wanting to create a purely Jewish or predominantly Jewish state in Arab Palestine in the 20th Century, could not help but lead to the development (completely normal, sociologically speaking) os a racist state with a racist state of mind, and in the final analysis to a military confrontation between the two ethnic groups." (Rodinson, 1973, p. 77).

Chapter 6

Phyllis Bennis

Phyllis Bennis is a Fellow of the Institute for Policy Studies. Her most recent book is *Before and After: US Foreign Policy and the September 11ᵗʰ Crisis*.

SF: There's one viewpoint, among some critics of Israeli policies like Lerner, that Israel was basically acting in accord with ethical norms, if not always with U.N. resolutions or international law, until 1967. And that was the watershed in which Israel fell from grace. What would you say?

PB: I have a different take, because I think if we look in a consistent way at international law, we can see violations by Israel right from the time of its creation. The partition resolution of 1947, Resolution 181, identified 55% of historic Palestine, the British Mandate territory of the Palestine Mandate, to become what was identified as a Jewish state. The other 45%—well, slightly less than 45%—was to become a Palestinian state. The partition resolution gave 55% to become a Jewish state and 45% to become a Palestinian state with the understanding that all of Jerusalem would become what was called a *corpus separatum*, meaning a separate body that would be under international jurisdiction. By the end of the war, in 1948, Israel controlled 78% of the land, including half of Jerusalem. And whatever I think about that resolution—and I happen to think it wasn't based on justice anyway; the Jewish population in Palestine at that time was slightly under 30%, and the land ownership was only slightly over 6%—so in my view it wasn't a just decision to begin with. However, it was made, it was the decision that was made, but by the end of the war, the Israeli control of land was then vastly more than had been authorized by the United Nations. So there was already a violation there.

The other point: From 1949, when Israel entered the United Nations, it was based on the acceptance of all earlier resolutions, which included at that time Resolution 194, involving the right of return of Palestinian refugees. Israel since that time has refused to even...not only have they refused to accept and implement the right of return, they have refused to accept Israeli responsibility for what Palestinians call *al Nakba*, the catastrophe, of 1948, which means the effect of the Israeli war of independence, as it's known in Israel, was the catastrophic massive collective dispossession that affected the Palestinians at that time, when 750,000 Palestinians were displaced from their homes by force, by fear, by war. The overall international law on the question of the rights of refugees in times of war is found in the Fourth Geneva Convention, which allows all refugees to return to their homes. It's a basic human right, regardless of which side you were on, regardless of whether your side started the war or not, regardless of whether you won the war or not. The addition of Resolution 194, which speaks specifically to the question of the particular rights of Palestinians refugees was put in place because the U.N. largely understood its role as having created the State of Israel, so it had a very particular responsibility for those who were victims of the war that followed that declaration. So there's particular violations of international law and U.N. resolutions that go right back to 1947, 48, 49, way before 1967.

SF: By the way, you didn't mention the Universal Declaration of Human Rights. Doesn't that include the right of return also?

PB: It does indeed. I mean, it's an understood part of international law that refugees in time of war have the right to return. The model of course in the contemporary period that we can look at is the situation in Rwanda. After the genocide in Rwanda, when there were over a million Hutu refugees who had fled the country, afraid of possible retaliation from the new Tutsi-led government in Kigali, the international community intervened and said, well, we will support the transfer back to their homes of refugees that had fled. Those who espoused the position of the Tutsi-led government could have been, well sorry, we're not going to let those refugees back, because it will change the demographic composition of our country. They didn't say that, but if they had, it was clear that the United Nations would have said, Sorry, you don't have the right to deny people their right to return because you don't like the effect of the demographics of your country, any more than the Israelis should have the right to refuse the right of return on the grounds that they don't like the demographic impact it's going to have on their country.

SF: Well in 1949, or was it 50, they promised, as you said, as a condition for admittance to the U.N., that they would repatriate.

PB: 1949, exactly.

SF: And I read an exchange with Abba Eban in which—I guess you're familiar with that exchange?

PB: Yes.

SF: He solemnly promises that they will do that. He was equivocal on one of their other conditions, I can't remember what it was, but.... Now the people on the left who say that, now, who defend the decision in 49—say that the Israeli state would have been destroyed. The Israeli government said, these people fled, and their act of flight was to aid the Arab countries who wanted to push Israel into the sea? Therefore we don't have to take responsibility for their flight.

PB: No, they actually claim that they fled because the Arab leadership abroad told them to and told them that they would be able to come back in two weeks. As far as I know, it's not based on the claim that it was to aid the Arab leadership. It's just that they were responsible for it. On the other hand, that's been found to be not true. The broadcasts, particularly the BBC broadcasts that were originally cited turned out to be non-existent. But the point is that under international law that doesn't matter. Even if that had been the case, even if they had fled under the misapprehension that they would be able to come back in two weeks, they still would have the right to go home. It doesn't matter the reason they fled. Their right to return is not conditional on having fled for the right reason.

SF: Another rationalization used for not allowing them to return—used by people now who defend it, even people who are critical of Israeli policies—is that had they been allowed to return, they would have threatened the security of the Israeli population.

PB: Yeah, all of this is based on the idea that Palestinians who were displaced from their homes would have all come back as terrorists. The problem is, there was opposition. Nobody asked the Palestinians what they thought about the partition agreement of 1947 in the first place. If they had, there's no doubt that there would have been massive opposition to it. The reality was that Palestinians were by far the majority of the population, controlled the vast majority of the land—although much of the land was owned by absentee owners—and had a historic tie to not just the idea of that land but very particular garden plots, agricultural land, homes, etc., and would have refused, would have rejected the partition agreement precisely because it was not a just agreement. That does not translate into the notion that there was a military threat, particularly to civilians, if they had been allowed to remain. The reality was that in the earlier stages of the 20th century in particular but especially in the 19th century, the tensions between the small Jewish community in Palestine and the indigenous Palestinian Arab population were very, very slight. There had been...there were riots in 1929, again in 1936, but that was very clearly in response to particular influxes of European settlers at the time. The opposition to the indigenous Jewish community, which had lived there, as Joan Peters liked to say, "from time immemorial," they had been there forever, and they were very much a part of the Palestinian community: they spoke Arabic, they were indistinguishable except in religious practice from the rest of the population, and the tensions were minimal.

SF: Actually, the question that's been on my mind lately, and I think it's most relevant today, I don't know how well it will be five months from now, is that there's been a lot of talk of an attack on Iran [August, 2005], and I've read numerous articles, including a quote from an article by Chomsky that wasn't published in America, in which he stated that the United States has dispatched 100 F-16s, advanced jet bombers, with a very specific announcement that they can reach Iran and return, and are versions of the F-16s that Israel used to attack the Iraqi nuclear reactor in 1981.

PB: Do I think the U.S. is going to attack Iran?

SF: Yeah, under Bush, or under Kerry?

PB: I would say that the possibility exists. There certainly is precedent in

1981, when Israel took out the Iraqi nuclear reactor at Osireq—the French reactor. Whether they intend to use military force against Iran remains a question. What's certainly true is that it would be consistent with the political policies that were put forward by the current members of the Bush administration, who drafted in 1996 a paper called "Making a Clean Break Defending the Realm," which was drafted by people like Douglass Feith, Richard Perle, and others, who went to Israel to work with the campaign then of Bibi Netanyahu, who was running for Israeli prime minister, about how to craft a campaign framework, and what would become a framework for Israeli foreign policy if they were...if Netanyahu were to win the election. Now that paper was very much a reflection in my view of an Israeli version of...a regional version of the role that Israel should play in the Middle East region that was parallel to the proposed role that the U.S. should play in the global arena that was drafted by the same group of people that became known as The New Project for the American Century. In both cases, there was a call for the U.S. in one case globally, the Israelis in the other case regionally, to act in a military fashion primarily, and only secondarily to take up the question of diplomacy. So in both cases, it involved the issue of how to build up the military capacity. It endorsed the Israeli nuclear ambiguity and the maintaining of the qualitative edge by Israel over any combination of neighboring Middle Eastern countries in conventional military capacity. The U.S. was clearly prepared to, and has, supported that capacity both in financial and military and diplomatic means of support, so it would be consistent with that. Whether the Israelis actually intend to carry out a policy as reckless as an attack on Iran remains obviously unknown.

SF: If they did that, it would obviously, or presumably be with the blessing, if not the instigation, of the current administration, if it takes place...

PB: We can assume that Israel is very careful to keep in mind the consequences for its primary patron when it makes strategic decisions. That doesn't mean that it is fully...at all times accountable to the tactical demands of particular forces within the U.S. It has its own foreign policy and is dependent on U.S. support but not, in my view, on a tactical basis, meaning that Israel will do what the Israeli ruling circles believe to be in Israel's interests as a regional superpower and a regional military hegemony—whether or not they have a green light from the White House or Congress.

SF: These kind of policies—attacking Iran or attacking Iraq—are widely viewed, at least by the peace movement, as severely exacerbating the likelihood of international disasters and international anarchy. I presume you agree with that?

PB: Yep.

SF: Do you think there's a reason to anticipate as aggressive a policy among... if the Democrats, if Kerry were to get into office?

PB: I think that U.S. strategic ties with Israel, which go back particularly to the Cold War period of post-1967, have been pretty much a bipartisan reality. There have been differences. The Republican Party historically has been less accountable to the domestic pro-Israeli forces in the U.S., but that was at a time when domestic pro-Israeli forces were primarily coming out of the Jewish community, the opposition of the traditional components of the pro-Israeli lobby. In the 1990s, the emergence of the particular power of the right-wing Christian fundamentalist component of the pro-Israeli lobby became much stronger, and they have a much more powerful base and political resonance within the Republican Party. And we've seen that particularly throughout the years of the second Bush administration. So I think that, at this stage, we can say that it is a pretty non-partisan or equally partisan component of both parties.

SF: Yes, you said that obviously the Republicans have a base of Christian Zionists who are more aggressive. Is Kerry likely to pressure Israel to negotiate any kind of treaty with the Palestinians, and the second question which is a genuine puzzle to me is, is Kerry as likely as Bush to implement the neoconservative agenda of attacking Iran and attacking other Arab countries?

PB: I think that the question of whether any president is prepared to pressure Israel at all has everything to do with the strength of a popular movement in the United States demanding that they do so. Absent that, I don't see any particular difference between the two parties in their willingness to support Israeli violations of international law and U.N. resolutions. With a strong popular movement—and it's a huge, important gain for the peace movement that since, I would say the spring of 2002, the centrality of Palestine and the ending the U.S. support for the Israeli occupation has been a central component of the U.S. mobilization for peace and justice in a way that it had never been before—that transforms that reality, so it makes it possible to hold the U.S. accountable in a way it never has been to opposing U.S. support for Israeli occupation. The second question, clearly the people around the Kerry campaign are not the same people usually identified as the neocons who have a very particular set of policies (the drive toward Empire). That doesn't mean that there's particular tactical differences. The tactical approaches are very similar in many ways on the Israel/Palestine front, but the overall ideological drive is not the same between the people that are around the Republican party–At the least the wing of the Republican party who have come to power since 9/11 with enormous popular ability to implement their fear-based, ideologically driven agenda is very different from those, what we might call pragmatic imperialists who are now somewhat around the Democratic party, and the question of what policies each will put forward on the immediate level on this issue may not look very different, but what drives them is really quite different.

SF: My question was, do you consider...do you agree with what most of the left says that Bush is a greater evil? I ask specifically in terms of the Mideast.

PB: I think that the policies of the Bush administration have been the most reckless policies of this...of the last fifty years.

SF: There are people who have said, though, that argue that now the whole dynamic has pushed the Democratic party to right, and so...: And if you look there, as you have done—-the Democratic Party campaign platform is more rightwing, it mentions attacking Iran, and some on the left would argue that we'd be in as much danger now if a Democrat would get in power.

PB: I told you my answer. The Bush administration policies are the most reckless in fifty years. I'm not going to do an assessment of Kerry right now.

SF: You say you wouldn't make any predictions on the future based on if Kerry got in power or...

PB: No, it's all going to depend on the strength of the popular movement.

SF: Do you think that popular movement, UPFJ, will have the...can develop sufficient power?

PB: I think this is the strongest movement we've seen since Vietnam. It's broader, it's deeper in mainstream American families and communities. The cost of the war in Iraq to American communities, to American families is higher than ever before, and people are coming to understand that. So yes, I think there's enormous potential for this movement.

SF: Chomsky has recently been saying that...speaking about the importance of the two-state solution. At the same time, other people—on the left, anyway (Tony Judt's article)—have abandoned the whole idea that a two-state solution is feasible—they argue that its appeal was that it was more practical but that now it's clear Israel will not compromise.... Chomsky seems to think that it is still feasible. Once again, he seems to make that contingent upon the development of a potent movement in America. He seems to think there can be a movement that will force the United States government to pressure Israel to negotiate on the basis of the Geneva Accords or something like them. Could you say what your opinion is on that?

PB: I've never believed that a two-state solution represents a comprehensive basis for peace and justice. Without justice in the region, there is no peace. I think, and I've written since the late 70s, that real justice in my view would come from the creation of a state based on equal rights for everybody. One person, one vote. And frankly, that's also the basis...if there's two states, there needs to be equality between states as well as within both states. I think that, realistically, the possibility of getting to a one-state solution will have to go through a two-state period, not least because that's the basis of this stage of international legal norms. Resolution 242 speaks to a two-state solution, and others. It is the consensus of the international community. So I think that is more likely. I don't think it's going...certainly if the Israeli creation of the Apartheid Wall continues, it will become visibly impossible to implement. Even without the wall, the nature of occupation and the creation of a distorted body politic based on what, in a very creative use of words, Sharon has begun calling the transportation contiguity as a basis of creating a Palestinian state, is not going to be viable. And that will become very clear. If there were to be a viable two-state solution, it would have to be based on a contiguous Palestinian state based on all of the West Bank, all of Gaza, and all of East Jerusalem. That might be viable, at least for a period of time, perhaps more permanently. .... In fact, to the contrary, U.S. posture is now officially rejecting that notion and accepting long-term annexation of large swathes of territory throughout the West Bank as well as virtually all of East Jerusalem. So it's clearly not a viable version of a two-state solution that is being proposed. So given that, it's almost not even worth it to talk about, Could it work or could it not work, when we know that, abstractly, maybe it could, but we're not being presented with what would be the minimum requirement for a viable two-state solution.

SF: So you don't think a movement around the Geneva Accords, which is...

PB: I think the Geneva Accords have some serious problems. I've written about the Geneva Accords and I think that, while they reflect some appropriate approaches, they are seriously flawed. They're flawed in a couple of ways. Number one, they don't come out of civil society, despite the fact that's often the claim that's used to justify them. They were put together by out-of-work diplomats. That's very different from civil society. There was not transparency, there was no consultation. And without transparency and consultation, you can't say that something reflects a civil society initiative. Significantly on some of the specifics, there are serious problems as well, most particularly on the right of return, which is one of the most difficult issues in the international arena. What Geneva poses as the likely settlement, I think it may well be accurate in terms of what Palestinian refugees, particularly those in Syria, Lebanon—most particularly Lebanon—and Jordon are likely to choose, but only *after* the right is acknowledged.

Until the right is acknowledged, there will be no choice by Palestinians. The choices that I think people would make if they were given the right to make their own, individual choice—and that is the basis of 194 and the right of return, it's an individually held right which cannot be negotiated away by any force, whether it be the Geneva negotiators or Yassir Arafat in person: no one has the right to give up anybody else's right of return except their own—given that, I think that while it may be an accurate reflection...I'm guessing that there's somewhere between two and three and four hundred thousand refugees who would choose to go back to Israel at this stage, to their homes, the vast majority would not. They would choose compensation, they would choose to get citizenship where they are, they would choose to go to a Palestinian state, they would choose to go to Canada or Australia or somewhere else, but they would probably choose not to go live in Israel as currently Israel...to live as second-class citizens inside Israel. That doesn't mean anything, however, until the right is acknowledged, the responsibility of Israel for having created the refugee crisis is acknowledged, and Palestinians are individually given the right to choose whatever they want to choose. Then I think the proposal in Geneva may well be a relatively accurate anticipation of what they might choose, but none of that is relevant until there is the first acknowledgment, and that's what has to happen first.

SF: You made a distinction somewhere between the right and the implementation of the right.

PB: Rights are absolute. Implementation of rights is thoroughly negotiable.

SF: For a long time, there was the idea of Barak's generous offer at Camp David, and recently there was an intelligence scandal in Israel, which a lot of people said undermined further the idea that Barak had made a generous offer and that Arafat was intent on not making any compromises. Do you have any comments on that?

PB: I'm not familiar with any new intelligence on it. I think it's been clear since the time of Camp David that the offer that Barak made was not generous at all. It was, in fact, significantly more generous than any Israeli prime minister had ever made before, but that's quite irrelevant; it's the wrong standard. The right standard is not how it compares to earlier offers by other occupying forces, but how it compares to the requirements of international law. And by that standard, it's not at all generous. The proposal that was made was for a set of bantustans that would be collectively...might include as much as 90-92% of the land of the West Bank for the Palestinians, but the division would be not only the settlements themselves—and it wasn't even clear that all of the...major settlement blocks would be included: the implication was they would not be. But even if they were, the division, the land in the 8% or so that was officially excluded, was not one single chunk of land somewhere where there could be an exchange or anything like that. It was in the context of roads, bridges, tunnels, all of the ways in which the separate bantustans of Palestinian land and Palestinian control would be separated from each other as well as from Israel, so that there would be no viability for anything remotely resembling a Palestinian state.

SF: You put that succinctly, that's very useful, but I was referring to something I don't have right in front of me—I thought you might know—that recently came out a couple months ago: the intelligence that Israel was getting since Camp David that said Arafat didn't want to compromise and wanted to destroy Israel was erroneous. The intelligence had in fact been politicized. And a number of previous heads of Shin Bet said that there was no evidence of what...

PB: I'm not familiar with it.

SF: I'll go on. It seems like the International Court of Justice corroborates what people on the left have been saying about the Wall.

PB: It's not only people on the left. People around the world and governments around the world...

SF: Well, in America on the left...

PB: ...have been saying that the Wall stands as a major violation of international law and a violation of U.N. resolutions. The ICJ opinion was a very, very important recognition of that. It was a huge victory that the General Assembly was able to unite to ask for the advisory opinion. It was even more significant that, following the issuing of the advisory opinion, which said that all of the Wall that is built in Occupied Palestinian Territory, which is about 90% of the Wall, is illegal and should be taken down, that there was another resolution within the General Assembly that included one of the strongest votes ever in support of Palestinian rights, in specific an endorsement of the ICJ opinion and a commitment to seeing that it be implemented. That vote had 150 countries voting for it; only 6 voted against it, including the U.S., Israel, and Australia, and three small island states, and only 10 abstentions, which is...that's where the problem usually lies. Where the Europeans in the past have often abstained on these issues, undermining the sense of unanimity and global unity that the General Assembly implies. This time around they didn't. Europe came through, and the 10 abstentions—at least, I think, 4 of them were also small island states, the only major countries, Uruguay was one, I believe, and Canada.

SF: Do you have a comment about the American Congress immediately meeting to condemn the ruling?

PB: Yeah, what was interesting about that, see, it was a classic sort of, knee-jerk congressional response. When anything happens in the international arena that looks like the rest of the world is standing up for international law and, in this case, Palestinian rights, the knee-jerk reaction of many in Congress is to immediately vote to condemn that action, in this case, condemning the court for issuing the report, condemning the General Assembly for endorsing the court. It was a kind of wholesale rejection of international law. What was very interesting about it this time around, was that unlike other instances where there's been that kind of a knee-jerk reaction, there was significant opposition, and 60 members of the House voted "no" or voted "present" on the resolution, which is a huge increase, including people who have historically been very close to Israel: people like John Lewis from the Black Caucus and others, maybe because there has been significant public education work and pressure brought by community organizations all around the country, organizations like the U.S. Campaign to End the Israeli Occupation, that has been mobilizing to provide the kind of education for alternative viewpoints that members of Congress almost never get access to.

SF: Do you think it will have any long-term impact, then?

PB: I think it's already growing!

SF: What about the American judge?

PB: The ICJ judge?

SF: Yeah.

PB: Well that was interesting, too. Everyone assumed that the American judge—because judges on the ICJ, despite the fact that they are international civil servants and are ostensibly independent, they tend, when it's an issue of significant importance to their own country to reflect the interests and perspectives of ruling forces within their country. It doesn't happen all the time, but it's not unusual, either. In this case, it was assumed that the American judge would be the holdout on any decision that was seen as supporting international law, U.N. centrality in dealing with the issue of the Israeli occupation of Palestine, and Palestinian rights in general. And in fact, that is what indeed happened. But again, it's very important to recognize what the opposition's positions actually said. The American judge did not condemn the decision, did not disagree with the decision. He said he believed that more information was needed before an accurate assessment could be made. That's a very different posture than I think many people anticipated, and the same was true of the Dutch judge who joined in the opposition position in one of the numerous areas, the one that had to do with the obligations of signatory powers to implement decisions like this. So in both cases, there was a significantly less knee-jerk, if you will, pro-Israeli reaction than many people anticipated.

SF: Yeah, I looked at the decision. I was a little surprised. Are they allowed to do that? On the one hand he can say they have no jurisdiction, and on the other hand he says he agrees with half of what the court said?

PB: Well, they can say whatever they want: they're judges. I mean, that's... yeah, the jurisdiction question is a separate legal question, which is, you know, it's determinative if the court had found that they had no jurisdiction. That was what many people were afraid of...

SF: And that's what the American judge said, right?

PB: The American judge said that he wasn't sure there was jurisdiction, but he didn't directly oppose it. So it's a very significant, virtually unanimous decision.

SF: Chomsky seems to believe that Americans should be campaigning for something like the Geneva Accords. As a basis for negotiations.

PB: My position is that people in this country should focus on U.S. policy. U.S. policy has supported the Israeli occupation of Palestine since 1967. It's U.S. money, U.S. diplomatic support, U.S. arms that make the occupation possible. So in the context of what should Americans be doing, we should be working on our government, trying to change the policies of our government. That's precisely why we established the U.S. Campaign, it's to bring together all of the organizations around the country that are focusing on many different areas. Some of the them are focusing directly on Israel, some of them are focusing on building Palestinian civil society organizations, but where everybody comes together in the U.S. Campaign is the focus on U.S. policy, and that's what the Campaign is all about. And I think that's what Americans need to be focusing on, is what our government is doing with our tax money with or without our consent but in our name.

SF: So therefore you wouldn't advise organizing around the Geneva Accords as an alternative?

PB: I think that the Geneva Accords, as I said yesterday, are fundamentally flawed. They represent a significant sector of the Israeli left, and among some Palestinian diplomatic types, certainly if something that looked like the Geneva Accords were implemented, it would be better than the situation we have now. Having said that, I don't think we need a new Road Map. We have a Road Map: it's the road map of international law that exists, it's the road map of U.N. resolutions that exist. We don't need a new one.

SF: What Noam Chomsky says is it's not the Geneva Accords per se, but it provides a basis for negotiations. You would disagree with that then, wouldn't you?

PB: I just said what I said about Geneva. Noam says what he says.

SF: Well, okay, I think any other questions I ask would get into...well, I guess I'll ask one more controversial question on the left: To what extent do you think American foreign policy vis-à-vis Israel is influenced by America's assessment of its strategic interests as opposed to influence by—?

PB: The lobby.

SF: Yeah, the Israel lobby, the pro-Israel Jewish organizations.

PB: This is an old question within the Palestine solidarity movement, within the movement for Palestinian rights and for international law and human rights. I've always come down on the side that says that policy is made by policy makers, not by lobbies. Part of the reason the pro-Israeli lobby has historically been as influential as it has is precisely because what it's asking of the U.S. administration or the U.S. Congress at different times does not contradict what the administrations and Congress want to do anyway. So when you're not asking them to do something that goes against the direction they're already heading, you appear to be much stronger, more influential, than perhaps you are. What's different now...

SF: Today.

PB: ...is that the traditional part of the pro-Israeli lobby that was made up largely within the Jewish community organizations, particularly AIPAC and the Council of Presidents, has been not supplanted but supplemented in a significant way by the right-wing Christian fundamentalist component of the pro-Israeli lobby, which has far more influence within the Republican party than the Jewish contingent of the pro-Israeli lobby ever did. The Jewish contingent is far more influential within the Democratic Party than the Christian fundamentalists are, the Christian Zionist movement. That movement, particularly in the era of the Bush II administration, have become far more powerful, and they are a key voting block. So in the run-up to the 2004 election, as was true in the 2000 election, they represent a major area of emphasis for the presidential campaign.

SF: Does that mean that, obviously, at times they would be lobbying for policies that are not obviously in the interests of the US ruling class?

PB: Yeah, I mean the traditional...the one clearest example of who calls the shots is in 1981, when they were lobbying very hard to prevent a sale of U.S. AWACs planes to Saudi Arabia. The Pentagon wanted those sales to go through, and they did. So it was designed...it was a direct challenge to the trajectory of U.S. foreign policy, and when it was that kind of a challenge, they lost.

SF: Do you anticipate they'll lose now that you said the Israel lobby is so much stronger, augmented as it is by all these Christian Zionists?

PB: Do I anticipate what?

SF: That they'll continue to lose...

PB: Well they don't lose very often. They don't often want to do things that don't go in the direction of U.S. policy.

SF: Even now that it's been augmented by Christian Zionists?

PB: Even now. They still are moving in the same direction as U.S. policy makers are, so even now they rarely are asking for anything that they don't already want.

SF: When you say there was a split in terms of U.S. policy makers, not in terms of between this administration and the last one but in terms of the policies of the last couple years, obviously a large segment of the ruling class thought it–such as the war on Iraq—was a policy that was reckless and dangerous, but the Israel lobby was totally behind it.

PB: The Israel lobby has moved onto the side of neocons that in my view represent the most reckless component of U.S. policy of the last several decades.

SF: So then that augurs more dangerous possibilities in the future.

PB: I think it's very dangerous that the reckless neocons that are now at the center of the U.S. administration have support from any significant sector of U.S. society, particularly an influential lobby sector like the pro-Israeli lobby.

SF: So in the future, they will be able to influence whatever administration...

PB: Absolutely, they will have enormous influence on any administration that comes in.

SF: So this is, in general, a very destructive development.

PB: I don't think it's a new development. This has been true...it's been increasing since 1967.

SF: Well, I appreciate your taking your time.

Chapter 7

Adam Shapiro

Adam Shapiro is an activist with the International Solidarity Movement and a doctoral student at Georgetown University. I am reprinting by way of an introduction a scurrilous attack on him that appeared in the *New York Post*. It illustrates the misinformation process to which critics of Israel invariably are subjected by the mainstream media. Note the disparity between Peyser's comic-book description of Shapiro's position and the sophisticated analysis he presents in our discussion.

PLO'S JEWISH PAL DISGRACES VICTIMS

Andrea Peyser. **New York Post**. New York, N.Y.: Apr 1, 2002. pg. 006

(Copyright 2002, The New York Post. All Rights Reserved)

IN THE eyes of many Jews, Brooklyn native Adam Shapiro is Israel's version of American traitor John Walker Lindh. The Jewish Taliban.

"He is a traitor," Shayna Levine, one of hundreds of protesters who gathered outside the Israeli consulate yesterday, told me. "A self-hating Jew." Shapiro is the self-styled humanitarian worker who boasted of eating breakfast on Saturday with Yasser Arafat after holing up in the PLO chief's compound in Ramallah overnight as Israeli forces attacked.

As he emerged, unscathed, Shapiro described to the media his harrowing 26 hours spent under Israeli gunfire. This made some Jews gathering by the hundreds yesterday outside the Israeli consulate highly uneasy, to say the least. "When all the Jews were being blown up, where was he?" asked Lester Goldsmith. Shapiro plays at best a minuscule role in the bloodshed. Unlike Lindh, he did not raise a weapon against his people. But like Lindh, he provides a human face onto which Jews, unified in their horror over suicide bombings, can funnel their anger and frustration. Some called for a rally on Shapiro's home. Others, like Ziva Belkin, warned not to give Shapiro too much attention. "He's a publicity-seeker," said Belkin. "He deserves a lot more than protest, but he's not worth my heel."

You would think that, six months after suicide terrorists visited mass murder on New York, our country would get it. Arafat has shown himself for what he is. He and his forces have ceded any claim to moral superiority by their appalling unwillingness to halt the insanity. Even as he condemns the suicide bombings, Arafat calls the reign of terror a reasonable reaction to Israeli "occupation." Blowing oneself up is not a reaction. It is a tactic. The suicide bomber dies knowing that his memory will be revered, his family taken care of. And fear will be struck in the Israeli psyche. The bombings will not stop until

Israel is destroyed. Or the terrorists are brought down. It is time for America, so recently wounded, to stand strong beside Israel. But even as President Bush supports Israel's military, the United States votes with the Israel-bashing United Nations Security Council to call for Israel to withdraw troops from Ramallah. And a Brooklyn Jew works against Israeli interests during wartime, comforting the enemy who is Yasser Arafat. When will we learn?

[Illustration] ADAM SHAPIRO "A self-hating Jew." (S, lcf)—TIRED OF TERROR: Demonstrators march in support of Israel at the U.N. yesterday. Helayne Seidman—SIGN LANGUAGE: A protester shows his fury at Yasser Arafat's role in suicide bombings. Helayne Seidman (m)

* * *

SF: Now I read this article…it struck me, I read it just recently: In 1949, you know, there was the refugee resolution?
AS: 194.
SF: Yes. And that was the condition for Israel to be admitted into the U.N.?
AS: Correct.
SF: In the book by Francis Boyle he was quoting Abba Eban, who was president of Israel and there is a dialogue where Eban in 1949 or 1950 is swearing his solemn oath to the United Nations that they would repatriate the Palestinian refugees.
AS: That's right.
SF: You know that, that he actually said that?
AS: One of the long list of broken promises, indeed.
SF: Now they talk about it like it's just some academic bullshit.
AS: Right.
SF: But I was looking over the Geneva Accords, and Beilin was saying about it.
AS: Yossi Belein.
SF: And he's supposed to be very liberal....
AS: Supposedly.
SF: And he speaks about Palestinians…they have to be realistic about one thing: we're not going to give them he used these words;" their so-called right to return", like it was…
AS: Like they made it up out of thin air.
SF: Or like some kind of Marxist dogma—The smugness: "their so-called

right of return." —as if it's not a fundamental tenet of international law. Anyway, I had mentioned to you the Geneva Accords, you agree that with many critics of it, one of the big flaws is that it doesn't guarantee…it's not based on international law.

AS: Correct. Not only is it that it not based on international law, but it doesn't try to pick up from any of the agreements from the past, of the UN resolutions, of the international law. And it doesn't mention human rights at all as a basis for this, which, on top of everything else, if nothing else, this conflict shows a complete disdain and disregard for human rights, and to try to pronounce the Geneva Accords as something new and fresh and liberal and all these things without taking into account any sort of consideration for basic human rights—it's really a travesty, it's ultimately just another attempt at Israel—certainly by, maybe not by the right wing or the Ariel Sharon camp of Israeli politics but still within the overall framework of Israeli politics—attempting to consolidate what it has gained and stop any movement toward receding what it has gained. So it's still within that mindset.

SF: What about people who argue like Michael Lerner that it would stop the bloodshed and it would force Ariel Sharon…

AS: The Geneva Accords don't redress… it accepts occupation in some form. And this is part of the problem. You have all these people today, including the Geneva Accords signatories but others who are working in this country supposedly for peace: They're jumping the gun. Because you cannot make peace unless you first…everybody is free. And so…and I often use the example of South Africa. In South Africa, they could only discuss how a future South African might look in terms of a government, in terms of a social system, in terms of institutions after they already agreed that Apartheid was going to end and they actually started taking steps to end it. So, the same thing with occupation: you cannot continue occupation and talk about peace. You have to end occupation in order to get to peace.

SF: Now how would you reconcile the determination of the Israelis to have a Jewish state and maintain a majority with the internationally guaranteed right of return of the Palestinian refugees…Nobody knows how many refugees—although there was one questionable study. No one really knows though how many refugees would actually exercise the right to return…I would think the majority of them would not want to go back to Israel.

AS: It's debatable. There are certainly…the large number of refugees who live in Lebanon, for instance, live in terrible conditions and are made to be just as unwelcome as they have been made unwelcome until now in Israel. So, it's a difficult call as to how many would actually return, but regardless, no matter how many return to Israel, the question is, If Israelis want to continue living in a sheltered, pre-modern mindset of "we have to live only with our own kind"—and basically, it's self-ghettoization. It's saying that we have to be the majority for ourselves, only for ourselves and we cannot in any way share with others who might be somewhat different from us. And these differences that are created are also exaggerated—there isn't really much difference between Arabs and Jews, and even the languages are similar, even the cultures are fairly similar. So these exaggerated notions of difference are somewhat politicized.... If Jews insist that they have to have their own state, then there are other ways of creating a state that would be part of a greater whole. You could have a federated system where you have a superstructure of a joint state, a binational state, but then local, municipal services and local...just the way we have in the United States: state services and federal services. And then they could have their own state within a federated system that would be binational, or multinational. So I think there are many options even if Israelis want to keep this sort of Jewish character or Jewish majority, basically

SF: What about a two state solution if it **was** a way to bring about a...some kind of reconciliation?

AS: If establishing a separate Israeli state based upon Jewish identity and a separate Palestinian state based on Palestinian identity...a two-state solution in which the refugees were allowed to return back to either place with guarantees for rights...because also, we have to keep in mind, it's not a panacea in the Occupied Territories under the Palestinian Authority. Refugees who live in the Occupied Territories under the Palestinian Authority face discrimination also from within. Since the PA's been in control, it's not that refugees living in Gaza and the West Bank have been equal with non-refugee Palestinians. There are systemic forms of discrimination against them as well. Palestinians who are refugees who live in camps in the West Bank and Gaza are also discriminated against within their own society by the Palestinian Authority.

SF: As opposed to ones who are non-refugees?

AS: As opposed to ones who are non-refugees.

SF: You mean... refugees from 1948...

AS: No, no, no. There were Palestinians who lived in Ramallah since centuries ago. So you have a situation where, if refugees from Lebanon, for instance, were to return to the West Bank or into Gaza, we need to make sure that they are treated also with equal rights and equal protection under the law and equal opportunity with their fellow Palestinians, which is something we'd have to work toward. So if that was going to be the outcome of the two-state solution as well as generating equal rights for the minority Arab population in Israel, I would say fine. But I don't have a preference to what kind of option...

SF: You mentioned of course since Oslo... Edward Said and people like that said that Arafat and the PA had basically become a—despite the criticism of them as a fomenter of terrorism—a quisling of the Israelis, policing the Occupied Territories for the Israeli government...sometimes brutally.

AS: Right. If you look at how the Palestinian Authority was created and who brought Arafat into the Occupied Territories: it was Israel –and the United States basically, through the Oslo Accords, through these agreements—who created the Palestinian Authority. It's not that in 1991 and 1992 and 1993, that the Palestinians living in the Occupied Territories were clamoring for the creation of an authority that would police them. No, rather they were clamoring for democracy, they were clamoring for civil rights, they were clamoring for independence, none of which they received as a result of Oslo. And so yes, it's true, the Israelis had a great interest in establishing a Palestinian Authority that could certainly police the Palestinians for them, that would also take over the areas that were costing Israel a lot of money. You have to remember that the Occupation pre-1993 cost Israel tremendously in terms of dollars. And so, they took over health care—Israel, had no interest in providing health care for Palestinians. So they generated the Palestinian Authority and allowed the Health Ministry to develop, and so, they divested themselves from this cost. Same thing with education. Israel saw no interest in continuing to provide schools and education for Palestinians, so they gave that over to the Palestinian Authority. And some other municipal services like trash collection and all this kind of stuff. So in all of these ways, Israel found it very much within its interests to create this authority, and still, despite all the rhetoric, Israel has an interest in maintaining a Palestinian Authority, and we will see…

SF: Despite…including Arafat, despite the demonization?

AS: I think perhaps they're willing to wait now until Arafat passes from the scene, but—which I think they expect to happen some time soon—but ultimately, they do want to create another system where Palestinians take over control for their own expenses, basically.

SF: In other words, you think as many on the American anti-Zionist left or Zionist left … that they still have this vision of an Apartheid system rather than, as some have argued, actually wanting to get the right opportunity to get rid of the Palestinians altogether?

AS: Well, I mean, it's a little bit of both. It's sort of like, which option is going to end up costing you the least in the long run and also achieve what you want to achieve in the long run. Is there an effort to make things as bad as they possibly can for the Palestinians so that many of them choose to leave? I think so. Is there also a realization that, you know…you have to remember, this idea of ethnic cleansing of the Palestinians and pushing them to Jordan…many people think that this is what Israel really wants to do. It doesn't necessarily make sense. Because if Israel is concerned about these Palestinians, pushing them to Jordan and allowing them basically to take over that state then means that the Palestinians have a state by which to attack Israel. If that's Israel's fear that they're going to attack them. Now they have a state, and they have territory, and they have territorial depth, and they have potential for building up armaments and all of these kinds of things. So it's not necessarily in Israel's interest to push all these Palestinians out into Jordan. It's certainly more within Israel's interests, I believe, to take over as much land as possible without Palestinians, and those that are left, keep them imprisoned, keep them in Gaza-like conditions.

SF: Bantustans.

AS: Yeah, pretty much. But in a Bantustan unlike South Africa. In South Africa, you did not have the establishment of a Black South African governing structure. The government of South Africa was still, minimal as it may have been, providing the basic services in a sense to the Black populations. In Palestine, Israel has realized, we can do it even one step better. We can have the Bantustans, and we don't have to provide medical services. We can create a Palestinian Authority that will do that for us.

SF: There's a quote from that Tanya Reinhart book—have you read that one? This is a minister in the Cabinet of South Africa who visited Palestine and he says…South Africa was never as bad as what we have in Palestine. Here it is, "For all the evils and atrocities of apartheid, the government never sent tanks into black towns. It never used gunships, bombers or missiles against the black towns or Bantustans." He says we had curfews but they didn't go on for days after days, we didn't have a policy of "deliberate starvation." Anyway, I should get back to your own narrative, first how did you end up going to Jerusalem in the first place? How old were you then?

AS: I was twenty-seven.

SF: And it wasn't particularly…it was for ISM…?

AS: Yeah, no, it was before the Intifada began, and…

SF: So this was not particularly a time when many internationals or progressive Jews were going to Palestine?

AS: Yeah, for the most part—not entirely, but for the most part—in the 1990s, there was this sort of idea of, Well, the peace process is working, and especially, there was a lot of hope when, in 99, when Barak was elected, you know, that—yeah, for the mainstream, I would say. There were certainly some groups and some people who were more aware of what was going on, even under Oslo, who were active. But when Barak was elected, a lot of people did hold out some hope that this would be the end of the conflict.

SF: Did you, at that time?

AS: No, I was already there when Barak was elected, and I knew.

SF: How did you get interested in Israel…?

AS: I was working for an organization called Seeds of Peace, which was working to promote youth dialogue from children from all kinds of regions of conflict. And I wasn't specifically working on the Middle East issue. I was working on that as well as the Cypriot issue as well as in the Balkans. And so, I was sort of, in my job, dealing with all three as well as some logistic aspects of my job.... I was asked to go to Jerusalem to establish a youth center that would be not just for Israelis and Palestinians but, being in Jerusalem, could serve the whole region. And then of course for Israelis and Palestinians in 1999, it was possible for people to meet fairly regularly. So I was there to set that up and to get that up and running, and I ended up staying there as the director of this youth center. And then, when the Intifada began, I saw what was really happening, and one of my friends was killed—a Palestinian boy—and somebody who I knew...

SF: Somebody who you had met fairly recently?

AS: No, no, I had known him for about four or five years, and he was shot and killed... I knew him from 1996, I would say...

SF: You were there, you were?

AS: No, had met him here in the States. He was part of the Seeds of Peace program. I had met him and became friendly with him and his family, and he was shot in one of the demonstrations inside Israel by the Arabs...he was actually an Arab citizen of Israel, and so...

SF: Shot in a non-violent action?

AS: Yeah, unarmed civilians protesting in their village, and the Israeli police responded with lethal force.

SF: And this is something, by the way, I would say most Americans are not aware of...

AS: True.

SF: Most Jews don't want to, you know... They want to believe Israel has the most humane army–the whole "purity of arms" stuff ... I even heard a refusenik speak, he was a good guy—about a year ago he said, Israel has the best army in the world, so still...

AS: Right, this is still this myth that's out there. I don't know how they measure this. Yeah, I would say you don't see from the Israeli army what we have seen from...through what the Serb army did, for instance. But when the Intifada began and I started...I was regularly traveling in and out of...well, from Jerusalem into the West Bank. I was living in East Jerusalem, eventually I moved to Ramallah. From 99, I was living in East Jerusalem, and then in...

SF: Was this the first political thing that you got involved with? What was your first interest?

AS: Before?

SF: You went to high school? Were you a normal high school student or what?

AS: I was a very typical high school student. Very typical. I was into sports, I wasn't into politics....

SF: Did you read Marx?

AS: Not in high school. I would say that what motivated me…

SF: Were your parents leftists?

AS: I wouldn't call them leftists, although I would certainly call them progressive.

SF: Are they professionals?

AS: Yeah, they're both teachers in the inner city in New York, so they know…

SF: Oh, they're professors, so they're intellectuals?

AS: No, they're high school teachers… In the inner city. So we grew up in a neighborhood where they were Puerto Rican and Cuban kids that were my friends and African Americans were my friends and Irish and Italian…

SF: How old are they?

AS: In their fifties….

SF: Oh, so actually they're closer to my generation; they're in the 60s generation.

AS: My dad, luckily he wasn't drafted for Vietnam, but his plan was that if he was drafted, he would go to Canada or something, I guess. But he never had to face that…

SF: So you were a normal high school student, interested in sports….

AS: Yes then I went to Washington University in St. Louis… And I had friends—that I grew up with in my neighborhood—who were serving in the U.S. military in 1991, and they were sent to….

SF: Which neighborhood are you from?

AS: Sheepshead Bay. So I knew some people who were sent over to the Gulf to fight, and I didn't know anything about this region, I didn't know anything about the Middle East really except what the ancient Egyptians…

SF: Did you support the war at that time?

AS: I didn't really know anything, and so I didn't take a position. I knew my friends were there but I wanted to learn, so I started taking courses in college about the Middle East, about the culture, about the history, about the peoples, about the politics. And by 1992, 1993, I was starting to become active against…well, by this time, the war was over, but already they were talking about sanctions against Iraq. And so, I was starting to become active against the sanctions. I thought the sanctions were a very bad idea. And then of course at that time was also the…

SF: The effect on—

AS: On the civilian population, basically that is was…you couldn't give…. We did a big thing in my school highlighting how you couldn't even send pencils to children because the UN decided that the lead in the pencils could be used to make nuclear weapons or something. So there was that, but then by 1993, of course, was the Oslo Accords, and there was a great hope, supposedly, and everybody seemed to be on the bandwagon of pushing for peace. And even looking at the images from on the ground, the images coming home were Palestinians giving Israeli troops roses as they left their cities and redeployed. And so it seemed like things were going to be going okay, and so…but I wasn't very active on that issue

SF: I think you said, you didn't have much religious upbringing at all, right?

AS: No…

SF: Were you bar mitzvahed?

AS: I was. My family…when my grandfather was alive, it was more out of tradition than anything. It wasn't out of any deep religious conviction. On the holiest holidays, I guess, we would go to the synagogue…

SF: They continue going on the holidays?

AS: These days? I don't think they go anymore. I think they haven't gone for a while. But…

SF: Would they go now? Would there be controversy?

AS: They probably wouldn't even be welcome because of me. By the time I finished college and going on to graduate school, I became much more educated about the Palestinian issue, and by 1996, I would say, I became much more aware of what was going on, Although, to be honest, I still wasn't, even by 1997 interested in Palestine…. My first trip to the region…. In 1996, I went to live in Yemen for a year, because I was.

AS: About the culture, about the people, the history…I was fascinated, and I really wasn't interested in the Israeli-Palestinian conflict. I really…I was much more interested in other parts of the Arab world.

SF: Was it that you felt it was too much to change—with all the suffering in the world?

AS: It wasn't even so much about suffering, it just, I found it far more comfortable in the sense to live and be intimate with other cultures. But by the time I started working for Seeds of Peace and was actually on the ground in 1998 and then in 1999 when I was living there and became a member of the community in East Jerusalem, I realized that not only was I living here and working, I also had a responsibility as an American citizen, and that I was contributing to this conflict in some way and contributing to the suffering.

SF: Also as a Jew by background?

AS: I don't really identify myself as a Jew, so to me that never mattered in terms of my own…

SF: Even though it's done in the name of Jews?

AS: It's done in the name of Jews, and I definitely am opposed to that, but for myself, that didn't motivate me. It was more as an American citizen that I was…and just personally, living there, being there… these are people who are my neighbors.

SF: If people ask you your religion what do you say?

AS: Nothing. No, I just say I'm nothing.

SF: Would you say you're an atheist?

AS: I don't even say I'm an atheist, I say I'm nothing.

SF: You never thought about the issue, or God, or is there a God?

AS: I really don't care. The way I see, it doesn't really affect my life in any way. If there is a God, and I do or don't believe in him, it really doesn't matter. Or him or her…. I don't think anyone else necessarily needs to believe in this or think this way. I have a great respect for people who have faith and who believe, and my wife Huwaida, she's Catholic…

SF: She's Catholic?

AS: Greek Catholic, it's an eastern form of Catholicism.

SF: I knew there were a lot of Palestinian Christians; I didn't know there were Catholics…

AS: There's a Greek Catholic church…

SF: Orthodox?

AS: It's not Orthodox. It's sort of between the Orthodox and the Catholic versions of faith. It combines both. It's fairly interesting—it's called the Malakite church. And she's not a big churchgoer, but she believes, she has faith. And I totally respect that, and…

SF: You don't think religion is the opium of the people or anything like that?

AS: It could be if it's used by politicians or by religious leaders, but… But I totally realize that it's also something very personal and spiritual for many people, and that's up to them. So I would say that by the time I was living there on the ground, I became much more active and interested. And even when I was working for Seeds of Peace, I was very much in tune and in touch with my community, starting in East Jerusalem and then, of course, branching out further into the West Bank. And I was going into Gaza just about almost once a week. And so I really… you know, I love Gaza, I think it's a great…I love the people there, and it's a terrible place to have to live.

SF: Since the last intifada and Sharon?

AS: Even before. Even before, Gaza was…is like being in a prison.

SF: Even before, even in the?

AS: Even in the 90s, absolutely. Gaza is a very difficult place to live, and yet, I found I had such wonderful experiences there, and…. What I was first doing is writing home and to my friends and my e-mail contacts and to my network of people and in my job through Seeds of Peace, trying to work in such a way to promote a better understanding of what was happening actually on the ground and why some of the assumptions that people in the peace community make are false assumptions. And so I was dealing not just with my own organization but also with other organizations, both American-based organizations and organizations based on the ground.

SF: Assumptions about—?

AS: Assumptions about Israel, assumptions about peace, the assumptions about occupation. Most people believed, by 1999, even Israelis believed that occupation was almost finished, when in fact, actually, it was quite the opposite. It was becoming strengthened, it was becoming more endemic.

SF: Would you say that was the plan all along of the Israeli government?

AS: No, I can't say that it's the plan all along, because I don't think anybody in 1967 or 1973 or 1975 or 1982 envisioned, We'll make a deal with Yassir Arafat, and create an authority so that we can make more occupation. I don't think anybody thought that.

SF: I mean since Oslo began?

AS: In 1993, did they think that? Well, did they think they could establish in 1993 an authority by the Palestinians that would allow them to divest responsibility? Yes. Did they expect necessarily that so many right-wing Jews would choose to become settlers? Because you have to remember, up until 1993, the total settler population was only about 200,000 people, which is still a lot, but in less than ten years, from 1993-2000, it doubled. So that rapid expansion I don't know if anyone could have envisioned. If in 1993, they were thinking about continuing the settlement project, they probably thought of it terms of continuing at the pace that they had be growing up until that point, which was rapid, which was taking over a lot of land, but it wasn't as rapid as it became over the next ten years.

SF: Are they actually intent on expanding to greater Israel?

AS: No, there are people who wanted to go with the idea of Greater Israel. There are no Israeli politicians or governments that are willing to give up Israel's ascendant role vis-à-vis the Palestinians and the other countries in the region, nor are they willing to give up anymore—or perhaps ever have been willing to give up—any sort of strategic control not just of the land, but of the resources of the land, which include water—probably most importantly water. And so those are two things that are things where Israel's not willing to compromise. Are there Israeli governments and politicians who over time have been willing to compromise over the amount of independence or self-rule that Palestinians might have? Yes, but even that has always been limited to some extent in terms of foreign affairs, in terms of maintaining their own self-defense forces, in terms of ownership over the airwaves over the West Bank. All kinds of things.

SF: No one willing to go back to the 67 border region?

AS: There is not a single Israeli government that has yet to express that desire.... The problem is two things since then. After 67, you saw the settlements expansion grow...develop. So that changed the whole dynamic of who the people were in this territory.

SF: Yes and that's when the Gush Emunim and the racist messianic movement...

AS: Right, but that was together with the settlement movement; that's where the settlers were. So you have...

SF: There was also the people who went there because it was cheaper places, cheaper land etc ... When you mean in the settlements, you refer to the right-wing zealot...?

AS: I mean the whole settlement project however for cheap housing or for also ideological reasons. So you have a change after 67 as to which people are actually now in these territories. You also have now Jews living there. So it changes the security considerations. Additionally, the impact of...looking at water issues became much more important after the 60s than it had been previously. Plus, you also have, in 1973, Egypt, through the one maneuver it was able to make by costing the Suez Canal, changed—and capturing Israel by surprise on the Yom Kippur War—changed the confidence that Israeli generals had that, Oh my God, wait a minute, there could be a sneak attack.

SF: In 73?

AS: In 73. So that also changed the confidence in terms of those who were pushing for—like Moshe Dayan even thought that they should return the territory and not hold onto this vast chunk of territory. That started to change into this idea that maybe we need to hold onto it in some way, and we can broker with it. And then of course, that's what we've seen since 1973 is this idea that we can exchange the Sinai Peninsula for peace with Egypt. With Jordan, even, there was some land given back to Jordan as a result of the peace treaty there. So things have developed over time as conditions have changed.

SF: Anyway, how did you get from Seeds of Peace to Arafat's compound?

AS: Well, after the Intifada began, a lot of us...the story of the ISM is basically that a lot of us foreigners were living there who wanted to do something...

SF: Did you have a commitment to this whole idea of non-violent philosophy, Martin Luther King and Gandhi. You were steeped in it or something?

AS: I don't know about "steeped in," but I was very familiar with the history of the Civil Rights Movement in this country. I was very familiar with the Gandhian movement, and I had done a lot of reading, and I had always considered that non-violence was a very viable means of social change. ...I had a lot of friends in Palestine who had been very active during the first Intifada, and hearing their stories and learning about how the first Intifada was organized and how the communities were mobilized and all this—it just seemed to me, and certainly in talking to other people and just sort of looking at the strategic assessment, that non-violence…massive non-violent movement, direct action, would be the best use of the Palestinian…whatever resources they had at their disposal. So that was the idea behind forming the ISM: by bringing in internationals and having them participate with the Palestinians, this is adding yet another resource to what Palestinians could use to achieve end of occupation, to achieve freedom, to achieve independence, whatever.

SF: You got involved after the suicide bombing in 2000 or 2001?

AS: No, we started ISM long before. It wasn't in relation to any suicide bombing. It was actually in relation to seeing Palestinians protesting in the streets and being shot at. That's what it was in response to. So, that's the idea behind forming the ISM. In terms of getting into Arafat's compound: although it was as ISM that we were doing it…

SF: Did I read in the paper that you and a bunch of other people snuck into the?

AS: That was another time.

SF: Oh, there were two separate?

AS: We actually entered Arafat's…we had people enter Arafat's compound three times. The first time, which is when I went with just one other person—we were on an ambulance, and this was sort of a…it became what ISM did at that time, escorting ambulances. But that really was not the mission of the ISM. In that time period, what we were doing was really responding to a crisis situation or crisis on top of a crisis. So we were escorting ambulances because otherwise, ambulances were not allowed to move. The drivers were being arrested…

SF: What about all of that Israeli propaganda that the ambulances are all used to carry explosives…

AS: They were transporting terrorists and all this bullshit. It's bullshit. I mean, there's no proof, it's just an allegation. I think there was one ambulance….

SF: So what happened after Arafat's compound…was that pretty much your last…you were banned from Israel? How did you find meeting with Arafat, by the way?

AS: Well, I give Arafat credit for this. When the heat is on, it's true what they say about him. When things seem hopeless or when they're more intense, Arafat seems to be more calm and in control. So I think what he did, though, at least for the time I was in the…he was very reassuring…There were some older people who were…who had been through similar things before who were definitely calm and more under control. You also had a lot, a lot, a lot of young men who were in their twenties who were policemen who just worked at the compounds. There was even a 17-year old kid there who was…who did all the cleaning. And so you had a lot of young people who didn't know what the hell to do, who were very unsure. And the second day that I was there, Arafat came down and just walked around and met everybody and just talked to everybody and asked them where they were from, and maybe he knew a lot of them already, maybe not. I don't know. But just talking to everybody was a big boost in terms of moral and in terms of just everybody feeling a bit more calm about the whole thing. And so I give him credit for that, but otherwise, we didn't have much interaction

SF: By the way, does it bother you when the press calls you anti-Semitic and a Jewish self-hater all the time?

AS: It doesn't apply to me, so if they want to call it, I don't care. Whatever. I think it doesn't change anything one way or another, so….

SF: You say you don't feel any identification as a Jew in any sense, culturally or anything?

AS: No, not really.

SF: Do you think that it's unfortunate that Jews in the past had a history of being an oppressed group in America and then become more and more conservative?

AS: Well, I think Jewish Americans still are…I think there's a large part of the population that still is progressive.

SF: You mean Jews on the far left?

AS: Not even so much…even some of the mainstream are still somewhat progressive on a lot of social issues, and if you take…If you look at like, civil rights for gay couples and on gay and lesbian issues, Jews tend to be more liberal, more progressive than the mainstream. But when it comes to Israel, it's true, there's sort of like this contradiction…. But that's because the way the mainstream Jewish organizations and synagogues in this country have framed the issue. They have basically framed the issue that you have to support Israel no matter what. And this is a problem, this is a problem I think even for Jews to identify with, because it basically says, On this issue, we are going to be completely uncritical, and we're not going to…we don't care what Israel does, we just support Israel. And I think that's problematic even for Jews, and I'll put it to you this way: there is tremendous support continually…ongoing for Israel, despite the fact that there is a very active and very dangerous sex slave industry in Israel. Women face…

SF: Literally?

AS: Literally. Women face a tremendous amount of violence in Israel.

SF: You read about physical abuse, but that's only….

AS: There's also a sex slave industry in Israel that is quite violent and quite abusive. And it's basically sanctioned by government, so you don't find a critique of that here. There is tremendous violence in Israeli schools. I remember in 1999, there was a study conducted of the top fifteen industrialized countries or something like that, and Israel ranked far higher than everybody else in terms of violence in high school. You don't find any sort of critical discussion about that among American Jews. There is…and of course, every society has problems. There's no perfect society. But this idea that all of this money and all of this support is going continually to go to Israel without questioning at all what's going on…. And let's face it, American Jews can have a very big role to play in Israel in shaping the future of Israel, in shaping the policies of Israel, and they simply choose to give money and step away.

SF: Why do you think they do that?

AS: Because those are the terms that most Israeli governments and most of the people who try and fund raise from Israel, those are terms that they want.

SF: Why do you think organized Jewry is so willing to go along with that?

AS: Because they've bought into this basic notion that this is our last safety valve.

SF: Oh, that Jews are still jeopardized after the Holocaust and all that?

AS: Yeah, exactly. That anti-Semitism is just around the corner, and the ovens can start up any time soon. You don't have to be extremist about it.

SF: Is there any truth to that?

AS: I do believe that there is anti-Semitism. I don't believe it's new. I believe it's the same as the old one. I think it's a bigger problem and a bigger issue in Christian countries than it is in Muslim countries, to be honest. I think any anti-Semitism that you find in Muslim countries today is the direct result of the policies of Israel vis-à-vis Palestinians. I think the anti-Semitism you find in Europe has much more to do with Christian-Jewish relations and the Jewish history inside Europe.

SF: But is there any more harassment of Jewish immigrants than there is of Muslim immigrants?

AS: There's different types, there's definitely different types. Obviously Muslim immigrants have their own issues, and we shouldn't look at these as like, Well, there's more of this and less of that, so we deal with this first and that second. No, I think we need to deal with all of these issues. Europe, I mean France is a great example. Today, France has a lot of issues to work out with regards to minorities, with regards to identity issues, and not just of Muslims or North Africans but of lots of people in their society, of Africans, of all kinds of people. One of the things I would say about organizing around anti-Semitism is that Jews want to see anti-Semitism as a thing in and of itself, and they want to see this phenomenon as simply about Jews. They don't want to see it as part of a broader context of the rise of right-wing politicians in Europe that are against immigrants, that are against any diversity, any sort of identity that is non-white. And they try to…the effort is under way to take anti-Semitism out of the overall social context and say, This issue needs to be dealt with by itself. I think that breaks the strength that you might have in co-organizing, for instance in France, with Muslims, with Africans, with Southeast Asians or Southwest Asians....

SF: The Jewish organizations in the US claim any criticism of Israel is an anti-Semitic—

AS: Right. This is a secondary thing, and this is totally bullshit. This idea that you can't criticize Israel. We're allowed to criticize…even when we're allowed to criticize in this country our own government as much as we want, and given the amount of money we give to Israel, we have a right and a duty to criticize and to say what's right and what's wrong.

SF: Do you think we also have a responsibility to criticize something done in our name?

AS: For those people who identify as Jewish, absolutely.

SF: But what if others identify you as Jewish?

AS: Oh, I refuse to accept somebody else identifying, so that's a bigger social issue. But no, I think absolutely, for anybody who accepts the identification for themselves as Jewish or accepts a communal definition for themselves as Jewish, then absolutely, it's important to be critical of anything being done in your name. We expect that…one of the great things that we blame the Germans for in World War II is that they didn't criticize what was being done in their name, and so we can't accept the same thing for ourselves.

SF: A lot of people have spoken about the poignancy, the irony of the fact that the Jews who were so oppressed for so many centuries and have now become one of the greatest oppressors.

AS: I don't see why this is surprising to people. Again, this is human history. Over and over and over in human history, those who have been oppressed have turned into the oppressors. This is…I think it's sad, and I don't think it's something natural. I think it's something social that happens.

SF: It's pretty much recent with Jews.

AS: Well, it's recent in the sense that this is the first time that Jews have had a state and have had a military and have had power vis-à-vis another people, so it's new in that sense, but it's also the first time they've had the opportunity. It's not like they had the opportunity in 1500 and didn't exploit it. It's not they had the opportunity in 1850 and had the opportunity and didn't exploit it.

SF: So you don't think there was there something about Jewish tradition or ethical tradition that kept them moral for all these years and that is somehow weakened by the…?

AS: No, if you want to use the Bible as history, or ancient Jewish history as an example of how…with these supposed Jewish values, Jewish morals, and all that stuff…you read the Bible, look at how other peoples have been treated in the Bible by Jews. It's not very pretty. The Caananites, all these people who were there...who was it, the Philistines were totally wiped out by Solomon...no not Solomon...

SF: Joshua—following God's command, right?

AS: Supposedly. It's a nice excuse to say, Oh well, you know God commanded me.... But the funny thing is...

SF: I don't think that's really a historical event though...

AS: Well one way you can look at it is if you can say that Jewish people in the Bible were operating according to God's command, then you sort of devolve yourself of responsibility for it.

SF: In America, what do you think of the demonization of Palestinians, that they're all terrorists and so on and so forth? You don't encounter that all the time?

AS: You do encounter that. Part of the problem in dealing with that issue... this is not just for Palestinians, it's for all Arabs...and this has to do with how Hollywood produces movies and all this kind of stuff. But that is not...I mean, there's a political project behind it, but there's also, let's face it, in the 1960s, you did have Arab groups that were wearing ski masks and hijacking airplanes. It's not like these images...I believe they're socially constructed, they have a political purpose, but they weren't completely constructed out of thin air, either. Because if you look at the 1950s, and you look at the 1940s, at the way Arabs were portrayed in movies, it wasn't very positive. They were seen as being somewhat savage and backwards or uneducated or maybe even conniving and evil, and that has helped create the foundation for creating Arabs as these mass terrorists and all that stuff. But let's face it: Osama bin Laden does exist, and Al Quaeda does exist. There are people who are doing very bad things which only help to push these images. So at least here in America and the way the images are produced, while there is a political aspect to it, they're not completely unconnected to something that's happening on the ground.

SF: Do you get any kind of prejudice against you and Huwaida as a couple from American Palestinians?

AS: Only from the same people who are prejudiced against me anyway.

SF: And her family doesn't have any prejudice—?

AS: Her family was very welcoming.

SF: What is their class background?

AS: Her dad is a blue-collar worker. He works on the transmission line at GM, and her mom's a nurse. So they're both working class.

SF: So what happened after your...after Ramallah?

AS: After Ramallah, Huwaida and I actually both left, and we came back here and we got married, and then we went back there a couple weeks after we were married, and we got in without a problem, and we continued our work with ISM through the summer. And in August of 2002, during the march with Palestinian villagers from a little village near Nablus, we…the people had been under curfew for, I don't know, three weeks, and we…they asked us to come, and they wanted to break the curfew, and they wanted to march out of their village and march all the way to Nablus. And Nablus also had been under curfew and under siege at that time. So the idea was to break the curfew in their village and march to Nablus and break the curfew there. And the idea would be, once we got to Nablus, that we would be joined by more people in Nablus, and it would become a really big march. So we did that, and then, as we were on the road to Nablus, we were about a kilometer and one-half away let's say from the checkpoint, we were stopped by the Israeli army and tear-gassed and all that stuff. And ultimately nine of us were…

SF: Just you and the villagers?

AS: Well no, we had about fifty foreigners with about two hundred and fifty Palestinians. And so the army…they fired some ammunition in the air. They didn't fire at any people, which was the idea of the ISM—that you put foreigners in and they won't shoot at the people. And nine of us were arrested. All of us were foreigners. There were five French people, three Americans, and one Irish guy. And we were all arrested, and because…I really think that the others would have been let go except for the fact that I was arrested with them, and by now, the Israelis knew who I was, and they wanted to get rid of me. We were in jail for about a week, and then we were sent away.

SF: Why did they single you out?

AS: Because of the whole Arafat thing, and because the saw me as the… because I was doing all the interviews. Even Ha'aretz newspaper did an interview with me, a full interview with me. So I was the one seen as like the leader of this group, even though I wasn't the leader of the ISM, they saw me in this way. So they figured they would make an example of me and all this stuff and get me out, even though I wasn't charged with anything. When they arrested me, the police chief told me I was under arrest for disturbing the peace. I said, "There's no peace here." He laughed…you know, we had a good laugh, and it was totally bogus all their charges. And ultimately I could have gone to trial with it. I could have brought it into court. It would have meant I would have had to spend probably a lot more time in jail, it would have been a lot of expenses for ISM that we didn't really have, and ultimately, even if I had won the case…the way the judges have found more recently is that, they'll let the people go but with the condition that they don't return to the West Bank or Gaza. And you can stay, but only in Israel. And I wasn't interested in that kind of ruling.

SF: So now you're banned.

AS: Currently banned. I'm actually on the top of the list…

SF: From Israel and Palestine?

AS: No, no, any country has the right to stop anybody they wish from entering their country. That is one of the principles of sovereignty. The problem is, I'm not trying to go into Israel, I'm trying to go into the West Bank and Gaza, and Israel doesn't maintain sovereignty over these places. This is actually something even Israel will admit to. They have not formally annexed any of this land, so they do not possess sovereignty over the West Bank and Gaza. So this is the question. The way they could keep me out is because there is no direct way to enter the West Bank and Gaza from another country. In order to enter the West Bank or Gaza, you have to first enter Israel. So this is the way they can keep you out. It's a technical matter.

SF: You're not going to contest it?

AS: I tried. There's no way to really contest it. I appealed to the Minister of the Interior; it's his decision. The current Minister of the Interior was apparently willing to listen and hear my case. I had a lawyer who was presenting it, and I had a member of Knesset also advocating for me, but the Shin Bet has interfered, and they have me, really, on the top of their list, and they refuse to consider anything different.

SF: And your wife?

AS: Well Huwaida is applying to law school for next year.

SF: In here?

AS: In the United States, so hopefully next year we'll be together, and if not, we'll see. Otherwise, she will also be making a decision as to how much she in terms of…for the next few years, what are the prospects for the work she's doing and whether it's worth continuing to stay, or, depending on what's happening politically, it might not be the work that she's trying to do, which is promoting strategic non-violence, working with Palestinian communities, might not be possible or feasible. Who knows? I can totally envision a time when a re-empowered Palestinian Authority would not want even for people like Huwaida to be active, or for the ISM to exist. And we already know that Israel…

SF: What kind of?

AS: A re-empowerment of the Palestinian Authority.

SF: You mean like…

AS: The 90s. And we already know that when there have been previous negotiations, for instance with Abu Mazen, one of the things that the Israeli government has tried to impose on the Palestinian Authority is that the ISM will be a banned organization in the West Bank and Gaza, and so, at this point, the Palestinian negotiators are unwilling to meet that demand, but who knows? Maybe they would be willing to meet it at some point if some sort of political constellation changed. I don't know.

SF: So you don't think it's going to get worse? Better?

AS: Oh, I think things are going to get much worse before they get better. I think what we'll see is a further imprisonment of the Palestinian population and further confinement on less and less land. And ultimately, the conditions will get so bad, that the people who can leave, as they have been, will probably continue to leave.

SF: Why do you think of the people like Tony Judt who say, 30-40 years from now, it will be better but not now. That the time of the two-state solution is already over, etc.?

AS: Oh, the time of the two-state solution has been over for a long time. That people like Tony Judt are only coming to this realization today…you know, they're behind the ball. The two-state solution option has been over for a long time. It's not to say that a one-state solution is really an option at this point. We can just look at the way that there's nothing written that says a minority population, as the Jews might be vis-à-vis Palestinians in a one-state solution…it's not written anywhere… we have ample evidence from history and recent history that a minority population can keep a majority population under its thumb; it absolutely can. So to think that a one-state solution will be a panacea of equal rights and civil rights for all people there is a false hope and a false premise.

SF: You got an award recently?

AS: The Marshall Meyers award…

SF: He's dead, right?

AS: Right.

SF: He was a Rabbi who was sympathetic to the Palestinians?

AS: Yeah, he was fairly progressive, apparently. I don't know much about him. The event was co-sponsored by JATO and by Jews for Racial and Economic Justice, and it was supposed to be held at, I guess, Bnai Jeshrun. …. Once it was announced publicly that this was going to happen at Bnai Jeshrun, and the New York Sun, an extremely right-wing and small-minded and small circulation newspaper wrote a hate article about it, Bnai Jeshrun revoked its hosting option, and said they knew nothing about this and had never been consulted. And that's just totally bullshit. And so, they pulled out from hosting the event, so the event was shifted to a church down the street, and they hosted it, and it turned out to be a very nice event, and from I heard—I wasn't there, I was overseas at the time—My brother and my family accepted on my behalf, and I heard it went off very well, so too bad for them.

SF: People claim you were supporting some suicide bombers.

AS: That's what the claims are. My position and the position of ISM is very clear: we do not…

SF: Your position is the position of ISM, right?

AS: Yeah, we're similar…. We do not support the targeting or killing of innocent civilians or non-combatants in any way by any party anywhere.

SF: What provoked B'nai Jeshrun?

AS: No, what's gotten me into trouble is that I wrote an article whereby I acknowledge...I was making the case for non-violent resistance, and what I basically said was this: Those who use suicide bombing consider the people who die in doing these things as martyrs. They way that, you know, if you are killed during a suicide bombing, you are a martyr. And my position was this: even for those people who consider them martyrs, they would, by their own standard of what a martyr is, if you die in a non-violent activity, you are also a martyr. And so then there's no difference between someone who becomes a martyr this way and somebody who become this way. So there's no reason why there shouldn't be support for people to use non-violence, also. People have twisted my words to say that because I accept that somebody who dies becomes a martyr, therefore I support suicide bombings. It's a total twisting. But if you read the article, it's quite clear that...you can probably find it online at the *PalestineChronicle.org*, and you can read it. .... This is the other part they don't tell you when they criticize it. I wrote the article, it was called "Why Palestinians Can Be Non-Violent," because it was a response to an article that was written which said—but by a Palestinian who said why Palestinians can't be non-violent—so we were refuting him—

SF: Advocating non-violence?

AS: He was sort of showing the conditions under which Palestinians live and saying, When all of this is happening, when all of these people are being killed, when all of this violence is being used against Palestinians, you shouldn't expect or you shouldn't advocate for Palestinians to be non-violent and you should expect violence. What we were saying was, Okay, even if Israel's going to use violence against you, that doesn't pre-determine what options you have. You're not like Pavlov's dog, where you respond simply to a certain type of stimulus. You are a thinking human being, and you are a thinking community, and you can decide how you want to respond.

SF: Ironic. You write an article in support of non-violence and the press and the synagogue attacks you as a supporter of terrorism! ...What are your plans for the future?

AS: I don't really have any. First I have to finish my Ph.D. and I have to...

SF: What's your thesis on?

AS: I'm looking at why is it that women in postwar reconstruction situations in general...well, I'm looking at three case studies: Afghanistan, Iraq, and Haiti... why is it that women have been less secure during this time when liberation of women and women's security is often used as justification for war in the first place. So there's sort of a quandary there.

SF: So do you have a continuing commitment to Palestine?

AS: Yeah, of course. I continue to speak publicly around the country, and I continue to organize for the ISM here in the States.

SF: It doesn't look very hopeful.

AS: I've been pessimistic before I started the ISM, but pessimism is no excuse not to do something. The only way to overcome your pessimism is to be active and do something that creates new situations and new conditions and change whereby you might become optimistic.

SF: Gramsci counseled pessimism of the intellect and optimism of the will?

AS: That's exactly, I think, my perspective.

SF: So do you remain committed to other political?

AS: Yeah, I feel, especially nowadays as an activist, as an American citizen, I feel particularly strongly that we have to do more with Iraq, that we have to do more to help the Iraqi people as citizens, as a civil society, and not only offer Iraqis the occupation and the occupation forces and companies like Bechtel and Halliburton to represent America in Iraq, that we have a responsibility to the Iraqi people for what we've done there, not just through this war but over the last 35 years, first in supporting Saddam, and then in turning against Saddam and imposing sanctions and all of these things. We have a historic responsibility to the Iraqi people. And I'm committed to…I'm active in many different ways on other issues like the Free Burma movement. I'm very interested and supportive of the Iranian student movement…

SF: Islamic reform?

AS: Well, the position in this country is that it's Islamic reform. Basically the students are looking for what certainly could be terms democratic reforms. It's all depending on what word you want to use. It's a Muslim country, so they're all Muslim. What they're looking for is basically…what most of the students are looking for are democratic reforms about dealing with representation, dealing with legitimation, dealing with participation.

SF: Are you going to vote against Bush or do you—

AS: Well, interestingly enough…

SF: think it doesn't matter…

AS: I vote…I live in Washington, D.C., and Washington, D.C. is not a state, and so we don't have…it's an interesting situation. We get to vote, but we don't have a delegate at the Electoral College, so our vote is worthless. So I'm actually working for two states, a Palestinian state and a Washington, D.C. state. I personally believe we have to get rid of Bush. Not that I…. I don't necessarily think that many of these guys are better on the Israeli/Palestinian issue, but I do think that certainly removing not just Bush…I think its more important to remove people like Ashcroft and Cheney and Rice and Rumsfeld and Wolfowitz. That's more important.

SF: They've got a plan, too. I think Iran and…

AS: Yeah, sure. They have much more, greater aspirations. But those are the people we have to get rid of. And so I support anybody who will get rid of them.

SF: Would you also say you're anti-Zionist?

AS: Somebody asked me last night, actually, when I was speaking, and it depends what you mean by Zionism. If you mean by Zionism a sort of historic or cultural and religious claim to the land at the expense of other people, then I'm against any type of nationalism like that, be it in Israel, be it in Serbia, be it wherever. But I know people who define Zionism much differently. They define it as sort of a love for the land, and they don't really care who controls it. They...

SF: Cultural Zionism as opposed to political Zionism which claims state-sovereignty?

AS: Political Zionism, the way it's been expressed, I have a big problem with it.

SF: So you don't think that left wing Zionism is much better than...and Michael Lerner?

AS: No. No. I totally, fundamentally disagree with Michael Lerner's position, and I think his position is dubious at best.

Chapter 8

Daniel Boyarin

Daniel Boyarin is the Taubman Professor of Talmudic Culture, at the University of California, Berkeley

Some quotations from books by Professor Boyarin

"As we begin to look at the Jewish culture of late antiquity, we can begin to construct a genealogy for the nineteenth century antiphallicism of European Jewish culture and its resistance to their culture of violent male sexuality that was endemic, even acutely so at this time...

Whereas European aristocratic culture despised the submissive male, both early Christian and early Jewish cultures frequently valorized 'him.' Both early Rabbinic cultures and early Christians performed resistance to the Roman imperial power structure through 'gender-bending,' thereby marking their own understanding that gender itself is implicated in the maintenance of political power. Through various symbolic enactments of 'femaleness'—as constructed within a particular system of genders—among them asceticism, submissiveness, retiring to private spaces and circumcision...were adopted variously by Christians or Jews as acts of resistance against the Roman culture of masculinist power wielding" (*Powers of the Diaspora*, pp.77-78)

"Rabbinic culture defined ideal men as peaceful, gentle and nurturing. It is here that we find the origin of the notion that Jewish men do not beat their wives." *(Unheroic Conduct*, p.162)

...."[W]e see at the foundation of the rabbinic value system the obverse of the 'manly' Roman values in the Masada foundation myth of Jewish heroism.... The Babylonian Talmud's Rabbi Yohanan prefers life and the possibility to serve God through the study of Torah over everything else...While the Josephan zealots proved themselves 'real men' by preferring death at their own hands to slavery, the Rabbis prefer slavery to death" (*Powers of the Diaspora*, 2002, p.52)

Goyim naches (games Gentiles play) can now be defined as the contemptuous Jewish term for those characteristics that in European culture have defined a man as manly: physical strength, martial activity and aggressiveness, and contempt for and fear of the female body" (*Unheroic Conduct*, p. 78)

"In Christian culture.... the feminized male was de-eroticized, while in Jewish culture he was projected as the husband par excellence, and even...as favored object of female desire." (*Unheroic Conduct,* p.64)

"The cult of the tough Jew as an alternative to Jewish timidity and gentleness rests on ideals of 'masculine beauty' health and normalcy that were conceived as if there validity were obvious and natural. They [Muscle-Jews] have...internalized the physical and psychological ideals of their respective dominating cultures. In doing so they forget that, far from being self-evident cultural universals, those ideals are predicated on a series of exclusions and erasures—of effeminate men, pacifism, Arabs, gentleness, women, homosexuals, and far from least, Jews." (Paul Breines, cited in *Unheroic Conduct*, p.xxi)

"For Herzl, it was conversion to Christianity, radical politics, and dueling—another variety of the Aryan/Teutonic cause–that Zionism replaced as the means to Jewish masculinity, to Jewish assimilation. If, in other national movements, 'manliness' is made to serve nationalism, for Herzl nationalism was an instrument in the search for manliness." (*Unheroic Conduct*, pp. 301-2)

"The Jews as colonists, constitute themselves both as natives and as colonizers. Indeed it is through a mimicry of colonization that the Zionists seek to escape the stigma of Jewish difference.... Among the first acts of his foundation of Zionism was the establishment of the Jewish Company—under that name and in London. Herzl had finally found a way for the Jews to become European; they would have a little colony of their own." (*Unheroic Conduct*, pp. 304-5)

* * *

SF: Most people I've met in the anti-occupation movement, are not Orthodox.... In San Francisco where you are I guess the radical group is the Jewish Voice for Peace? You're familiar with all that?

DB: Yeah, I'm on their advisory board.

SF: Here, it's Jews Against the Occupation. I think they're similar in that they both tend to be (without getting into long, complex things) they both tend to be anti-Zionist, you said, among other things, Orthodoxy is the best place to preserve Jewish alterity. Could you say a little bit about that? Besides Neturei Karta, there are very few Orthodox involved in social causes. Correct me if I'm wrong.

DB: Relatively few, but there certainly are. I mean I'm Orthodox because I'm Orthodox. I was Orthodox before I was anti-Zionist.

SF: But didn't I get the impression that you were not raised Orthodox?

DB: I wasn't. It's true, but nevertheless I was Orthodox before I was anti-Zionist.

SF: Well that's a stronger argument, from my point of view, against Zionism, as you say, as a deviation from. Judaism—

DB: Yeah, no, I agree. I'm just saying that the question is not, Why Orthodox? I'm Orthodox because I'm Orthodox. I'm Orthodox because I'm committed to historical Judaism. I believe in it, whatever that means, but that's a complicated statement, but that's who I am religiously.

SF: You spoke of your attraction to the Talmud. By the way, I was raised in a secular Jewish home.

DB: So was I.

SF: Oh you were? Completely secular? Huh! But I'm a 95-pound weakling, so in that way, I am more in conformity with rabbinic Jewish ideal.

DB: Yeah, I understand. So I mean it's not a question for me, Why Orthodox?

SF: Do conservative Jews study Talmud, too, or not really?

DB: I'm sure many do, I mean, probably not many conservative lay people.

SF: Oh I see. So it doesn't have the same hegemony as it does within Orthodoxy?

DB: Uh, yeah, that would seem to me to be obvious. The vast majority of conservative lay people barely know anything about the Talmud.

SF: But you still wouldn't want to say that's why you became Orthodox?

DB: Well, that could be, you could say it that way if you want to. If conservative Judaism were like Orthodoxy, than I'd be conservative. I think this is historical Judaism as I understand it. And this is what I understand that Jews are called upon to do: to study the Talmud and keep the mitzvahs.

SF: Is there not a difference between rabbinic Judaism and Orthodoxy today which, according to what I've read—for example Kaplan and others started with neo-Orthodoxy. In other words, correct me if I'm wrong, does not Orthodoxy today mostly have more in common with the neo-Orthodox movement associated with Samson Hirsch, and isn't there a difference between that and rabbinic Judaism?

DB: Of course, modern Orthodox Judaism is not identical to the Judaism of Babylonia in the year 500. I mean everything develops historically?.... And I think the various forms of contemporary Orthodox Judaism are the historically organic development out of the Judaism of the rabbis of the Talmud.

SF: You describe Orthodoxy in both *Powers of Diaspora* and the other book as quite at odds with the exaltation of the cult of violence in what you describe as Roman in some places and in other places, Greek. Could you elaborate on that a little, because I'm...?

DB: Yes. But this has nothing to do with Orthodoxy. Well, I mean, Orthodoxy is only a relevant term since the 19th century, so before the 19th century, it doesn't make sense to speak of Orthodoxy. But what's important is to say that I think that there is an important strand in historical Judaism that promotes a very different model of masculinity from the macho violent kind of masculinity that we're familiar with from most of the European tradition. Now, I'm not saying that this is always the case or essentially the case. I'm saying that this was one very important strand, particularly in Europe, of a kind of antithetical masculinity that developed within the Jewish rabbinic high culture.

SF: And you would, I guess, argue that we could recapture that, one should recapture it?

DB: You know, that's an interesting question. I don't know what we can recapture or not. Generally projects of cultural recapturing seem to me to be doomed to fail. What I would rather say is that by putting ourselves in touch with these powerful strands and experiencing them, we might be moved to discover slightly different courses of action and ways of being in the future. That's different from recapturing the past. It's more a question of opening up possibilities.

SF: Do you see that specifically related to American Jews' kind of knee-jerk pro-Zionism?

DB: Well I think that there's a lot more respectability to anti-Zionist positions in the United States now than there was 20 years ago. Certainly in the Jewish academy, it's now possible to be anti-Zionist, whereas 10 years ago it was like being a space man or something.

SF: I didn't know you could take an actually anti-Zionist position without being ostracized.

DB: Well, I've taken a direct and unequivocal anti-Zionist position, and I was given an award by the National Foundation for Jewish Culture for service to the American Jewish community through scholarship in teaching just a year ago. I think that that would have been unthinkable a generation ago.

SF: You're certainly the only person I've read who's written on the sexual politics of Zionism.

DB: Well I'm not the only person who's written. I may be the only person you've read.

SF: Oh. Who are the other people who've written?

DB: Mickey Gluzman.

SF: I'm sure there may be people in Israel. Is he an American?

DB: No, he's in Israel.

SF: Oh, that's why, because I'm not a scholar on this topic. In fact you say for Herzl, Zionism was a means to...overcome his insecurity about being a feminized Jew. Could you elaborate a little on that?

DB: Yes. Well, there's been a lot of scholarship, starting initially with the work of Sander Gilman...

SF: Yeah, I read a couple of book by him.

DB: ...showing that one of the major components of anti-Semitic discourse in Central Europe, by which I mean primarily Germany and Austria, in the 19th and early 20th century, with some earlier historical roots, had to do with an ascription to Jewish men of a damaged masculinity or even a feminization. Now one of the major arguments of Unheroic Conduct is that at least initially...that there really was a positively different ideal of masculinity being perpetrated by the high culture of the Jews of Central and Eastern Europe which has, moreover, Talmudic roots, and that Jews were pretty comfortable with it until some time in the 19th century, when, with the rise of the regime of sexuality and the classification of people into categories of heterosexual and homosexual, the characteristics of male Jews—again, ideal characteristics, partly lived, partly not—were categorized as homosexual and via of course the vilification of homosexuality, Jews in these countries...societies became uncomfortable and responded in various ways. So I argue that, on the one hand, Freudian psychoanalysis in some of its characteristics is a response... and that Zionism is another response, that by gathering various citations from Herzl, from various kinds of writing, including his diaries, I try to show that, for him, one of the major motivations for the foundation of a Jewish state was to demonstrate that Jews were real men.

SF: And that he had an insecurity, I think you show, that he wasn't a real man and that a real man was associated with violence and dueling, etc. You use dueling as a metaphor pretty frequently.

DB: Yeah, it's not only a metaphor, I mean it was so central in both Austrian and German society. Dueling clubs and the practice of dueling was considered absolutely essential to the establishment of masculinity. And in fact, Jews were excluded from dueling after a certain point, were thrown out of the dueling clubs, and this had to do, again, with their exclusion from the masculine order.

SF: Yeah, and they were basically considered, you used another term in your work, deficient or lacking or pathological, and that this one particular norm of masculinity has hegemony over the western world, at least—and over most of Orthodoxy today, or not so much, or what?

DB: Well, I don't know. You know, I don't even know what we're talking about when we're talking about Orthodoxy. If we're talking about Zionist Orthodoxy, I think that so much of the worldview is so dramatically changed from what it was even just a generation ago, like...

SF: ... You actually, in one of your revolutionary formulations, say that the position of powerlessness that Jews were in didn't invalidate their stance. If anything, it gave them an insight that they might otherwise have lacked because it was assumed that what was normative in Europe etc. etc. was normative for humanity. But would you say that some of what we would consider the better or more pacifistic, less violent, more social traits of Judaism that you describe, since they're less macho, less violent, would you say that's solely a function of their lack of power? How much is it a function of particular values that they chose and that were embodied in the Talmud?

DB: That's a complicated question, because values always come from somewhere, also. Let's put it this way: we see how quickly those values have disappeared.

SF: Yeah, with Zionism.

DB: Right. Which, even a decade ago, 15 years ago, there was still a large traditionalist, anti-Zionist Orthodox community in Israel. It's now just a remnant of what it was. And that's a transformation over only the last 15 years.

SF: Most radical Jews, in Jews Against the Occupation, they celebrate various different Jewish holidays (I'm kind of on the margins of that group, it's a new group), but the people I've talked to, for most of them it 's more a matter of maintaining cultural continuity more than it is a spiritual or religious thing. But they have been influenced by Shahak, who describes Judaism basically before the Enlightenment as mired in superstition, fanaticism, and ignorance, and filled with just hatred, as if it came sui generis, for Gentiles. And he claims that the Talmud sanctions stealing from people as long as they're not Jewish, and that it interprets "Thou shalt love thy neighbor as thyself" as meaning only one's fellow Jew. Could you comment on that?

DB: Shahak hated Jews and hated Judaism.

SF: He was a survivor...

DB: He was a bitter, nasty, unpleasant person. I thought...

SF: Did you know him?

DB: I agreed with him politically and disagreed with him in every other way. The book is a scandal, it's a slander, it's the sort of thing that the worst anti-Semites could write. If I had the time, I could take the trouble to contextualize every one of his claims. Now my point is not to whitewash anything. Judaism, like every other tradition, has much that is ugly in it, but I think no more and probably no less than any other tradition.

SF: Well, wouldn't it have less than Constantinian Christianity?

DB: Well, by staying out of power, you avoid the worst of your baser human instincts.

SF: Ill read a paragraph from Answer in the Mail, in your book on Paul: "The solution of political Zionism...seems to me the subversion of Jewish culture, not its culmination, in that it represents a substitution of a European western cultural formation for a traditional Jewish one that has been based on a sharing—at best— of political power with others and which takes on entirely other meanings when combined with political hegemony." So it's been based on a sharing with others, you say, so there was that moment, that utopian moment that was realized or almost realized—you do talk about there was still the oppression of women—but almost realized before the rise of Zionism.

DB: That the utopian moment was almost realized, I wouldn't go that far. That would be a gross oversimplification, but certainly there was a kind of political ideal or ideal politics in opposition to the idea of the ethnic nation state that was possible, that was generated in the context of a diasporic national existence.

SF: And do you think that had a lot to do with the rejection of what's called the Roman ideal—by preserving a more traditional community?

DB: Yes.

SF: You speak about Herzl, I don't know if you've written anything, maybe you've written an essay—I would have liked to have read some more about Ben Gurion and the...

DB: No, I have nothing to say about that.

SF: Is there a reason you have nothing to say about them?

DB: Yep, I'm not a political writer, I was studying a particular cultural moment... I didn't write about anything after the very beginning of the 20th century.

SF: Well, it seems to me just reading a little bit that what you said about—I don't know if you would comment as a lay person on this topic, it seems to me similar to Herzl, there was certainly Ben Gurion had a contempt, that even his biographer wrote about, for diaspora Jews, the negation of the diaspora...

DB: This is what Gluzman writes about. He writes about what comes after Herzl and how it works out in the Israeli context.

SF: Would you agree with the critique that's Yoder's picture of rabbinic Judaism? Although he seemed to overlook its dependence on the Talmud, he says it's an actualization of the Jeremiac vision.

DB: Yeah, look, obviously to a certain extent, his presentation is the presentation of an outsider. On the other hand, I think that there's much that he understood and that, in one way, Yoder's political religious theory is something along the lines of what I'm calling for at the end of the Paul book: for identities, both religious and ethnic, that are disaggregated from sovereignty. So to the extent that Yoder and Mennonites in general and other communities similar to them are vigorously resisting temporal power, I think was not inappropriate for a theoretician, for a theologian like Yoder to appeal to historical rabbinic Jewish existence as a model. Of course if he had been a scholar of rabbinic Judaism, I think he could have made the argument richer, but he wasn't. That's not what he was called to be; he was a Mennonite theologian.

SF: In fact he wasn't even published—I don't know if you read it, *The Jewish-Christian Schism*—it wasn't even published until after he died.

DB: No, I didn't, I haven't read it.

SF: What's your reaction to his quote here? "Occasionally, privileged after the model of Joseph, more often emigrating, frequently suffering martyrdom nonviolently, Jews were able to maintain identity without turf or sword, community without sovereignty. They demonstrated pragmatically the viability of the ethic of Jeremiah and Jesus."

DB: Yeah, I like...I mean, I think it's a little perverse to see Jews as a exemplifying the ethic of Jesus, but only slightly so, but on the whole I find the sentiment appropriate.

SF: Do you see Jesus as—I know you're not typical Orthodox—would you see Jesus as a great Jewish prophet?

DB: I don't think we know anything about Jesus at all.

SF: Oh, so all the work on the historical Jesus, you don't...

DB: I don't buy any of it.

SF: So okay, then one couldn't say anything.

DB: You know, my Jesus would be an anti-Zionist intellectual, somewhat alienated from his Orthodox community, you know, everybody makes up a Jesus like him—or herself.

SF: What do you think could have been—I know you've described yourself as a binationalist and identifying with Buber and Magnes and those people—what do you think could have been the alternative to Zionism at the time?

DB: Well, you know, I don't what to second-guess what happened 70 years ago, particularly right after the war. The alternatives at the time of Herzl? There were alternatives, of course. The Bund was the primary alternative. Now some would say that the fact that there is no more Bund, because of the dual ravages of Nazism and Stalinism, is itself an argument that argument that Zionism was right. I would not accept such a point. But there have been alternatives; at every point in history there were alternatives. At the time in the late 40s, the alternative was the Magnes-Buber ideal of a binational state, and they were considered Zionists. Today calling for a binational state is anti-Zionist.

SF: Yeah, Chomsky points that out. Do you like Chomsky's work, by the way?

DB: Yeah, very much.

SF: What about the Neturei Karta idea that Jews shouldn't have sought sovereignty at all during any time before the Messiah, just continued living in the area as part of the Mideast....

DB: That's my theological position, that's my religious position.

SF: It is, even during the 30s and 40s?

DB: Yeah.

SF: You're familiar—I know you make some reference to it, but I don't know how familiar you are with the working showing how Zionists went out of their way to prevent any kind of rescue mission toward the Jews, didn't...

DB: I don't know whether...how extensive that was. The fact that there's any evidence in that direction was shocking enough, but I don't know the...you know, I'm not a historian, and certainly not a historian of the 20th century.

SF: You said you were Orthodox before you were anti-Zionist, but you described growing up feeling yourself as odd or queer or whatever.

DB: Yes.

SF: Were you a political activist, a leftist, a radical first?

DB: Yes, I was.

SF: In the anti-war movement or what?

DB: Yes, certainly.

SF: And are you married now?

DB: Yeah.

SF: You have kids too, don't you?

DB: I've been married for 37 years.

SF: Wow, that's a long time.

DB: Yeah, same woman.

SF: Do you attribute your successful marriage partially to your embodiment of the kind of Orthodox...

DB: I attribute my successful marriage to having chosen the right wife.

SF: You know Leibowitz, I was reading an interview with his grandson, and I read a couple books by him—I found them rather dry and not particularly inspiring—but he saw no connection between morality and Judaism, and he said basically man can be religious and just adhere to the food blessing, daily prayers, and various other things that are commanded, and then of course his grandson—you know about his grandson?

DB: No.

SF: That he's a lawyer, Orthodox and an anti-occupation activist in Israel?

DB: Yeah, I don't follow that stuff, so.

SF: Anyway, first the grandfather, Leibowitz, felt that you didn't have to adhere to moral precepts to be a Jew, and the grandson said, I'm quoting him here now, "A religious Jew must also adhere to the precepts of not oppressing non-Jews, not humiliating and not detaining people without trial." In other words, it was not just a matter of a universal morality, but it was a specifically Jewish thing that obligated him to do that. Do you have a stand on that as between the...

DB: Oh, I think that Yeshayahu Leibowitz's position was extreme and fundamentally wrong.

SF: Could you elaborate on that?

DB: Because there are lots of mitzvahs that have to do with what we call *ben adam l'chaverot*, with being decent to other human beings.

SF: And so you agree with the grandson, obviously.

DB: Yes.

SF: Do you see any possibilities where you speak about the preservation or recovery of Jewish alterity within Orthodoxy? Do you see any possibilities of that within other forms of Judaism

DB: It's a question of what you invest, first of all. If Judaism is something that occupies two or three hours a week, then it's not going to be very transformative. So the fact that there are—and I'm not saying that there aren't—communities certainly of Conservative Jews and, as far as I know, no reason to think not Reform Jews who dedicate themselves to study and to practice and to sort of constant attention to the Torah—but by and large, I think that you find that kind of a life in Orthodox communities much more.

SF: Well you said "much more." What about someone like Abraham Heschel? Would he be someone you would consider the exception?

DB: Yeah, I mean I have some arguments with various aspects, yes, but of course, he was Jewish when he woke up in the morning until he went to sleep. He was studying, he was thinking, he was doing mitzvahs.

SF: Very interesting. But you would say—obviously, Buber was not an observant Jew, but could you characterize him?

DB: No, I don't want to get into personal stuff.

SF: I didn't mean that to be personal.

DB: Well, kind of in an ad hominem sort of thing, what am I going to say about Buber? If I had a choice which Buber to meet, I'd want to meet his grandfather.

SF: His grandfather?

DB: Yeah, Solomon Buber.

SF: Here's another theological thing, if you could answer it. A theologian who said, "A literalist interpretation of the Torah avoids with difficulty descent into attitudes of racism, xenophobia, and militarism." Of course there's in Deuteronomy and Joshua... And Shahak claims—of course you disagree with him—that those commandments to genocide are repeated by the Talmud.

DB: But that's just rank nonsense. It's absolute nonsense.

SF: What does an Orthodox do with God's commandments in Deuteronomy to show them no mercy, etc.?

DB: Well what the Talmud does with it is to say that those people that it was talking about are all gone. They don't exist any more. Well the commandment doesn't exist anymore.

SF: I know, but how could it be justified?

DB: I don't have to justify it. Thousands of years ago under a particular set of conditions.... (Pause)

SF: But were those really God's words, or could that be man's interpretation of God?

DB: If it's in the Torah, it's God's words.

SF: So then the only thing one could say is that we don't know why God commanded genocide.

DB: Of course not. But to say that it's repeated in the Talmud is ridiculous. That's precisely what the Talmud does is to say it's not relevant anymore.

SF: It's not relevant anymore?

DB: And a lot of the militaristic stuff is precisely interpreted in the Talmud not literally.

SF: Yeah, I know that.

DB: So then what's the point?

SF: It seems to me that the kind of God I would worship would never have commanded genocide.

DB: Well, I don't know. I don't if it's genocide or it's not genocide.

SF: Oh. The Talmud doesn't say on that issue whether it was genocide or not?

DB: Genocide is a modern term. I don't know if it applies or it doesn't apply. The rabbis defined those commandments by saying that the peoples involved don't exist anymore.

SF: Some of the people on the left are angry, were hostile (at least one) that I even included Neturei Karta. In fact Rabbi Weiss gave me one of the most eloquent interviews. He didn't seem to be that knowledgeable about theology when I asked him about theology, but he seemed to be quite knowledgeable about Zionism. What would you say to someone who says that, Well, Neturei Karta doesn't belong in your collection, or it doesn't belong....

DB: I would say that they don't belong in the collection!

SF: Yeah.

DB: I mean, what kind of nonsense...? First of all, who are they to decide who belongs in your collection or not? They have a choice to decide whether they belong in your collection, but not whether somebody else does.

SF: Yeah, she described them as reactionary, but she, by the way...she must have been somewhat familiar with your work, she said, Well that's fine, because you were clearly leftist and anti-phallic etc., etc.

DB: You know, what do I care what such an idiot thinks?! That's just idiotic prejudice as far as I'm concerned. She doesn't know them. She probably doesn't know anything about them. She's probably never talked to a member of Neturei Karta. I doubt very much if she's read through the Satmar writings. She might not even be able to read them, for all I know. So she looks at a Jew wearing a black suit and a black hat and having a beard, and she thinks she knows everything about him already.

SF: You think there's a prejudice against traditional Orthodox Jewry on the left or among...

DB: I don't know if there is on the left. I mean, of course there's a kind of traditional leftist anti-clericalism, right? Which is not only Jewish, it's part of the left. On the other hand, the Catholics at least—the Catholic left—have managed to realize that there are genuine leftists who are religious Catholics, right?

SF: Yeah, well Daniel Berrigan was also one of the first critics of Zionism.

DB: Daniel Berrigan, Dorothy Day. I mean, so, but it's...I'm not saying that I know that the opinions of any particular or many or all or most Neturei Karta are ones that I would agree with on every point. Of course not. That's not the issue. The issue is whether they have something genuine to contribute to our particular conversation, and whether they have to pass some kind of bona fides in every possible area of political correctness before they're allowed to articulate their principled anti-Zionist position. I didn't notice any leftist Jews who were part of the PLO delegation to the peace talks in Washington. I did notice that there were three Neturei Karta who came as part of the Palestinian delegation.

SF: Yeah, the Neturei Karta, I don't know, would you say—it seems to me—that they transcended the traditional boundaries of Orthodoxy as it existed a century ago in terms of their political praxis?

DB: No, I would say that they're the only Orthodox Jews left. I mean, the only truly traditionalist Jews left.

SF: Because specifically of their position...

DB: Simply because they haven't adopted the heresy of Zionism...which as far as I'm concerned is out-and-out heresy from a theological point of view.

SF: Many people on the left trivialize Neturie Karta's critique by saying that it all hinges just on a matter of a doctrine, whereas—you know, the doctrine that you shouldn't force the coming of the messiah—they trivialize it by saying that it's purely theological reasons, but it seemed to me that Rabbi Weiss—and from the readings of Neturei Karta—that they have a moral, spiritual critique of...

DB: They have a moral, spiritual critique, a theological critique. It's very, very brilliantly developed in their writings. They speak of the Palestinians as the indigenous people of the land. They object to going to the Western Wall because it was taken by force and by blood. Now, of course, some people on the left will say, oh, that's all just hypocrisy; they don't mean it. So that could be said of everybody.

SF: Yeah, that could be said of everybody.

DB: Anybody who articulates a position could say, No, no, it's really masking some other position, no? So, I really object to those ascriptions of bad faith.

SF: Well I wanted to make the book as pluralistic as possible, but since I could only include ten people, most of them are leftists, because most of the people critical of Zionism...

DB: Right, so therefore there has to be some balance.

SF: Do you agree with Rabbi Elmer Berger's argument—in the little essay in which he has an introduction by Toynbee—in which he said that the land– this may be similar to the Orthodox position—the Jews have no claim upon the land; it's not the land that makes them holy, it's only by being holy that they're entitled to the land.

DB: You know, I don't know if I would subscribe to every single detail, but that doesn't matter. The point is that, basically, we've got a complex of opinions that are related to each other.

SF: Well it seems in your books, which I found inspiring—as I said, I just happened across it—you use the different gendering of Jewish culture to critique the Roman or masculinist, sexist culture of the times and of modern society—and I know you don't have to say, of Zionism, because you said you don't write on the 20th century, but certainly most people have made that critique of modern-day Zionsim, that it's become more martial than Jewish people ever were.

DB: Yes, well no. I mean of course there's an implicit argument that a lot of what's going on today is a result of it sort of being a continuation of what happened then.

SF: And in fact, obviously American culture, as evidenced in the Democratic convention and the so-called war against terrorism, there's becoming more...

DB: Yes.

SF: To use the Lacanian term, modern western culture is becoming more phallic.

DB: Yeah, yeah.

SF: Do you think that, then...you said that Orthodox Jewry is open to women participating in Torah readings and...

DB: In study.

SF: ...and to homosexuals.

DB: In study of Torah. No, no, no. I said many things. You're mixing things, different things. In general, in modern Orthodoxy there has been a revolution with respect to women learning Torah. It's now virtually everywhere accepted that women learn Torah. We now have women who are leading yeshivas for women and are very important scholars, and that's having halakhic impact already in various ways. And the other thing I said was that traditional Judaism, as opposed to certain phenomena of modern American Orthodoxy, was not particularly homophobic.

SF: Yes, you didn't say in which way you felt that it had changed.

DB: Well, there's a kind of modern American Orthodoxy that is virtually identical in its social ideas to Bush. But that's a product of some American cultural phenomena as much as anything else. Genuinely traditionalist Judaism was not homophobic.

SF: Would that include Neturei Karta?

DB: It would include everybody.

SF: Today?

DB: It would include the Neturei Karta. They only become homophobic under the impact of European and American culture. Now, of course I'm not saying that there isn't a reprobation of certain homosexual sexual practices, but they're not singled out from the whole complex of other practices that are forbidden.

SF: You mean pre-marital sex among heterosexual...?

DB: Or...yeah, or certainly adultery among heterosexuals, or, for that matter, eating on Yom Kippur. So as far as I'm concerned, what constitutes homophobia—I mean, this requires a long and complicated discussion—is precisely when the whole system of Torah is abandoned, as it is by the Christians and by many so-called liberal Jews, but specifically, all of a sudden, one pufruk in Vayekreh 18 is the commandment of God.

SF: Isn't that Leviticus?

DB: Leviticus, yeah!

SF: You're saying that's developed a particular charge...

DB: I'm saying that when Southern Baptist preachers say that the whole Torah is abrogated, right, and you can eat chazer and you can eat b'tsah b'cholev and eat on Yom Kippur, and everything is permitted, and then all of a sudden they say, they pull out one thing and they say, This is the commandment of God, this is an abomination: that's homophobia. When the rabbis said certain homosexual practices—by the way, not all—when certain homosexual practices are no worse nor better than sleeping with a niddah (with a menstruant), that's not homophobia.

SF: You also said somewhere that you think, to some degree, that the rejection of masculinist culture is preserved in Judaism today. Somewhere you said that, do you remember that?

DB: No, I don't. Well it is here and there, but it's becoming less and less.

SF: Would you say, for example, that Woody Allen movies...

DB: Well that represents a kind of debased, popular version.

SF: Now he's been vilified...

DB: Yes, of course. All right, let's take a somewhat less problematic...

SF: In the 60s and 70s...

DB: An example would be Philip Roth, who has, I think, quite a clear feeling about this. A clear sensibility.

SF: And you also think he represents a resistance against the Roman culture...?

DB: Well he articulates it, he describes it. And I think he describes it with a great deal of understanding and empathy.

SF: Are you talking about...

DB: Not so much in *Portnoy's Complaint*, but more in the later books. Also in *Portnoy's Complaint*, but *Portnoy's Complaint* is a satire. But some of the later novels are more...or less crude.

SF: I remember Woody Allen movies. Of course he presents himself in the 70s as both a klutz and as physically inept, not possessing the kind of virtues of masculinist or phallic culture, and yet he's an intellectual.

DB: Right, right.

SF: There were all kinds of articles in pop viewer magazines in the 1980s about women who were having sexual fantasies about Woody Allen, somewhat reminding me of the passage in *Unheroic Conduct*, where you describe the sexual object of the Orthodox female as being pale and thin, a Talmudic scholar.

DB: Yeah, so this is a kind of vulgar, popular remnant of that. Yes, I agree.

SF: Do you see it as a positive thing, as a kind of holdout against...

DB: Yeah, insofar as it...that we remember something, yes.

SF: In your critique of Herzl you argue that Zionism rather then being the end was a means for his assimilation to the phallic values of western culture. That being a colonist and a fighter against the natives was a way for Jews to prove their manliness—to prove they were like Christians.

DB: Yes.

SF: Yeah... do Jews have a particular obligation to speak out against Zionism?

DB: Yes, I mean, I certainly hold that there's a particular obligation when something is being done in one's collective name, when in some sense precisely one identifies with the people who are doing something, then one has a particular obligation to resist if one thinks that that's wrong. Yes. Some of these people say, why am I always demonstrating and writing against Zionist oppression of Palestinians. What about the Rwandans or Senegalese...not the Senegalese, the Sri Lankans? We have a particular obligation [Hebrew phrase]: first you take care of the poor of your own people before the poor of other people, and that includes the poor behavior of your own people before the poor behavior of other people.

SF: Is that from the Talmud?

DB: The Talmud says, Take care of the poor of your own city before you take care of the poor of other cities.

SF: And that part now would include the Palestinians?

DB: Absolutely, but I'm saying something else. I'm also saying you have to take care of the poor behavior of your own people before you worry about the poor behavior of other people.

SF: Okay, I just asked you one last question, which are of the quintessentially Jewish values that are now endangered by Zionism and modern western culture and the Zionist...

DB: You know, I don't believe in quintessentially Jewish values. That's a problematic conception for me; it sounds triumphalist. What I think in terms of particular constructions, ethical and political constructions that were available to the Jews in particular historical situations owing to a combination of the positive content of the Torah and the particularities of their material existence. And that's something different than saying "quintessential Jewish values." And I think that a particular set of values that were constructed in a particular historical situation were explicitly...Zionism set out explicitly to destroy and reverse those values, and insofar as I hold with those values and admire them and think that they're very important, that dictates a lot of my political position.

SF: You're referring to what you discuss in *Unheroic Conduct*? The ideal of the male as gentle and nurturing?

DB: Yes, and notions of, if not pacifism—Judaism was never pacifistic (there I disagree with Yoder)—but certainly of an abhorrence for violence and a seeking of nonviolent solutions whenever, whenever possible as opposed to a European culture—and again, not monolithic—for which violence was exalted as romantic, as manly, as somehow genuine and deep, vital, vitality.

SF: In Nietszche...

DB: Not only in Nietszche, you find it all over. You find it even in my beloved Verdi, in the Sicilian Vespers: "Long live love, long live...." Oy, I can't remember.

SF: I remember that quote, "Long live love, long live war," or something like that.

DB: ...I forget the exact quote, but "Long live war": what kind of a Jew would ever say "Long live war"? You know?

SF: And then to pair it with love!

DB: Yeah, exactly, the notion that these are the two realms of vitality.

SF: Well as you remember, in the 1960s, one of the popular adages was, "Make love, not war."

DB: Exactly.

Chapter 9

Rabbi David Weiss

Rabbi Weiss is a member of Neturei Karta, a group of Orthodox Jews, who have opposed Zionism since before the creation of the state of Israel. At that time virtually al Orthodox were opposed to a Jewish state, but since 1948 most have accepted Zionism and made their compromises, as Rabbi Weiss explains.

SF: I think not many Jews are even aware that the majority of Jews in the most of the beginning part of the twentieth century were opposed to Zionism.

R: Yes, true. In fact, basically, maybe I could give you a short overview of what Zionism is and what Judaism is…

SF: Yeah.

R: …to differentiate between the two. Judaism is a religion. It was the patriarch of Abraham, Isaac, and Jacob. Abraham had it from Isaac, Isaac got it from Jacob, and they have the twelve tribes. Jacob had twelve children: twelve tribes; and twelve children *haleynu* who were reconsidered the heads of the twelve tribes: the children of Israel–their children and grandchildren accepted the Torah (the Bible) from G-d on Mount Sinai, and…which, actually, G-d had promised Abraham that he would give to his great grandchildren, whatever offshoots, that he would give them the Land of Israel. Now there was two issues here. There was people living in the Land of Israel called the Canaanites… Well basically, G-d promised Abraham the Land of Israel for his grandchildren, because he was the one person who recognized that there is one god over the whole world. At the same, there was other people living there: the Canaanites, and G-d said to Abraham…but actually that's later…. G-d said to the people that the Canaanites were being sent out of the land at that time, because they had defiled the land. Israel, the Land of Israel, is a very holy land….it's like G-d's garden. In other words, it is a land that is chosen by G-d to rest his spirit more than all the other parts of the world. G-d is all over, but he rests in a certain manner, in the chosen Land of Israel. Now he promised…being that the Canaanites were defiling the land, they were not holy, G-d said that they had to leave, and he had promised it to Abraham's grandchildren, to the children of Israel. But he promised them, when he gave them on Mount Sinai, he gave them the Torah, he stipulated very clearly with the Jewish people that they can remain in the land as long as, again, they are very holy people. If they are not very holy, then the land, which is a holy land, will actually reject the people who are living there. And that's said many times in the Bible.

SF: Prophets say it, don't they mostly?

R: Well, in the Five Books of Moses it does state that also. [Hebrew]; "The land shall regurgitate you when you defile the land." So, there's many times things like that in the Bible. And the Jewish people accepted from G-d, they accepted to be servants of G-d, they accepted that they will be…G-d said before he gave the Torah, [Hebrew]; "You should be to me for a kingdom of priests and a holy nation." It was to be accepted upon ourselves the yoke of the service of G-d more than other people. Every human being has to serve the one G-d: not to kill, not to steal, not to commit adultery—idol-worship: to serve G-d. But the Jewish people accepted upon themselves the yoke of being priests, in other words, to be in total servitude to G-d, meaning that they should constantly have to study the books, the holy book, to watch the sabbath, eat kosher, family purity, whatever else is involved. Now this is a yoke…

SF: Where did I read somewhere that other people were asked and turned it down and the Jews…

R: Yes, yes.

SF: Is that in the Talmud?

R: Yes one of the books in the Talmud, yes, that G-d went to the other nations, and everybody, like each one, said, according to their character, they said, What does it say in the Torah, what does it say when it says that thou shalt not kill? So one nation that was pretty much part of the tendency to kill, they didn't want to accept it. The other one says thou shalt not steal, so they turned it down. And each one had its individual reason for turning it down, while the Jewish nation said: "We will do and will adhere." In other words we will accept…whatever you require of us. So G-d made this vow with the Jewish people, and the connection between us and G-d is the Torah. And the Jewish people accepted to watch the Torah as one. In other words, we believe that all our souls were there. In other words, of all the generations, every Jewish soul was standing on the mountain side—and I bet anyone who converts to Judaism, his soul was also there. And we all as brothers and sisters accepted together, we were responsible one for another. That was one of the issues, that we accepted to be responsible for one another, that we are all as one, that we accept the one G-d, and we are ready to serve him. And we accept, no matter if we consider it hard or not, we are ready to accept G-d's teaching.

Well, one of the issues was that G-d stipulated, as I say, that we can go to the Land of Israel, in fact we should go, and there is commandments and mitzvots, obligations, that we should fulfill in the Land of Israel, but he stipulated at the same that if we will not be holy enough to this land, that we will have to leave the land. And then, you go into, you say, the books of the prophets that speak about after the Temple was built at the same as King Solomon and afterwards, that the Jewish people were found not to be worthy enough of staying in the land, and the prophets warned the Jews that they should repent. Eventually, ultimately, they were sent into exile. Now when they were sent into exile, the Jewish people accepted this as…we have certain phrases, like it says that G-d spilled his anger on wood and on stone.

In other words, instead of punishing the Jewish people directly, he punished them by destroying the Temple, letting the Temple be destroyed, and basically, he had compassion on the people, and he did not kill them totally, and they were dispersed into different lands, and the Jewish people accepted this lovingly, because we know it's from G-d, it's like medicine from G-d, so medicine sometimes is bitter, be we know this is ultimately what's good for us because it's from G-d. .... We understand that it wasn't a physical weakness that put us into this exile... It's not like the Zionists say: if only we had a stronger army...

SF: Yes.

R: ...it was, on the contrary...many times the Jewish people are very, very strong, and the reason why...it's clear that we were only sent out because of our metaphysical, because of our spiritual weakness.

SF: There are a couple of points I just want to make now. You make, I think two main points. The first point about the covenant and the land, I think is actually against the Zionist as well as many Orthodox Jews today who seem to think that the land confers holiness, whereas you're arguing the exact opposite, that they're only worthy of the land insofar as Jews are holy.

R: Exactly. In fact, I'm going to come around to that... Basically, this was the concept of exile. In other words you consider it medicine from G-d, and two issues are involved here. I'm sure there's more, but two main issues here: When a person is in exile, he's humbled, and G-d wants us to repent and, and then, when G-d feels the Jewish people are worthy—and we don't know when that will be or whatever—what is in his wisdom, when he understands what we have to go through, but the time will come he will end this exile. I want to backtrack on one thing. I want to show that it has nothing to do with physical weakness, our test that we go through in/by the exile is what by the walls of Jericho they sunk, right? Because it says that the Jewish people went seven times around the wall, and the walls of Jericho sunk–despite our strength. It had to do with G-d. When G-d wanted that they should be victorious, they were victorious. There was a time when there were some...a tribe decided to leave exile ahead of time, and they tried to go into the Land of Israel. They were not successful, they were wiped out. It was before G-d told Moses that they could go. So they were wiped out.

SF: So the Zionist's idea of compensating for this idea of putative weakness by military strength is contrary to the divine will...

R: Exactly, that's what I'm getting to. Now our concept of redemption is exile-redemption. Oh, one other issue here: in the exile, we know that when G-d sent us into exile, he put us under oath. Now this is stated in the Talmud on page 111 of Ketubot, which we can get back to (you won't know the exact), but it says there that when G-d put the Jewish people into exile, he put them under oath and said that there were three things: they should not rebel against any nation; they shall not take up arms…they shall not go back en masse to the Land of Israel; and they shall not try to end the exile. Because basically, G-d put us here; he doesn't want us to try to rebel against his wishes. So he put us under oath and he warned us that if will try to basically break these oaths, then what would happen is that we would severely punished.

SF: Listen, can I ask a question here? Many Jewish philosophers and writers, maybe Orthodox and non-Orthodox, emphasize exile as a time of mission, as an opportunity for Jews to fulfill the mission to "the nations"—as they call them.

R: Exactly. That part, I was saying there's two issues here. One is for us to be humble, and secondly, because G-d is perfect, so whatever he does has a lot of issues involved, he wants us to be a light unto the nations. A Jewish person is, like I say, a priest. He has many commandments to follow, and he has to emulate G-d. Just as G-d is compassionate, you should be compassionate. We try to change, correct our characters, that should be perfected in the service of G-d. And every person has his weaknesses. One person has a bad temper, one person is stingy, and everybody has things. The work of a Jew is to perfect himself as best as he could, to serve G-d and to emulate G-d, and he should be a light that… unto the nations…

SF: An example.

R: Right. Now the goal and the duty of a Jewish person is the yearning and the praying for the redemption. What is the redemption? It doesn't mean that we shall return as a strong and mighty nation. That is not the concept at all of what we all are striving for. Our suffering…our biggest problem, our only problem is that when we went into exile, G-d's glory was dimmed or somehow…in other words, G-d's glory is not respected or known throughout the world, and we bring and yearn—and we say this in our prayers every day—we pray for the day when G-d's name will be known throughout the world and everyone will serve him together. In other words, our yearnings toward the end of exile is for the day when the world, the total world, not just the Jews, will recognize the one G-d and serve him in harmony. So there will be a metaphysical change to this world, and it's quite well known, like on the Dag Hammerskold Plaza, on the wall it states there that they will beat their swords into plowshares, and the wolf will rest with the sheep. In other words, there will be a total change to this world.

SF: An end to war and death?

R: There will be no more war. In other words, there will be a recognition of G-d throughout the world, and everybody will fear him and serve him.

SF: And the resurrection and eternal life?

R: Yeah, things like that. So this is a concept which we yearn for. That is what we yearn: to return to the Land of Israel. We don't yearn to return to become a mighty nation. This concept is totally strange to Judaism. Judaism's yearning is

for the glory of G-d... So these two issues here: he doesn't want us to leave exile....
and of course as a nation of compassion, a nation who's supposed to serve G-d,
he doesn't want us oppressing a second person. So with both aspects, Zionism is
totally incongruous with Judaism, it's the antithesis of Judaism...

SF: In this Messianic state...would Jews remain Jews keeping the Torah or is
that unnecessary in the messianic stage? And would Muslims remain Muslims and
would Hindus remain Hindus?

R: That's interesting. In other words, what we believe is that everybody will
recognize the one G-d and serve him. In exactly what details, how the service
will be as far as the nations will go.... I mean, the Jewish people will uphold the
Torah, we believe, and how the other nations will serve G-d, I'm not quite sure.
But whatever is contradictory to the service of the one G-d, they will not be doing.
What parts they will be continuing upholding and what parts of their religious
duties that they've been doing, I don't know. But the point is only that, as I say,
first of all the coming of the redemption will be without any human intervention:
G-d will make it happen

SF: Two other things: in this state, one would call it the messianic age?
R: Yes.
SF: Would there be a Jewish state? What would the political forms be?
R: That we'll get to next. When the time will come there will be a messiah,
and everybody will go up to serve G-d, will there be a concept of a state the way
you see it? No, definitely not. There will be a court system, there will the messiah
who will lead people in service of G-d, but there will definitely not be like this
concept of this Jewish state. Exactly how the details will be, I'm not ever certain,
because there's many different...

SF: There won't be privileges for Jews in this state that Muslims don't have
and that Arabs don't have?

R: Everybody will be trying to serve G-d, so exactly how the details of the
service of G-d is, that we have to see when it comes around. Maimonides says that
we should not delve into how it will be. We just have to know that it will happen.

SF: Don't most Muslims you talk with about this find it an appealing
alternative from what they're used to hearing from Jews?

R: Of course, of course, they certainly do. They're shocked to hear it, and of
course this is not a new teaching of the Jewish people, this is rather the teaching
of old time Judaism: this is the way the Jewish people thought, and this is the way
of their philosophy, this is their Talmud and so forth. Now let's understand where
Zionism came from. Zionism was actually born out of reform Judaism basically. In
other words, around 200 years or some-odd years ago, a movement came and...

SF: Yes but of course the first Reform Jews in America totally rejected
Zionism at the Pittsburgh Convention in the late 1870s.

R: Let me step back. The Reform, around 200 something years ago, a movement started that said, you know, instead of believing that G-d gave the Torah, they said, you know, it wasn't G-d, it's like a man-made thing from Moses or something. If we're not obliged to follow this teaching, you can pick and choose to what you want. And what was their goal? Their goal was to change the picture of the Jews. If a Jew suffers from anti-Semitism; we believe it's a spiritual happening, you know, everything is from G-d. G-d wants us to understand, to remind us that we're Jewish. Maybe through anti-Semitism, a Jew remembers, oh yeah, I'm different, I have to study to come closer to G-d. While these other people, the Reform movement, said, look, you're suffering and suffering. It must be because you're standing out, and you're too noticeable. What we have to do is assimilate. And if we'll assimilate, then nobody will call us Jew anymore, dirty Jew anymore, you're not a backward person, you'll be cultured, and all the problems will fall away. Now for over 100 years they tried this, and they became very successful in becoming assimilated, except they weren't successful in wiping out anti-Semitism. It didn't work. So Theodor Herzl was around 100 years ago, he was affected by the Dreyfus Trial, who was a French soldier and he suffered very severe anti-Semitism. Theodor Herzl walked in and he became very upset. He said, look, the guys are assimilated, these guy's are not noticeable as Jews, and they're still persecuted— we can't run away from the fact that we're being persecuted. So we have to look in another direction for another solution. He took G-d out of the equation, and he said, well, let's try another angle, let's make a 180° turn. Instead of assimilating, let's make a strong nation. And that way we won't suffer anymore... So his solution: he looked at our problem, and the problem that we were sent into exile instead of as a metaphysical, he looked at it as a physical weakness. Oh, 2000 years ago they say Jews were physically weak, we were thrown out of the land. And the solution is a physical solution: we'll just be strong, we'll make a strong army, and we will stop suffering. The land was just one of the main offsprings or, would you say, facets of Zionism. The main issue was to actually transform this religion of Judaism from a religion into a political nationalistic entity. In other words, a land-based entity to have...that we should be a nation amongst nations. In other words, instead of calling it a religion, call Judaism a nationalistic entity.

SF: And of course, Jewish people were a race or a nation in Zionism rather than a community based on a particular religious faith.

R: Yes, but really the Jewish nation is what bonds us to...what pulls us Jewish is because of religion. Jewish is a religion. It has nothing to do with race or creed or color; it has to do with religion.

SF: That wasn't Ben Gurion's viewpoint.

R: Right.

SF: Let alone Herzl.

R: So these people simply really transformed Judaism and convinced the Jewish people to transform themselves ...gut themselves from this religion to become a G-dless people but a nationalistic, strong powerful people. Why he couldn't just convert and drop everything, why he had to grab the whole Jewish nation with him is beyond me, so that I know it's the work of Satan.

SF: So if it was the work of Satan, it would actually be *postponing* the day of the messiah, right?

R: You are so astute that I can't begin to tell you. In the Talmud it says that the messiah cannot come until that there's not even a small kingdom amongst Jews. In other words, this is exactly what you're saying: it's postponing the coming of the messiah. Now, Herzl and all these people sat down and he said, Look, we have to have a land, we have to have a base, we have to have a place where to go. So at first they wanted to go to Africa, you know, Uganda, where there was rich soil, and that made sense. But then turned around, Look, who are we going to fool? The Jewish people are not going to follow us; we'll have a few individuals, fine, but it's not going to be really a nationalistic movement. So they turned to Palestine. Because as I told you before, every Jew yearns to return to the Holy Land.

SF: Well for many years not too many Jews actually, literally returned to... literally returned to Palestine, not until German persecution.

R: Well interestingly enough, the community that was living in Palestine, which was, as you say, not many, but throughout the world, it still turned out to be like well into the tens of thousands were moving there. Now these people were as a...almost completely they were very, very religious Jews. They were people who were not interested in...who didn't aspire to become rich or powerful. And they went there only to serve G-d in the holiness of the land.

SF As far as everything I've read, the first Jewish Palestinians had no desire to establish a Jewish state or a Jewish majority.

R: In fact they were opposed to this because they understood that this is not what we're allowed to do. So what they wanted to do is simply serve G-d. And they lived door-by-door with the Arab neighbors, they were our best neighbors, and we had people who attest to that constantly, they baby-sat each others' children.... So the Zionists turned to Palestine. Now, as I say, there was a Palestinian community of thousands and thousands of people all who felt opposition to Zionism. They wanted to live door-by-door with the Arabs. They went to pray by the Western Wall with the permission of the Arab leaders or without any problem, they went quietly, they did their prayers, they went home, everybody was happy. Now all of the Zionist movement started at the beginning of the twentieth century with aspirations to create a state. To have their nationality, it should be their land. And the Arabs had no idea who these people were, so they sold them land. Why not? They had good Jewish neighbors, why shouldn't they?

SF: I think it's probably noteworthy to say that there wasn't the kind of anti-Semitism in the Arab world that there was in the Christian world.

R: Of course, and that's a fact that people always knew—Jews knew that they had a safe haven as a general rule—of course, there were certain cases that were different, but as a general rule amongst the Arab land was a safe haven for Jewish people. So this was constant in all the countries, whether it would be Yemen or Tunisia or Morocco or Iraq or Iran: Jewish people lived, and they lived basically as a whole, peacefully. And now, all of a sudden the Zionists came—and they had to pick Palestine as the land because they had to get the Jewish following—and they told the Jewish people that this is the "beginning of redemption." This is what G-d meant by redemption. And they conned a lot of people. People were ignorant, they knew that that's what they yearned for—the land. And they had these people coming....

SF: Once again, was it not the reversal of Judaism? Instead of by keeping the covenant, you'll get the land, you go to the land, and that itself will bring redemption.

R: Yeah, right, that was also their idea. Supposedly, in fact, they had a few rabbis to go along with them. That majority almost completely around the world was in opposition. But they had a few. So they found this Reb Kook like you said, and now on the Sabbath, playing football in Israel or something is better than watching the Sabbath in America.

SF: His son was even worse...even more of a fanatic.

R: Now they came to Palestine, as we were mentioning, and they had to pick this land, but they had a technical problem, because there a lot of people living there. But of course this is only a technicality by them, because of course, they have no morals or scruples because they don't have G-d or Torah to command them what to do. So as far as they're concerned it's only a technical problem, and they have to get away this technicality at the cost of lives of non-Jews and of Jews. So be it that everything gets sacrificed on this altar of this G-dlessness, of this altar of Zionism, so people died for this struggle, and all against the rabbinical authorities...1947, that was a year there were, or some time before, when they knew there was going to be creation of the state, the chief rabbi of Jerusalem sent a letter to the United Nations, and it's in their files (we have the docket number and so forth), where he says, "I'm pleading with you. Do not take any action. Do you receive my letters? He says, I have sixty thousand people under me, and I'm the chief rabbi of Jerusalem, and we do not want to be included in the State of Israel,"—in the Jewish state, he called it. So you see the opinion of the great rabbinical authority. This was a rabbi, we have his picture, he was a chief rabbi, his name was Rabbi Vishinsky, he was the chief rabbi of Jerusalem, he was really the chief rabbi of the whole Palestine, and he was one of the greatest in the generation, and he said, We don't want to be a part of the State of Israel. You can see how people look at it, at the State of Israel as the legitimate representation of Judaism, when here you have the really Orthodox saying, we don't want to have anything to do with it.

SF: Well, of course now, almost all the Orthodox...I think you're the only exception now, aren't you? There used to be, what, Samar, or what was it called?

R: Well, let me explain something. It's very hard to classify, to say that there's very, very few, because the truth of the matter is that most Orthodox people, for instance, don't send their children to the army, and most Orthodox—almost the whole don't serve in the army, and they don't have flags on their school buildings, because...

SF: What about the Lubavitchers?

R: Right, the Lubavitchers. Because his father-in-law, the one who just passed away, who was the rabbi before him, and his grandfather: these were all anti-Zionists, very strong anti-Zionists.

SF: But the Lubavitchers were completely opposed to Oslo or any kind of negotiation process.

R: Well, they walked the line at that time but they were opposed to Zionism. They were totally opposed. Now when...

SF: Oh, so this was in the 40s and 50s?

R: Right. Now when he came along...

SF: The one who just passed away, I know he was opposed to giving up any land after 1967.

R: Exactly. But supposedly he's an anti-Zionist. That's the way their song goes. Their ideology is that he's anti-Zionist, but you can't change the way from everything that he's been taught. And yes, he doesn't change, so we weren't very happy with him. We're very upset, the Orthodox community, with him as a general rule.

SF: Are they opposed to the Occupation at least?

R: Yes, supposedly they're opposed to everything. But, they have a problem, because they say," Look, now, if we're going to give up the land, what's going to happen is that the Arabs are going to come and slaughter every Jew." So they have a problem because of fear of the lives of people.

SF: Many of the former chiefs of staff of the Israeli army say that the safest security measure would be to return the land.

R: Right, but of course they ignore that. And not only that, we Orthodox are not such great politicians. We don't know what really politically correct would be. But we know what G-d wants of us, and G-d wants of us that we should return the land. And that will definitely make peace, because if you listen to G-d, then G-d will protect you. So basically, the concept of not having the state is accepted by all, basically all Orthodox unless they're very, modern. But the really Orthodox…

SF: You would live in Israel now with the state in the hands of Palestinians or what?

R: Oh yeah. Yes, definitely. And this…the way…

SF: And it wouldn't be an Islamic…what kind of state would it be?

R: Oh, that's another issue. We believe that we have no right to dictate for the indigenous people of any land how they should…you know, as long as they're not idol worshipping. So we believe that they have the option, if they want a Muslim state, so be it. You know, if they want a democratic…

SF: So what, it would be determined by a majority?

R: However they decide to…

SF: Including the so-called Occupied Territories?

R: I don't know what to say. Depending however they decide to go about it, we have to be…a Jewish person…. That's another issue of exile is that we have to accept loyalty to every land where we are residing. That's one of the religious requirements of exile, whether you like it, you don't like it. In other words, that's part of the exile, that's what we believe. And people say, oh, you're way…you're backward people. No, we're not backward people; this is what G-d wants of us that we do. So we believe that we, you know, that it is forbidden to have this state, and we have to keep ourselves holy, basically. Now, so you have…so there's a very large amount of people who are in opposition to Zionism, and still and all, they're a part of the state, because they're afraid of being wiped out by the Arabs, right? You have the other section like us, the [Hebrew word], who…the 60,000 who were under this Rabbi Vishinksy in 1947, they multiplied, they were fruitful, they were never massacred. So where are these people? They're still there, the majority, and these people as a general rule—not as a majority, but as a general rule—still are in total opposition. Now they're intimidated so they don't go out and fight Zionism, because we have many pictures that we could show you at our site, you can see that many Jews go out and demonstrate, and they're all beaten.

SF: Have people from your group been beaten?

R: Yes, you can see this all on our site. I mean, through the times, you…

SF: You've seen it yourself?

R: No, I was never there. I mean, I was there for a month as a young boy, but everybody was there.

SF: Beaten by the army or by Jews?

R: By the police, by the army, by the police, and we have pictures, we have many pictures of that.

SF: Not by Gush Emunim?

R: No, no, no, by the police, the standard police, by the army. There were cops and people were killed, and almost everybody had been arrested at least one point in their lives by the Israeli police.

SF: Why?

R: Why? Because they're in total opposition what we care for. Now of course the general media does not talk about this. How much they know about it, I don't know, but they never write about it.

SF: Your group barely gets any publicity when you demonstrate in the United States.

R: Exactly...

SF: There's a Zionist apparatus.

R: They have a strong apparatus, they have a media watch, they threaten any newspaper that want to print anything, and the paper says, What do I need the problem? And even though they may interview us and it seems like they're going to print it, at the end of the day, they don't. It's happens tens of times....

SF: What do you say to people both critical of Zionism and Zionists who say that the actual seeds of the hatred for Arabs and Zionism is in the Torah itself, in G-d's admonition to utterly destroy the Canaanites and make no covenant with them and show them no mercy in Deuteronomy and then in Joshua, when G-d says, Leave no one alive, kill every man, woman, and child? And then you have Rabbi Goldstein (the guy who, as you know, slaughtered in cold blood all those Arabs praying in the mosque) quoting the Torah...

R: Yeah, but that's misconstrued. It's simply...they're simply...

SF: But those words are in Deuteronomy.

R: Oh yes. If I can explain to you. The idea of killing the Canaanites was before the Temple. That was a time when G-d said we should go into the land. And the walls of Jericho fell down. But it's quite, very clear that G-d said afterwards, that we are sent into exile, and then he clearly put us under oath that we are forbidden to do all these things that before that time we were told that we had to do, we were forbidden to do once we went into exile. It's a whole other set of laws and books that were set up once the Jews went into exile that we can't fight G-d. If G-d wants to take us out of exile, he will. We can't fight...

SF: Why would G-d before the exile say to kill the women and the children?

R: That's a good question, that's a good question. I mean, in fact, I don't know if I will try to, you know, present any reason why except that most, even the Muslims, agree that the Bible is a G-dly-given thing, and G-d is compassionate, and he is the epitome...he is the perfection of compassion, and he told us to kill or not to, whatever his reason is. But it wasn't that the Jewish people decided, now we want to kill other people. It was because G-d told us to.

SF: Do you think that G-d condescended to the low moral level of humanity at that time, or do you think, maybe...?

R: No. G-d is lofty…

SF: So, I mean, obviously killing everything that breathes, including women and children, today would be considered a horrible war crime.

R: True. But at the same time, not the Muslims and not the Christians and not the Jews consider what it says in the Bible war crimes because it's something from G-d. It's a good question, I mean, your questions, you're asking very intelligent, astute questions. But it's not my issue to try to answer for G-d why he would want such a thing which is in the Bible which is accepted. I could look and try to find, according to the Kabbalah, reasons, you know…that's secret as far as, you know, there's a deeper meaning for everything…

SF: Could it be interpreted symbolically rather than literally?

R: No, we don't…we definitely hold it was literal, and it had to do, maybe…each soul, you should understand … we were wiped out. But we believe that G-d…every human being who was saved and every human being who was destroyed was exactly as G-d wanted it. So even though the Nazis were the ones who deserve punishment because they are the ones who did it to us, ultimately we believe it came from the hands of G-d. And the one who was to be saved was saved, and the one who was to be destroyed was destroyed. Like we believe that there was a time at the destruction of the Temple that they tortured ten of the leading rabbis. Rabbi Akiva and others, and his skin was peeled from him with hot irons…I mean, terrible.

SF: So you're saying G-d sanctions these horrific acts?

R: And we believe, and it says in the Kabbalah books, that these rabbis were the gilgul—reincarnation—of the twelve tribes, these ten people who were killed were the reincarnation of the twelve tribes who sold Joseph into slavery. So you have to have their tikkun, their completion, their…

SF: Healing.

R: Tikkun, you know it's called tikkun, the… Tikkun means the fixing of the world…

SF: Mending?

R: Mending, exactly. Mending. And the mending of the twelve tribes had to be done with punishment…that they came again in the reincarnation to these twelve holy rabbis, and when they were killed, this is how they got their mending, their final rest. We believe people reincarnate, and maybe these people, the women and children…

SF: Oh like Hinduism. The rabbis were atoning for bad karma in previous lives. You believe actually in reincarnation?

R: 100%. Judaism…

SF: I didn't know Judaism believed…

R: Yes, yes. Judaism is full of this concept of reincarnation.

SF: In the same ways that the Hindus believe it?

R: We believe that many people…that our souls come until we finish doing our duties doing all commandments. Every Jewish person comes again and again.

SF: Well that's just like Hinduism.

R: Well, if it is, it is. Yeah, but it's there.

SF: Is that just Hasidism?

R: No, but it is more in Kabbalah written, and the ones who are knowledgeable in Kabbalah wrote about that fact,

R: So if you have these demonstrations, you have large demonstrations, sometimes you have small demonstrations, sometimes they are good even though they're part of the government, who will demonstrate against Zionism because they're so immoral… Sometimes the Zionists will make these decrees or put a swimming pool in the middle of the holy Jerusalem or they'll make archaeological digs. What they do, in other words, they dig up graves, because they can study the exact dates of the bodies, because they know it's when the rabbis died, right, from a thousand years ago. So then they would dig up graves and then the Jews run out there and they find out they're digging in a certain area, and they'll stand out there in front of the bulldozers, and they'll become a big fight, and they'll arrest the Jews and this goes on. And we have pictures of that.

SF: Oh yeah, that's another issue I should bring up with you, because that is one of the main things in the Neturei Karta literature that you emphasize: the obliviousness of the Zionists to the plight of the European Jews. Do you want to say something…?

R: Yeah. 100%. As I say, this is…we believe that to the Jews the Zionists were worse than Hitler. That's a very radical statement. But Hitler wiped out a few million Jews. The Zionists came and they took up all these Jews from all these countries, and they separated the children from the parents, and there's many…

SF: After the war?

R: After the war, before the war, in every…many different times. Whenever they were able to make these Aliyah [the "return" to Israel in Zionist theory] movements, you know? They took them up from different lands, they separated the children from the parents, they put them in non-religious areas, and they made them totally not religious. And we believe that if you make a person a sinner, you're sinning against G-d, so every day you're freshly sinning. In fact, there were Jewish people—and the Zionists make fun of the Orthodox because of this—because the rabbi said, Rather die in Europe than go up to Palestine.

SF: Wow. The Zionists didn't do anything to protect, or did little to protect the European Jews, because they were more interested in getting them to Palestine than in lifting immigration quotas in the West?

R: They were interested in getting sympathy from the Western nations, they said…one…that the more Jews raq b'adam: Only with blood will the land be born.

In other words, that if the people have compassion on the Jews, so they'll give them land, so if there's more Jewish blood, more Jews killed, it's better because people will then feel compassion. Then I have a quote...

SF: In other words, the more European Jews that are killed by the Germans, the better for the Zionist cause.

R: Exactly. Right. Then they said, one cow in Palestine is worth more than fifty Jews in Europe. They wanted to see...in fact they said, Let the Jews—I have a quote from Chaim Weitzman from his book—he says, Let the Jews be the dust of history. You know, see they were out...they said we want...only the cultured Jews.... We don't want them coming into Palestine and making it into a low-grade ghetto. That's a quote from him.

SF: Israel Shahak claims that in the Hatanya, the fundamental book of Chabad Hasidism, it says that all non-Jews are totally satanic creatures. Is that untrue?

R: The quotes that they take, I don't know if they took it from the Talmud or whatever...

SF: He claims that was from Hatanya, the fundamental book of Chabad Hasidism.

R: Hatanya, Hatanya, Hatanya. Oh, again, you see that's a perfect example of how you have to not take something out its context. Because if you would look in the Talmud, it says, Every Jew who is not living in Israel is an idol worshipper. And the Talmud was written in Babylon. So there you go. In other words, the Talmud and the Midrash speak very sharply about Jewish people and about non-Jewish people. And everything...you can't take it out of context. It says that every human being is an animal, or whatever, if you've not properly corrected your character...

SF: So you don't think it's a racist document, a Jewish supremacist document?

R: It's not, because we believe that there's levels in the service of G-d, and every person can elevate himself, and it's like they're speaking to the animalistic tendencies of Man, and it could say the same thing about rabbis, you know? I'm not going to disagree with him that there's a quote like that, but you have to be a scholar, you start learning, you see that it's neither here nor there.

SF: So anyway, so what is the mission of Neturei Karta?

R: There's two things here. First of all, the issue is that we should not be Zionists, we should be true to G-d and through prayer we pray to G-d for the speedy and peaceful dismantling of the state. We believe that we have to pray to G-d...

SF: Which also would be a prerequisite for the coming of the messiah, right?

R: Exactly. And we believe that prayer is the ultimate, because only G-d can accomplish. We can't accomplish; we can only do. So the first thing is prayer and to educate the people to understand that they should not equate Judaism with Zionism, to understand that Zionism is an ideological movement. It's not Judaism, it's the diametric opposite of Judaism, that is the first mission of us: that the Jewish people should know it and the non-Jewish people should understand it, because first of all, the Jewish people should not be caught up in this movement, and if the non-Jewish people understand that then G-d's name should be sanctified, that the name of Judaism, which is so stained and sullied, will be cleansed. ...The second mission is to take away also this anti-Semitism. Because we believe that Zionism is the creator of anti-Semitism, the factory of anti-Semitism throughout the world. And Jewish people are dying...I mean, besides that Palestinian people are dying, Jewish people are in terrible danger throughout the world and in Palestine all because of the actions of Zionism. So we ought to save Jews from death. Our rabbi, Rabbi Teitelbaum, who you were speaking about, kept on saying that it is a duty of us to sanctify G-d's name because it's being sullied by the Zionists.

SF: Your father was in the same order of Judaism as you are, right? Your father was Neturei Karta and your grandfather?

R: Oh, my father wasn't Neturei Karta, and my grandfather, no, but he happened to be a follow of one of the leaders of anti-Zionism in Europe. His name was Rabbi Shapiro, the Nunkatcher rebbe.

SF: Yeah, I read about him, too.

R: So my father was a follower of his. But all of Satmar, the really religious were anti-Zionist... How ironically they accuse us of being haters of Jews, because that's their defense to be on the attack. But they are the one's whose hands are covered in blood. For close to a hundred years, Jews are dying because of Zionism, because of the animosity that was created, all the deaths that were created in the land were all because of Zionism.

SF: How can it be defeated when it's so strong, not just in Israel but in America?

R: Well first of all, we are clear that they will not continue forever, because it says anything that is against G-d, it says in the Bible, it will not be successful—so it will eventually end. The question of when it will end, we don't know, and how much death and destruction and suffering and pain, we also don't know when.... We just have to do, you know what I mean? Secondly, the second issue is we are actively saving Jewish lives, because when we speak to the Arab people, and we...

SF: And you yourself have personally spoken to many Arab people?

R: Oh, yes. I've been on Al-Jazeera television.

SF: What was it like? I mean, your rapport with them.

R: It was very good. And they're very respectful. Sometimes they ask very sharp questions, and they challenge me with quotes of Rabbi Kook, and I have to explain to them that he's just the lackey of the Zionist state. It's easy to find one rabbi, but what about the thousands of other rabbis who speak the truth about Judaism. So they're paying this guy, and they make him a chief rabbi, so of course he'll speak like that. So that's…

SF: And you've been on Al-Jazeera. And have you met with various different Islamic leaders?

R: Well, I've met with many representatives, but personally, I don't travel to Israel, so I haven't met with…

SF: Do you meet with them here?

R: I meet with constantly, at conferences or whoever, whoever it happens to be: a spokesperson or this and that, whoever's there, we meet. I've had the occasion to meet with whoever was available at these conferences or whatever, spokespeople, many important spokespeople. Who is…Said, whatever his name was who just passed away?

SF: Edward Said.

R: Yeah, I met him.

SF: And you think there's little or no real anti-Semitism?

R: There is anti-Semitism. There's no question there's anti-Semitism. But anti-Semitism, because it's from G-d, you know that we believe came from G-d, you know that if G-d wouldn't allow it, it wouldn't happen. But you can't stand… we give a parable: You going to go burn down your neighbors house, and he's going to yell at you, and you're going to figure, You anti-Semite! You know what I mean?

SF: So you think the anti-Semitism is primarily a result of the Zionist injustice?

R: Well it's not "I think": It's a fact! You have to be blind not to see it. Of course, but they accuse the world of being blind, because they say, Hey, you can't say that—you're an anti-Zionist…

SF: So it's different from the anti-Semitism you'll find among Christians?

R: Exactly! The Muslims didn't have this anti-Semitism, and even in the Christian countries, you know, of course there is the anti-Semitism, but if you're going to go and cause them to be anti-Semitic by acting repugnant as a thief and do all the other things, well what do you expect? You can claim, it's no difference if I'm a good Jew or a bad Jew, because it's anyways anti-Semitism: that's ridiculous.

SF: So those are the two main activities?

R: Yeah, so like I said, first the prayer and let the Jewish people know that they shouldn't fall into the trap and snare of Zionism, and to educate the people, like I say, to sanctify G-d's name and to take away the anti-Semitism throughout the world which Zionism is creating throughout the world. And to save Jewish lives. So it's both…the issue is each one in itself is worth a whole lot of time and effort and it's a requirement of G-d. ...The imam, he invited me to speak in his mosque, and he turns around after I finished speaking, got up and he said, whenever I saw a Jew, I hated them.

SF: Really?

R: I have taped it, we have this tape...

SF: And how old was this imam?

R: He must be in his forties or whatever. But he's a very...

SF: Learned?

R: ...he's, besides that he's learned, but he's an influential person amongst the Arab community.

SF: In what country did you say?

R: In London, I was in London. They were there for a conference...

SF: But this imam was from which country?

R: He's also from London.

SF: What nationality was he?

R: Oh, I think, if I remember, if I'm not mistaken, he was either Afghanistan or Pakistan, I don't remember. But he has people in the...

SF: And you say he embraced you afterwards?

R: Oh yes, he did, and he invited me to speak in his school, which I spoke in his school; he has a school, he has a radio show. And it's commonplace. This happens to me all the time. This happens to me all the time. I just spoke in Boston this Sunday at MIT University...

SF: That's where Noam Chomsky is.

R: Yeah, right. And there was some sharp Arab speakers who were condoning the violence and so forth, say because they're freedom fighters and so forth...

SF: The terrorism, you mean the suicide bombers?

R: Basically. They didn't use the word, maybe, but they call them "freedom fighters." And they said that every Jew is basically responsible, and I got up and I spoke to them and I said, you're making a mistake. Do you have the whole picture? And they couldn't believe it what I was telling them; they'd never heard.

SF: Have you made friendships through this, actually become friends with some of these...?

R: I meet them at different...you know these people...at different conferences. There's some people you meet more often, you know. And they become very respectful and friendly. We don't play golf together, but there's no reason...

SF: Did they invite you for dinner or something?

R: They invite us of course...

SF: Kosher.

R: I could go to their dinners but I don't eat because we have different issues, kosher and all these things, but I go and I show them we have no problem of maintaining good relations.

SF: Wow.

R: We do this constantly. Like I say, two weeks ago, I was in London. I made a tour. Basically, I went to speak in two schools and two universities. And then… we were in The Hague when…about the Wall issue a few weeks ago. I just went to Boston last Sunday. We try, we try. Today I had a guy from Beirut come over and he's going to write this in his Arab papers. These are important, this is important to take away the hate against the Jewish person.

SF: Do you think ultimately it is hastening the coming of the messiah?

R: Anything that you do good for G-d, yes, and I can say, is hastening the coming of the messiah, that's what we…

SF: When we speak of the coming of the messiah, do you actually see one messiah playing a critical role in it or is that more…?

R: We believe there will come a very righteous person who will make people …serve G-d properly and repent and so forth.

SF: What do you think about the non-Orthodox or non-observant Jews who are also demonstrating against Zionism, you know, the International Solidarity Movement and the…?

R: Well of course it's a good thing what they're talking, but we believe that they're coming from not the right…. In other words, even human rights, according to us, is G-dliness. In other words, because G-d requires us to be human and proper, right, but when they come and they say that there's no G-d and whatever they have and they're just doing it because that's the feelings of a human being, we disagree with them, but you know, that's not where you should be coming from…. He's giving us to live and to breathe, he's giving us life. He wants us to be non-Zionist. He wants us to watch the Sabbath, he wants us to eat kosher. So it always hurts me that I see these people who are ready to stand up and fight for what's right and humane, and so they have a good heart. At the same time, they unfortunately they're not doing other requirements what G-d wanted. Like I say, we believe it's the responsibility of every Jew for every other Jew. A Jewish person has to watch…do G-d's requirement to watch the Sabbath.

SF: Is that the most important, would you say?

R: The Sabbath? It's one of the cardinal issues. Maybe it's because G-d created the world in six days, and the seventh day he rested. It's like we're bearing witness that we believe that G-d created the world… If somebody wants to become religious, we are always ready and willing to take them to our house, not just mine, but many, many Jewish people are willing to help and put a person on their feet, and it's not that hard once you know the rules, and it's very rewarding

SF: One more thing: how much hostility have you encountered from the Zionists? Have they made death threats and all kinds of…?

R: Oh yes.

SF: So how difficult has it made your life, actually?

R: Well, I ignore it, and we're finished. I just hope and pray that G-d should protect us and...

SF: They've never actually done anything, just talk, right?

R: No, we've been beaten... very seriously. In Israel, the...

SF: Beaten in America or in Israel?

R: No, I'm saying, the people who are in Israel have been beaten bad. But us, thank G-d, here, nothing very serious has ever happened. Thank G-d, G-d should watch us further. And basically, and then, of course, people lose their jobs, and people get different...people try to humiliate them. Every type of issue. They try all angles to stop people from being vocal against them.

SF: How old are you?

R: I'm 47.

SF: So you've been speaking against Zionism for, it must be, twenty years at least?

R: At least.

Chapter 10

Marc Ellis

Marc H. Ellis is University Professor of American and Jewish Studies and Director of the Center for American and Jewish Studies at Baylor University.

Since his writing is so powerful, I asked him if I could re-print a recent speech he gave at a forum sponsored by a Palestinian Christian organization.

5th International Sabeel Conference, Jerusalem, April 15, 2004—Holocaust, Christian Zionism and Beyond: A Jewish Theology of Liberation *After*

Marc H. Ellis

Marc_Ellis@baylor.edu

After my second visit to Israel—some twenty years ago—the idea of a Jewish theology of liberation began to resonate within me. During my first visit in 1973 that began before and continued during the 1973 Arab-Israeli war, I witnessed a fundamental disparity between Jews and "Arabs," as I then called them. The Jewish Israelis I met were European in background and were clearly transplanted from other geographic areas of the world. They were also dominant in politics and economics. The Arabs I met were Palestinian, clearly indigenous to the land, and on the margins of this newly created Jewish state.

It is remarkable how little I knew of the history of the state of Israel, let alone the history of Palestine and the Palestinians. Growing up in 1950s America, we were taught little of contemporary Jewish history; even the Holocaust was yet to be named and had yet to become central to Jewish identity. In retrospect those days of innocence were halcyon in their quality. At that time Jews were involved in the great African-American civil rights struggles. Could it be possible that elsewhere Jews were depriving others of their human and political rights?

Like most Jews in America, I was unaware of the divide in Jewish life, a divide that has deepened considerably in the past decades. But with that growing awareness, I was faced with a conundrum: how do I as a Jew speak about a contradiction in Jewish life that is unspoken, buried and seen as threatening to Jewish continuity and empowerment? This is especially difficult in light of Jewish suffering in Europe, an event that would wait until the 1960s to be named as "Holocaust."

The difficulty is compounded when one thinks of the enormity of the Holocaust and the pressures it places on contemporary Jews for empowerment. Could I criticize our newfound power when so recently and tragically we were without power? And since as a community Jews were grappling with a language requisite to the Holocaust, a landscape so terrible and unprecedented that words could hardly describe the suffering, could I, with other Jews, fashion a language that illustrated our own complicity in the suffering of others?

This difficulty has not changed over the years. In many ways it has worsened. Knowledge about the Holocaust has exploded in scope and detail; it has become the most studied event in world history. The situation in Israel and Palestine has become the most media-covered situation in the world. In the 1950s and 1960s neither Holocaust nor Israel was central to Jewish identity; today they form the core of our Jewishness. Without them, one wonders what Jewish identity would look like. With them, Jewish identity is becoming more and more fractured, almost schizophrenic. For if at the heart of the covenant is justice and compassion, what do Jews do with our suffering and the suffering we are causing?

It was in 1984 that I was determined to meet Palestinian Arabs and to see first-hand their plight. After this visit, which confirmed and deepened the intuitive understandings I had formed in 1973, I had to find my voice and words to articulate this division in Jewish life, which also was somehow a division in the covenant. Or perhaps better stated, I could sense that the division in Jewish activity on behalf of justice—in America for justice, in Israel against justice—was also a division within the Jewish covenant; Jewish history was at war with itself and thus inevitably Jews were at war with one another. Could Jews remain united when the entire history of Jews and Judaism was at stake, not only in the Holocaust but now in Israel and Palestine?

Constantinian Judaism/Jews of Conscience

These questions form the center of *Toward a Jewish Theology of Liberation*, a book I originally published in 1987. I extended these reflections in the 2nd edition published in response to the Palestinian uprising that began shortly after the 1st edition was published. The final chapter of the 2nd edition is aptly titled "The Palestinian Uprising and the Future of the Jewish People," for I ask in those pages whether, now completely aware of what I had only dimly perceived fifteen years earlier, we as Jews could continue on as if we are only victims of the Holocaust. In a short period, a little more than four decades, we had embarked on a project of empowerment that yielded new victims, the Palestinian people, *and that victimization continued to increase after the emergency years of the Holocaust were past.* I noted then a fact which is even truer today: we as Jews come after the

Holocaust *and* after Israel. After Israel means after what we as Jews have done and are doing to the Palestinian people.

After is an understanding in Jewish life that denotes tragedy and possibility. To Jews and others, the tragedy of the Holocaust needs little explanation. *After* is obvious: what can we say about God after the Holocaust; what can we say about humanity? After Israel, the gaze is turned inward toward us, our history, leadership and future. In the Holocaust, Jews were innocent. In the displacement of Palestinians in 1948 and beyond, Jews are culpable. With the Holocaust, Jews remember as a people; memory is not only for those who directly experienced death and destruction. We are called upon to remember collectively. So, too, in regard to Israel. Israel is a collective work hardly restricted to Jews in Israel. The entire Jewish world has been mobilized on behalf of Israel and therefore is culpable in the plight of the Palestinians. Lobbying for Israel and attempting to define and control the debate on Israeli policies has been the central work of the Jewish establishment in America over the last decades. Are they not as well responsible for Israeli policies toward the Palestinians?

This responsibility has increased as the situation in Israel/Palestine continues to worsen. It is not only the expulsion of the Palestinians in 1948 to make room for the creation of the state of Israel or even the conquering of the West Bank and Gaza in the 1967 war. Today the Jewish settlements in Jerusalem and the West Bank, settlements that threaten the very viability of a Palestinian state, have become permanent. Indeed, their expansion is taken for granted. A ghetto wall is being constructed in the West Bank to protect Israeli expansion; it will enclose a million or more Palestinians. A recent interview with Prime Minister Sharon calls attention to the possibility of the transfer of "tens of thousands" Palestinians within Israel proper once the wall is completed. Targeted assassinations continue apace. The Jewish establishment in America is silent and punishing of dissent.

For me the journey from 1984 to 2004 is immense and, though the seeds of my understanding were already there two decades ago, the reality is much starker today. Thus the need for a 3rd and expanded edition of *Toward a Jewish Theology of Liberation* which will be published in the fall of 2004. It carries the subtitle *Into the 21st Century*. This expanded edition continues the narrative into the 21st century with a more formidable question: the path of power has already been taken by the Jewish community in Israel and America: the conquering of Palestine is virtually complete; Jewish political and economic ascendancy is unparalleled in Jewish history.

As I relate in the new edition, the Jewish community is divided between those who support Jewish power without question and those who resist the use of that power to oppress and silence. A Constantinian Judaism has come into being, mirroring the empire-oriented Christianity that emerged in the 4th century and beyond. At the same time, Jews of conscience confront Constantinian Judaism and its collusion with power and the state. There is a civil war in the Jewish world that crosses geographic and cultural differences. There are Constantinian Jews in Israel and America; there are Jews of conscience all over the Jewish world. The civil war was already in evidence in 1987; in 2004 it is everywhere and, I think, permanent.

Constantinian Judaism is an assimilationist Judaism, an assimilation to power and the state. Jews of conscience resist that assimilation and in so doing are exiled from the Jewish community. Constantinian Judaism is becoming more and more powerful; the exilic community of Jews of conscience is growing. In terms of power the struggle is unequal; witness—a witness without power or reward—is the only avenue left for Jews of conscience.

Blaming the Jews and Christian Zionism

The struggle is difficult. The assault from the Jewish establishment continues and accelerates, impugning the very character of these Jews. Are these Jews self-haters, and in their critique of power, creating a context for another holocaust? There are other assaults, including from those who impugn Jewish empowerment as a cover for impugning Jews themselves or even the Jewish witness in history.

I include here those Christians who see colonialism as the essence of the Hebrew bible and Christianity in error only when it adopts these Judaic elements. I include as well those Christians who fight Christian Zionism as if somehow that form of Zionism is an import from Judaism. There is no question that Israel and Jews in general are culpable in the disaster that has befallen the Palestinian people. However, the culpability of Jews pales in comparison to that of Christianity, especially in its Western variant, in the creation of global violence. Perhaps this is simply a feature of the differential in size and power over the centuries. As it turns out, Jews may be as violent and empire-hungry as their Christian counterparts, but the historical record is clear. Christians should pay attention to their own misuse of power and from that vantage point enter into a critique and solidarity with Jews who critique Jewish power.

Is this also the case for Islam? After all, there has been historically and is today a Constantinian Islam. There are also Muslims of conscience. Like Judaism and Christianity, Islam contains elements of both beauty and violence. The continuum is shared, as is the struggle. One wonders if Constantinian Jews, Christians and Muslims should be seen as a community bent on power and exploitation while Jews, Christian and Muslims of conscience are gathered together as seekers of justice and compassion. Then the critique of all three religious perspectives can be internal and across boundaries. Aren't all people of conscience fighting the same battles within their communities and outside of them? All people of conscience are to some extent losing; they are involved in a witness that raises the possibility of an alternative path. Pitting one against the other is counterproductive: it is also false and self-serving, protecting the innocence of a "true" faith belied by its own history.

So why blame the Jews? There is no question that the Jewish narrative of innocence and redemption found in Holocaust theology and identity is the driving force behind the displacement of Palestinians. Since the 1967 war, that narrative has been joined by a Jewish messianism concretely embodied in the settler movement and a Christian Zionism that resides primarily in the United Kingdom and the United States. At the same time, a Christian Holocaust theology—one that emphasizes the need for Christian repentance in the face of historic Christian anti-Semitism eventuated in the Holocaust—has flourished. It is a repentance whose vehicle is Israel. Coupled with the weakness of the Arab world and the Palestinians themselves and the power of Israel and the United States, these Jewish and Christian narratives have been important, perhaps even decisive for the empowerment of Israel and instrumental in the Palestinian catastrophe.

September 11th has raised the stakes here; the narrative linking the terror visited on American soil with the "terror" visited upon Israel has been strong. Most critical thought on the issue in the Islamic world, especially relating to Israel and the Palestinians, has dissipated. The Jewish establishment has increased its call for unity and the punishment of dissenters and the Sharon government has used September 11th as a green light to re-invade Palestinian territory and begin construction of the Wall of Separation in the West Bank. On the one hand, this wall simply demarcates territory Israel already controls. On the other hand, the construction of the wall further limits Palestinian life and possibility. Symbolically and concretely, the wall being constructed on both sides of the West Bank is a ghetto wall, similar to the ghetto walls that at different points in history have been constructed to enclose Jews.

Christian Zionism is part of this narrative and real-time ghettoization and is now being called to task, and rightly so. By privileging Jews in their eschatological drama, and thereby making Palestinians invisible or demonic, Christian Zionists are participants in this crime against the Palestinian people. Yet seeing this as a Judaization of Christianity is wrong; seeking to distance Christianity from Judaism is also wrong. When a distance is created between the two faiths, we return to previous struggles within Christian history about the role of the Hebrew Scriptures in Christian theology.

To return there is to raise again the question of the influence of Jews in Christian texts and theology, even the Jewishness of Jesus. We re-enter here the terrain of heresy, declarations which throughout Christian history have led to anti-Semitism and intra-Christian wars. The internal struggle to define Christian heresy has often led to an anti-Semitism that eventuates in the murder of Christians by other Christians. The controversies surrounding Marcion come to mind, but also the Crusades. Who can forget the role Jews played in Luther's imagination and the status of the Jews in Christian theology in the Reformation and Counter Reformation?

Declaring Christian Zionism a heresy is the easy path. It has no political clout; it simply draws a line between authentic Christians and those in error. But after this long history of defining heresy and thus Orthodoxy, can one really declare what is and is not Christian? Christian Zionism is a way of being Christian just as those who oppose this sensibility represent a way of being Christian. Like the struggle between Constantinian Judaism and Jews of conscience, the battle is joined. The attempt to define Constantinian Judaism as not being Jewish—as being heretical— is foolish. Jews of conscience oppose this form of Judaism because, in conscience and in context, these Jews choose a certain path within Judaism and Jewish life. To struggle for definition is different then declaring the other side as being "not" Jewish or Christian in the proper way; it is to argue that the practice of faith always needs correction and vision.

There is little doubt that Constantinian Judaism is in debt to that which went before it, Constantinian Christianity. Does this mean that the Christian influence on Judaism needs to be excised or that Jews can blame Christians for this dangerous and "inauthentic" import? Would Jews return to innocence if this "Christian" influence was isolated and denied? Or should we say that the evolution of Constantinian Judaism has many sources, including complex and various interactions in history, and that those influences are part of Jewish history and in this sense are Jewish, whether we oppose elements of these borrowings or not?

Perhaps it is best to understand that Judaism and Christianity are not innocent, are not formed in purity and then distorted, and cannot be purified. Therefore there is no heresy *per se*, only a constant struggle within an impure, always evolving and constantly contested tradition we call Jewish or Christian. In the end, the standard cannot be belief, or how that is judged and it is difficult to see how it is important or even proper to change people's belief as a project. The challenge is to modify political practice that comes from certain beliefs so that conscience and justice are at least considered, if not at the center.

So, yes, it is possible for Jews to believe that Israel is promised to Jews by God: the Hebrew bible certainly has this as a major theme. And yes it is possible for Christians to believe that Jews are chosen by God and that their "return" is an eschatological sign. Do Christians have to see Jews only as a fossil replaced by the church at the time of Jesus? What we can say to these beliefs is that the movement of faith and theology into the public realm must be limited by the question of justice. Belief cannot be turned into action without restraint and the dislocation of peoples must be prevented. Belief must await another kind of power beyond the present and the human.

Perhaps better stated, belief must work within history with limitations and restraint. If belief oversteps these boundaries, it must be restrained, theologically yes but also politically. In politics the use of force is inherent and contested. Theological force, including the declaration of heresy, is counterproductive. It represents a violence against the internal life of the person and of communities. It also represents a simplification of history and tradition, itself a form of violence to diversity and culpability.

An Alternative Path

So the alternative path is clear: Jews, Christians and Muslims of conscience must come together, pooling the resources from their own, now-fragmented traditions into a broader tradition of faith and struggle. The broader tradition is a witness found throughout history but is as yet unnamed. Naming it in our time at least clarifies the stakes involved; it also can become a gathering place for all people of conscience, regardless of religious affiliation or non-affiliation. The exilic community grows until a new diaspora comes into being, a diaspora that honors particularity in the service of the universal.

A Jewish theology of liberation enters the 21st century humbled by the failures of the Jewish world. It is also buoyed by the emergence of Jews of conscience and people of conscience everywhere. The losses are clear; *the end of Palestine means the end of Jewish history as we have known and inherited it*. The end of Palestine is a tragedy that is already at hand, yet at the same time Palestinian identity and consciousness is stronger than ever. At this end, Jews of conscience are in solidarity with the Palestinian struggle as a way of testifying to a new beginning. In the Jewish and Palestinian diaspora creative and deep relationships continue to be forged; the situation on the ground in the Middle East is so terrible that more and more Jews and Palestinians recognize that their fate is common, interconnected, bound together in place and time. One wonders if the ghetto walls can contain this solidarity forever.

A Jewish theology of liberation is a prophetic theology, a return to the roots of the Jewish experience, a re-embracing of our most lasting contribution to the world. For if Jews do not practice the prophetic, who, then, will? It is true that the greatest gift is the one given to others, freely and without expectation of reward or attribution. And truly the prophetic is now everywhere in the world. Jews, especially those of the Constantinian variety, often have difficulty recognizing the prophetic, especially as it is now firmly pointed toward us, as a critique of unjust power.

It is of little solace to remember that the prophetic, our great gift to the world, our indigenous practice, has always been heard and rejected by the Jewish community. The prophets have always been persecuted within the Jewish world and one hears through the ages the cries of Aaron and Moses, Jeremiah and Isaiah, Amos and Jesus. They have always and everywhere been surrounded by darkness and violence. Is this the same darkness and violence that surrounded Archbishop Romero of El Salvador and Rachel Corrie of the United States, both of whom gave their lives in service to others?

One remembers the cry of Romero, who said that after death he would be resurrected in the history of the Salvadoran people. Is this not our common hope, to live as a witness for and within our own peoples and the peoples of the world? As a Jew, I think also of Edward Said, the late Palestinian intellectual, who embraced Jews as he embraced his own people. As a Jew I cannot withhold my embrace of him and therefore of his own people. That embrace must be given freely as a sign of justice and compassion.

I cannot embrace my own history or religion without embracing the Palestinian people. I cannot affirm the prophetic without practicing it in my own lifetime. The prophetic is not for the few or for someone else or for another time. It is the now deeply grasped, even in loss and at a cost.

In the end a Jewish theology of liberation is simply an expression of that prophetic voice in the 20th and now 21st century. May there be a time when the different editions of this book will only be a historical curiosity of the time *before* justice, *before* a reconciliation of Jews and Palestinians, *before* the broader tradition of faith and struggle became the norm rather than the exception. Then the *after* can take on a new meaning and substance: a time when misfortune and injustice come to an end.

Yet in the meantime the radical questions posed by a Jewish theology of liberation must be moderated by the political realities of our time. Justice would be extra-ordinary in our context and certainly in the Middle East. For the foreseeable future Israel will dominate and the Palestinians will be a subject people, not only in relation to Israel but also the Arab world. To survive, even the Palestinians will participate in their own subjugation: at the lower levels Palestinian workers will, as they have for years, help build settlements; as even today they are workers in construction of the Wall of Separation. Palestinian elites will sell land to Jews and also, on a corporate level, bid for settlement and wall construction contracts. Betrayal is everywhere, as is the simple need to feed one's family.

At the same time as the very survival of the Palestinian people in Palestine is at stake, a renewed call for the implementation of the right of return is being voiced. While understandable, even principled, the right has become part of a rhetoric that seeks a war onto death. Wars unto death sometimes materialize and those who speak in this ideologically way are free to do so; perhaps they are being faithful to their history and people. However, it is wrong to involve the collective, perhaps even force the collective, into a situation where all or nothing is the result. So often the nothing is the result, and no one remains to pick up the pieces of shattered lives and communities.

Of course it is the oppressor who is first and foremost to blame for the situation. One must never lose sight of this. Still the oppressed have a responsibility to think through and survive the disaster in order to struggle another day. Like religions, the history of a people is complex and the pretense to innocence, even when a people is being oppressed, is superficial and dangerous. The subversive is not suicidal and martyrdom becomes the seeds of a future beyond injustice rather than a call for a war unto the end. Martyrdom is the sign of a resistance that will be carried on over time; without compassion and the hope for a new world for the oppressed and oppressor, martyrdom becomes a form of suicide and violence. It fuels the cycle of violence that may engulf all.

The moderate course in Israel/Palestine is one where the hurts, complaints and hopes of both peoples are expressed and where a political framework of peace and stability is constructed within the parameters that are possible. Today is not forever and the psychological and physical borders and boundaries of one generation are not those of the next. The relentless land-grab of the Israeli government must be stopped and the Wall of Separation must be dismantled with force if necessary. Still, the immediate goal of this force is to reestablish the possibility of a future for Jews and Palestinians, not the radical implementation of a justice that will not come to fruition or a justice that to come to fruition would mean the dislocation of millions or even their murder.

* * *

Marc H. Ellis is University Professor of American and Jewish Studies and Director of the Center for American and Jewish Studies at Baylor University. His 3rd edition of *Toward a Jewish Theology of Liberation: Into the 21st Century* will be published in July. He can be reached at Marc_Ellis@baylor.edu

Conclusion

Marc Ellis, Jewish Constantinianism and the Emergence of the New Jewish Prophetic

M arc Ellis reports in a recent essay ("Jew vs. Jew: On the Jewish Civil War and the New Prophetic" 2003, p.139) that a rabbi and neighbor of his sent an email message to her rabbinic colleagues in the United States: "In Waco we have a similar situation to Michael Lerner, though on a local, not a national level. Baylor University, a Baptist University... has a professor who is unabashedly pro-Palestinian...Things came to a head last week when he was the only Jew interviewed by any of the television stations about the Middle East. We are contacting the media to let them know he does *not* speak for the Jewish community.... Slanted media coverage is trouble enough, but to have so much of this driven by Jews, who...get media attention...is tragic"(p.140).

The rabbi was only doing her duty as a low ranking member of the Jewish Establishment, and thus as putatively a defender of the Jewish people. After all, as Ellis comments wryly, "good Jews support Israel no matter what its policies are; Jews who dissent from these policies are hardly Jews at all" (2003, p.140). Considering the level of State terrorism directed at the Palestinian people, being a good Jew today requires either an extraordinary capacity for self-deception, and/ or an attrition of one's moral sensibilities. In an address given to a convention of American Muslims in 2003, focusing on the symbolism of Sharon's infamous wall—which Noam Chomsky wrote was "turning Palestinian communities into dungeons, next to which the bandustans of South Africa look like symbols of freedom [and] sovereignty..."(NY Times, Feb 23,2004)—Ellis stated: "There are no public comments on this wall by Jewish neo-conservatives or Jewish neo-liberals; perhaps the wall denied is a wall of denial...That denial is clear: the entire Jewish community is silent on this great crime, as if it is not taking place, as if terrorism is the reason for its construction, as if the occupation is not decades old and continuing, as if the expulsion, degradation and dispersal of a people has not taken place before our eyes and under our supervision, as if we as Jews are innocent"(2003c, p2). And in another recent statement on Sharon's policies, Ellis declaimed the "[g]hettoization of an entire people, a pretense to innocence when the actions involved are against international law and a moral tradition embraced for centuries by the Jewish people" and described his own "feeling of betrayal by my own community's participation in policies which were, in another age and in different circumstances, carried out against us" (2003d, p1)

While decrying the rabbi's inability to separate independent moral judgment from support for Israeli policies, Ellis ironically writes that she has her facts wrong—in some ways Lerner is in fact in denial about Israel, is in some ways an apologist for Israel. Doubtless it would not console the poor Rabbi to learn that Lerner is not as threatening as she thought, or rather that Ellis is even more of an "extremist" than Lerner in his critique of Israel. Michael Lerner, editor of *Tikkun* magazine, is probably the most well known American Jewish critic of Israeli policies–after Noam Chomsky. In this essay ("Jew vs. Jew.") Ellis brings together criticisms of Lerner's camp that he has made in his books (sometimes in passing) over many years. Lerner, or Rabbi Lerner as he prefers, is a "Jewish dissident" (to adopt the terms Ellis uses in his aforementioned essay) but there is another camp of critics–albeit a much smaller group. Ellis calls the latter in this essay (and elsewhere), "Jews of conscience" and believes that they are heeding the call of the "Jewish prophetic." His critique of the Lerner camp is excoriating, and it delineates the substantive issues, the philosophical/political commitments that distinguishes dissident Jews from Jews of conscience (to use Ellis' terminology).

I should add that although I agree with most of Ellis' criticisms and with the thrust of his argument I think Lerner's educational and organizing efforts actions has been successful in expanding the bounds of discourse about Israel among progressives and among American Jews in general–despite the limitations of his own critique his work and magazine *could,* and undoubtedly often does, serve as an *introduction* to critical perspectives on Israeli policies. Although Lerner has recruited a membership of 10–15,000 for the "Tikkun community" it is of course not surprising (for many reasons, discussed previously) that he has had no success in achieving his stated goal of pressuring the US government to try to broker a Mideast peace settlement; Lerner thought he could influence American policy by providing a counter-weight to the hawkish right-wing well-heeled American Jewish Establishment which in terms of Israel is the decisive Jewish influence on the Executive and Congressional branches of US government, and speciously claims to speak for the entire Jewish community.

The Establishment of Israel–The Myth of Zionist Innocence

Ellis formulates eloquently what is distinctive about Jews of conscience in the current era of Jewish empowerment. To sustain the prophetic tradition Jewish radicals must not seek the approbation of organized Jewry, or of the Jewish political or religious leadership. To the contrary, unlike Jewish dissidents, they must be willing to abjure the hope of any kind of relationship with the Jewish Establishment– and even of acceptance by the organized Jewish community. They must be willing if necessary to accept ostracism, to willingly embark upon a "new exile" (see below). Far too often Jewish dissidents have allowed their desire to be accepted by organized Jewry to lead them to adopt ethically compromised positions.

Unlike Jews of conscience the dissenters affirms the legitimacy of the modern Jewish "return" to Israel and are thus not capable of developing and enacting a profound critique of Jewish power, of Zionism, of Jewish Constantinianism itself, as Ellis terms it (see below).

Ellis describes the left Zionist position to which Lerner has adhered for years: "Zionism is something good, the national liberation struggle of the Jewish people. Israeli politics are sometimes wrong; these specific policies are aberrations and must be opposed. The opposition to certain policies is to bring Zionism and the Jewish state back into line, in a sense to recover their innocence... Thus the Jewish establishment and Jewish dissenters have been arguing over the same turf—Jewish suffering and Jewish empowerment as innocent. Jewish leadership proclaimed this innocence as self-evident, Jewish dissenters as in need of recovery" (2003b, p.142.). For Lerner, Israel's apostasy from its original idealism began only after 1967 with the Occupation of the Palestinian territories. But if Lerner is wrong, if Israel *is* like other nation-states, if the Jewish religious ethical tradition at its best is not in any way constitutive of Israel's identity (which Lerner thinks it is, or was) then "calling Israel to its Jewishness is a lost battle" (2003b, p.143). Lerner is pursuing a lost innocence which cannot be recovered because it was always an illusion, at least as soon as the Zionist state was created with the massacres and deliberate expulsion of close to a million Palestinians—it is a carefully cultivated facade that Israel's statesmen have always used to conceal from the world their political ambitions.

In Lerner's view Israel's crimes against the Palestinians are aberrations from the idealism of its founders, and are thus subject to rectification by the Jewish community if they are organized and educated by progressive Zionists like Lerner and his associates and proteges in the Tikkun community. (Lerner has succeeded in reaching thousands of people, presumably mostly Jews, through his magazine Tikkun, which claims a readership of over 50,000 and he has created a network of 15,000 Jews who have become "members" of the Tikkun community.) According to Ellis, Lerner and those in his camp are engaged in a "struggle to become the next Jewish establishment" (2003b, p153), presumably more humane, more "Jewish" in their prophetic sensibility as Lerner would see it. Ellis, on the other hands, rejects the legitimacy of the creation of the Israeli state in the first place, views the nation-state in general as inherently (or at least by predilection) oppressive and thus cannot and will not affirm Jewish empowerment as an unequivocally positive development.

The "redemption and return" to Israel is not founded in justice, contrary to Lerner. The modern return to Israel and expropriation of Palestinians is the "original sin," to cite the prominent Israeli scholar and psychiatrist Beit-Hallahmi (1993) that the overwhelming majority of Jews (in Israel and the diaspora) are unable or unwilling to face. Those who mention this sin, let alone condemn it, have stepped beyond the parameters of legitimate discourse as defined by the Jewish Establishment. Here Lerner and the Jewish establishment concur; as Ellis puts it: "In their view...Jews had no choice but to found a nation-state after the Holocaust.... They agree with each other that the undermining of Israel's raison d'etre and the power to maintain its existence is an unpardonable sin to be punished by ex-communication from the Jewish world" (2003b, p.152). Israel as a nation-state thus becomes the "litmus test for Jewish loyalty and Jewish empowerment"(2003b, p.142).

Ellis points out that at the time of the establishment of Israel there were renowned Jews who were opposed to the policy of establishing Jewish sovereignty on Palestinian land. Martin Buber, Hannah Arendt, Judah Magnes were only a few of the prominent Jews who were advocates of a bi-national state in Israel. But their arguments and pleas for compromise with the indigenous Arabs were opposed and ignored (blatantly in the case of the dispute between Buber and Ben-Gurion mentioned above) by the leaders of the Zionist movement whom Lerner reveres (e.g. Ben-Gurion) and have today been erased from Jewish history, and thus have no appreciable impact upon the Jewish collective psyche.

In the mind of most Jews the creation of Israel was a refuge for persecuted Jews, including survivors of the Holocaust. In fact an absurd but commonly believed fallacy is that Israel "was founded by Holocaust survivors" or "in response to the Holocaust." As Beit-Hallahmi puts it, "The uninformed develop this mental image of Holocaust survivors in Europe in 1945 creating a movement to leave behind the hated continent, to sail to the old homeland and then to build an independent state in record time"(1993, p.179). Of course this canard was useful to Israel as a means of deflecting criticism as only evil anti-Semites would criticize a state of holocaust survivors. Even those who realize the foundation for the Jewish state was built by Zionists who emigrated to Israel in the 1920s, such as Ben-Gurion and Chaim Weizmann, take it as axiomatic that the rescue of European Jewry after Hitler's ascension to power were uppermost in the minds of the Zionists in Israel. In reality the Zionists subordinated the salvation of the Jews to the creation of a Jewish state.

The maniacal nationalism of a Ben-Gurion was not compatible with a whole-hearted effort to save European Jews—that would have required at least a willingness to pressure other countries to open their doors to imperiled Jews in the late 1930s when it was still possible to escape (see Evron, 1995). But in 1938 Ben-Gurion warned his fellow Zionists, "If we allow a separation between the refugee problem and the Palestinian problem, we are risking the existence of Zionism" (Cited in Brenner, 1983, Chapter 13). When after Kristallnacht the British proposed that thousands of children be admitted into Britain, Ben-Gurion opposed the plan! Ben-Gurion explained his reasoning to a conference of Labor Zionists on December 7,1938: "If I knew that it was possible to save all the children of Germany by transporting them to England, but only half of them by transporting them to Palestine, I would choose the second. For we must weigh not only the lives of these children, but also the history of the people of Israel"(Ibid, Chapter 13). The Zionist plan hobbled rescue efforts because allowing all the Jews to emigrate to Palestine was infeasible. For one thing, the British did not want to take such a move because it would alienate the Arab countries, and risk undermining their support in the war effort. Furthermore the Zionists themselves did not want to provide refuge for all prospective refugees–they regarded older or unskilled Jews as a burden. (They only wanted to prevent Jews from going anywhere other than Palestine.) Chaim Weizmann, the future (first) President of Israel, wanted 2 million youth. He told the Zionist Congress in 1937 that the Zionist enterprise would be harmed " if Palestine were to be flooded with very old people or with undesirables"(cited in Schonfeld, 1992). "The old ones will pass; they will bear their fate or they will not. They were dust, economic and moral dust in a cruel world...Only the branch of the young will survive. They have to accept it" (Brenner, Chapter 13).

Ben-Gurion instructed his Zionists followers to ignore or attempt to undermine any and all rescue plans that were not tied to emigration to Palestine (see Brenner, 1983; Evron, 1995; Schoenmann, 1988). Thus the Zionists were able to sabotage the success of the Evian Conference convened on the eve of the war at the initiative of President Roosevelt to explore refugee options for European Jews. Weizmann was "particularly worried that it would move Jewish organizations to collect large sums of money for aid to Jewish refugees, and these organizations could interfere with our collection efforts"(Evron, p.260). Ben-Gurion was afraid that the conference "will open the gates of other countries to Jewish immigration..." Ben-Gurion and the other Zionist leaders decided the wisest course of action was "to belittle the Conference as much as possible and to cause it to decide nothing" (Evron, p. 260-1). (See also Evron's discussion of a number of books in Hebrew on this topic.) The Zionists succeeded in stymieing the Evian conference, largely as result of their status at that point and their reputation as spokespersons for international Jewry.

This topic is too extensive to do justice to in these few paragraphs, and students of the topic have unearthed a plethora of facts that undermine the Zionists claim of innocence; for example the efforts of several prominent Zionists (including Yitzhak Shamir, who became Prime Minister of Israel in the early 1990s) to form a pact with Germany based on cooperation in the Nazis war effort in 1941– the Nazis rejected the offer (see Brownfeld, 1998: cited in Schoenman, 1988,pp54-5). But the more important point here is that the Zionists believed that measures that could have and would have saved hundreds of thousands of European Jews were a threat to their own nationalist ambitions to procure support for an Israeli state.

Evron points out that even after the full scale of the Holocaust became known "the Zionist movement showed no interest in trying to save Jews outside Eretz Israel" (p160). He also states based on his review of studies in Hebrew: "The Zionist movement...interfered with and hindered other organizations, Jewish and non-Jewish, whenever it imagined that their activity, political or humanitarian, was at variance with Zionist aims or in competition with them, even when these might be helpful to Jews, even when it was a question of life and death" (p.259). One can speculate on the basis of solid evidence that had Zionism not existed, or had its leaders (particularly Ben-Gurion) not attained the deference of other world leaders, the international resistance to the persecution of the Jews would have been greater and more effective, the scope of the Nazi holocaust would have been far less broad, and would not have claimed the lives of so many Jews. Of course this subject is taboo among most Jews who insistently identify the interest of all Jews with that of Israel, a state which is regarded as the virtual incarnation of innocence, a state which owes its existence to the Holocaust itself.

In America the Jewish establishment that today serves as a lobby for Israel— that insistently identifies the interest of American Jews with that of the state of Israel–are determined above all to protect the myth of Israeli/Jewish innocence. This has entailed one of the most extensive public relations campaign in the history of the US. The level of denial involved in the media's manipulation of reality is extraordinary. The Israeli journalist Gideon Levy comments here on Israelis, but his description aptly fits American Jews also–and the US public at large: "More than ever before, the Israelis' ignoring of the Palestinians suffering is reaching dimensions that are difficult to comprehend...The only Palestinian still talked about is the suicide bomber, the only children mentioned are 'terrorist children.' Not poverty struck children, not orphaned children, not children whose homes were demolished before their very eyes, and not children whose fathers were taken, humiliated, in the dead of night, to detention without trial and did not return for months and years"(cited in Ellis, 2003c, p.3). Of course Americans' ignorance of the Palestinians' suffering is undoubtedly greater than Israelis'–as the American mainstream media (unlike the Israeli media which publishes a few critics of Israeli policies) proscribes any mention of Palestinian suffering while Israel is depicted as the innocent victim of deranged suicide bombers, terrorists whose acts have no context and emerge out of a void, or since September 11 out of the evil underworld of Islam. The word "occupation" (which is a legal concept denoting Israel's status in Palestine–as determined by international law) is not even used anymore, evidently because U.S. Secretary of Defense Rumsfeld decided "contested territories" sounded less invidious.

It should be added that while the suffering of innocent Palestinian victims of the Israeli Army goes largely unrecorded by the US mainstream media, the act of every single suicide bomber is described–often in elaborate detail. These facts do not exculpate American Jews who see Israel as blameless because it is obvious that many of them deliberately deny available information that does not fit their preconceptions and ignore the evidence the press *does* print (not to speak of the readily available alternative media) of Sharon's brutality—they are motivated by their desire to maintain what Ellis calls the myth of Jewish innocence. Any discussion of Palestinian suffering is taboo as it clashes with the determination of ordinary Jews to maintain their stance as perennially innocent victims of anti-Semitism–and now of Islamic terrorists. Ellis comments "Palestine is burning. The Jewish ethical tradition is coming to an end"(2003c, p.2)

Those Jews who publicly take positions like that of Ellis or the other interviewees in this book, may inevitably find that if they are going to be faithful to the Jewish covenant itself, to heed the Biblical command to "seek only justice," to heed the prophetic call, they must be willing to face censure, Jewish hatred, ostracism. (Even the *parents* of Adam Shapiro were deluged with death threats after the articles about his activism in Palestine appeared in the press.)

Those I had chosen to interview for this book are in fact opposed to (as they make clear in their interviews) the basic Zionist position embraced by those in Lerner's camp, i.e. by those who espouse a (leftish) *new Zionist* paradigm, to use my own term. Following Ellis I will frequently refer in this chapter to the dissidents outside the neo—Zionist camp as "Jews of conscience." In the first place the latter do not believe that the establishment of the Jewish state and the consequent ethnic cleansing of almost a million Palestinians (numbering several million today, 2 generations later) was morally justifiable. It should be noted that the Zionist founders of Israel were all (very discreet) supporters of the idea of the ethnic cleansing (or ethnic purification) of Israel (for a definitive survey of their views see Masalha, 1992)—a fact that Lerner tends to ignore. These positions have profound political and metaphysical/theological implications. As Ellis argues the modern left-wing Zionist depiction of the Jewish state as innocent is constitutive–thus the new Zionists believe that Israel unlike other apartheid states will respond to moral appeals. They posit the Jewish state as transcendentally good (unlike other states) despite its flaws, they valorize the Jewish empowerment and ignore its moral costs, and they attempt to theoretically justify the idolatry of Israel that is characteristic of the practice of organized Jews in America today.

This move to validate the formation of the Israeli state and its undergirding by Judaism or more precisely by a Judaic ideology (with the blessings of the representatives of Judaism) led inevitably to the acceptance of the "Constantinian" synthesis of religion and State, to Constantinian Judaism as Ellis terms it. The prototype for this constellation and ideology is of course Constantinian Christianity. Constantinian Christianity replaced the messianic universalist goals of the original

Jesus movement with those of the Roman Empire, just as Constantinian Judaism, in America as well as Israel, replaces universalist prophetic Judaism with the nationalist interests—as interpreted by Israel's ruling elites—of the "Jewish state."

Constantinian Christianity

A brief recapitulation of the development of Constantinian Christianity may be illuminating. As Elaine Pagels among others have documented, the early Christian movement was a socially radical egalitarian counter-culture, at its best. These Christians were not political revolutionaries but they adopted radical and egalitarian ideals in their own Christian associations; they were awaiting the imminent act of God which would establish his Kingdom on earth; this would entail the universal realization of the egalitarian norms that Christians had adopted in their own lives. But while they waited many Christians went among the poor and " into the slave quarters, offering help and money and preaching to the poor, the illiterate, slaves, women and foreigners –the good news that class, education, sex and status made no difference, that every human being is essentially equal to any other "before God," including the emperor himself, for all humankind was created in the image of the one God" (Pagels, 1988, p.57). This kind of message made the representatives of the Empire nervous, which of course is why Christians were persecuted for the first few centuries by the Roman Empire.

The "conversion" (he refrained from being baptized until he was on his deathbed) of Constantine to Christianity effected gradually the transformation of Christianity from the radical worldview held by a persecuted sect to the religion of the Roman Empire. It is revealing that Constantine's epiphany occurred on the battlefield when he appeared to be losing to his adversaries. Suddenly Constantine had a vision of a sign that resembled a cross and saw beneath it the inscription, "In This Sign Conquer." Constantine was instantly convinced that he could win the battle if he renounced his own god and solicited and accepted the assistance of the Christian God which he immediately proceeded to do. (Alistair Kee wrote that this was not conversion but "an exchange of divine patronage," 1982, p.16) This was only the first of many battles Constantine won, allegedly with the help of the God of the Abraham, Moses and Jesus. It is remarkable that the Zionists also interpreted most of their military victories as the results of divine favor.

Alistair Kee aptly termed Constantinian Christianity as "the Great Reversal." In the religion of Constantine (and of Constantinian Christianity) "God is manifested in kingly power, wealth, status and security"(p.151). Christian leaders "were now drawn into the imperial court as advisers...given status and power in the Empire so that they might in turn enjoy a little persecution of pagans" (1982, p.157). Christians as functionaries of the state religion exchanged their humble Christian dress for rich apparel.

Although Jesus would not even act as a king to his own followers, and exhorted them to be "servants" of all human beings, Christians now praised monarchy as the most ideal form of government; Bishop Eusebius, Constantine's Christian promoter and hagiographer believed an Emperor was necessary for "the salvation of the world" (p.135). Although Jesus asserted that no one was an enemy of God, Eusebius claimed that Constantine made war on God's "enemies." Jesus was no longer the normative human being—the Son of God. He had been replaced by Constantine. Kee puts it "Does the Emperor wage war on his enemies to destroy them. Then so does God. Does the Emperor carefully plan the downfall of his rivals and kill them their families and followers. Then so does God"(pp143-4). Did Constantine become subservient to the Church? "Far from it: the Church was incorporated into his grand plan and became an instrument in his unification of the Empire" (p.139). Constantine and Eusebius accomplished something unprecedented in the history of the Christian community: "the replacement of the norms of Christ by the norms of imperial ideology" (p.4). Kee comments astutely, "It is in this way that European history is determined by the values of Constantine, *as if* they were the values of Christ" (p140).

The first most well known critics in the modern era of the Church's Constantinian transformation were the congregations and denominations that constituted what came to be known as the *Radical* Reformation. The most coherent and abiding segment of this movement were referred to as Anabaptists because they eschewed infant baptism and believed Church membership should be the product of a voluntary decision. The (non-radical) Reformation itself was thoroughly Constantinian and had no qualms about using the power of the state to outlaw and persecute "heretics," including the Anabaptists who were pacifists and social radicals in the tradition of Jesus.

The Anabaptists argued that the corruption of the Church first took place when it subordinated its own witness to the goal of defending and advancing the cause of the Empire, now viewed as a "Christian" empire. The recently deceased Anabaptist (Mennonite) theologian John Howard Yoder explicates a modern Christian critique of mainstream Christianity based upon the premise that Christianity has still not overcome its Constantinian heritage. Only by separating itself from "the world"– which Yoder terms 'structured unbelief'(1994, p62) can the Church become a transformative force. Anabaptist Charles Scriven in his book on Yoder writes "the Church must be willing to accept the role of outsider in society, that precisely in that role it must exercise political responsibility"(p.146) This is of course analogous to Ellis's position: Jews of conscience must be willing to accept a new exile–an exile from the structures of Jewish power in the United States and in Israel. Otherwise the

Church–or modern Jewry—risks surrendering to Constantinianism and becoming co-opted by the existing power structure. (Need one mention that the new ghastly travesty of Christianity today–the "Christian" right–is rabidly Constantinian?)

Scriven writes that the radical vision is "awake to the massive defiance of the way of Jesus in surrounding culture and it is resolved to make a public witness against it" (1988, p191). As will be seen there is a striking parallel (albeit with some obvious differences) between Yoder's vision of a Church that seeks to influence the world by remaining separate from it, and Marc Ellis's concept of "practicing exile" or accepting a "new" Jewish exile–both seek to recover the prophetic dimensions of the Biblical covenants. But unlike Constantinian Christianity which is close to 2 thousand years old, Constantinian Judaism is a recent phenomenon. Marc Ellis might aptly be termed the first theologian and prophet of the Jewish Radical Reformation. (The first Reform Jews preceded by over a century the fusion of Judaism and state power, and thus their mission was not analogous to that of the Radical Reformation, although they opposed nascent Jewish nationalism.)

Constantinian Judaism and the Triumph of Zionism

Ellis writes, "Constantinian Christianity was a new form of Christianity that transformed its witness [to God, to justice, to community] to legitimation of the state and its policies in return for its elevation to respectability"(2003b, p.143). As Yoder put it, the two disparate realities "church and world were fused. There is no longer anything to call "world"; state, economy, art, rhetoric, superstition and war have all been baptized"–by the Church (1994,p57). And now Jewish religious authorities and the symbols of Jewish religious and ethical tradition have also been put to the service of Jewish power, used to cloak the Jewish state with an aura of spirituality purity, a Jewish nation-state as brutal and amoral as any other nation-state–and more racist than most. As Ellis notes, "[M]any Jews have been part of this history in an intimate way, as soldiers, politicians, bureaucrats, businessmen, intellectuals, rabbis and theologians...[T]o lay the blame solely on the state is to evade responsibility. The founding, building, defending and expanding of Israel have been a collective effort of the Jewish people. Most Jews take a collective pride in Israel; there is also a collective culpability. The return of Jews to power has mostly been seen as a miracle in light of the light of the Holocaust. Today it may also be recognized as a disaster"(1999, p.52). For Ellis the question becomes how to recover "the prophetic," if not within Judaism, at least by Jews who are willing to bear responsibility—first of all to acknowledge—as Jews for what they or other Jews have done.

Here we see the primary difference between Ellis and Jews like Lerner. Lerner not only accepts and celebrates the idea of a Jewish state, he not only defends Israel's refusal in 1950 to allow the Palestinian refugees to return after the 1948 war (see Lerner, 2003) as it promised the United Nations it would as the condition for its acceptance as a member, but he accepts unquestioningly the Constantinian synthesis of Judaism and political power—in America and Israel. His complaint is only that those who now wield the power—in Israel and America—have become corrupted, whether by power or (in Israel) by the influence of the right wing messianic settler movement. Lerner, Ellis alleges, aspires to become part of what could become a new Jewish Establishment in America, a new class of power brokers between the American state and Israel, whose use of power will–they believe—be tempered and kept pure by their reverence for the Jewish ethical-religious tradition. Ellis denounces the Jewish Constantinian synthesis–for him it represents the "fall" of Judaism. (He does not use this term which was commonly used by Christian radical reformers to explain the Church's condition after Constantine.) Ellis distrusts state power altogether and recommends a new exile and the severance of the intimate bond between Judaism and the Jewish state.

Zionists believe, as seen above, that the foundation of state of Israel was the realization of the Jews' ancient dream to return to their home–their God-given home, their metaphysical as well as physical home. Thus in the Zionist view the long period of Jewish exile has ended–the Jewish mission is essentially completed. All that remains is to eliminate internal or external threats to Israel's existence or expansion to its Biblical boundaries, and to "ingather" the exiles who remain in the diaspora—at least this is how the pure Zionists view the issue. The Zionist founders of Israel also believed that the return to Israel must be brought to completion by the process of "the negation of the diaspora," extirpating the diaspora mentality which is an adaptation to life in the diaspora and is thus ostensibly characterized by pathology, by fragmentation and incompletion. (See Weaver, 2003). Ben-Gurion used to refer to diaspora Jews as "dust"; future Prime Minister Yitzhak Rabin called them "misfits" (Shahak, 1988, p.302). The negation of the diaspora denigrated thousands of years of Jewish life and culture before the triumph of Zionism. As Beit-Hallahmi noted, it also rejected the image of the Jew, which represented that culture. "The almost total rejection of Diaspora traditions is the cornerstone and capstone of the new Israeli identity, the most tangible product of Zionist ideology"(1993, p.120). It is ironic that Zionists today accuse critics of Israel of being "self-hating Jews." Even in the United States many Jews adopt a modified version of this theory. They consider Israel to be, on Biblical grounds, the spiritual home of the Jews.

Reform Judaism, Prophetic Judaism
and the Struggle for Social Justice

But Zionism was rejected by virtually all Jews before World War Two –and did not become popular until well after the war had started. (For Orthodox the acceptance of Zionism took at least a generation after WWII.) The Orthodox originally rejected the Zionist concept of salvation because it eschewed the messianic-universalist interpretation of the return to Israel–in other words they maintained the Jewish exile could not come to an end till the Messiah came and brought peace to all humanity. (This is still the position of Neturei Karta.) Reform Jews' original principles included the rejection of a literal return to Palestine altogether. They argued that the early nationalist period of Judaism was a temporary necessity to prepare Jews for their God-given task of carrying the message of universal justice to all men—Jews were not a nation but a distinctive religious community (Mezvinsky, 1988, p.314) Rabbi Isaac Mayer Wise "the major spokesperson and organizing genius" (Mezvinsky, 1988, p.315) of the early American Reform movement wrote "the idea of Jews returning to Palestine is not part of our creed. We rather believe that the habitable become one holy land and the human family one chosen people" (Ibid, p.319).

In Rabbinic Judaism God's imposition of exile upon the Jews (as a punishment for apostasy) was viewed at the same time as a call to mission–to bring all the nations to God. The idea of a mission to the nations within the diaspora lacked valence among Jewry during the 100s of years of hegemony of Christendom when Jews were confined to ghettoes and subject to pogroms, but it burgeoned in gnostic form in the metahistorical writings of Kabbalists and in historical form in many of the great Jewish thinkers after the emancipation. Neo-Kantian philosopher and Jewish theologian Hermann Cohen did most of his writings in the last quarter of the 19th Century; he was the leader of the German Liberal Jewish movement and probably the most profound advocate of the notion of the diaspora Jewry's universalist messianic monotheistic mission, as well as passionately anti-Zionist. Cohen wrote that "the world marches toward prophetic messianism, and that the realization of Judaism is bound up with the Jewish dispersion among the peoples of the earth. This dispersion is our historical realization: "to be a light to the nations'"(cited in Melber, 2003,p.402). How quaint these words sound today when virtually the whole of organized Jewry worships at the altar of the nation-state of Israel. Only in Ellis is this idea of the Jewish dispersion given a positive prophetic-missionary interpretation redolent of theologians like Cohen. Cohen continues: "Hence the political nationalism of the Zionists runs definitely counter to the conceptual world of the prophets and must be rejected" (Ibid, p402). Cohen writes presciently (this was in the late 19th Century): "In the Jewish state we may vanish as the bearer of God's mission" (Ibid, p.401).

But surprisingly one finds that even Orthodox thinkers in the 19th century emphasized the moral and spiritual value of a Jewish mission to the nations. Samson Raphael Hirsch the founder of the neo-Orthodox movement (which like all fundamentalism regarded the Bible as the unmediated word of God) rejected Zionism as a crude form of nationalism that valorized violence. Hirsch wrote, "Abraham, the father of the Jewish people, was willing to give up homeland, fortune, fame and status—all things that people obtain by force–to ensure, in a peaceable way, that the world be governed by justice. The destiny of Abraham's descendants is to proclaim [to the nations] the victory of moral force over armed physical force." Hirsch wrote that Israel must "root out" from itself all traces of worship of physical power, especially "the cult of the hero," "the laurels that the nations in their blind enthusiasm bestow upon murderers." Fortunately for Hirsch he lived in the 19th century, and thus was spared the vision of the Jewish worship of the state, and of American and Israeli Jews bestowing laurels upon the soldiers in the Israeli Army (I.D.F.) who murder Palestinians, often wantonly, in the name of the Jewish people and the Jewish state.

One finds the idea of the hegemony of the diaspora mission in a positivistic form in American Reform Judaism as well as in more profound guises in original Jewish thinkers like Franz Rosenzweig, Although the Reform concept of a Jewish mission based on prophetic-messianic ideals galvanized the creation of Reform Judaism, it failed to retain its power as an inspiration for vigorous social activism—-probably because Reform Judaism itself embraced the middle class ethos and ideal of upward mobility of America itself, where most Jews lived after WWII.. In the 20th Century the Reform synagogue became a social center for Jews and an agency for liberal reform projects. Unfortunately when anti-Semitism began to fade in America after World War II and Jews achieved a considerable measure of power and status, Reform Judaism embraced Zionism (particularly after the 1967 war) and not long afterwards turned its back upon the radical ideals of prophetic Judaism. By the 1970s even liberal social activism was out of fashion among Reform rabbis–only Israel aroused their passions. In the 20th century as a whole movements for social justice were more often secular in their orientation and took place on the margins of the synagogue and organized Jewish society.

The theoretical foundation for modern social activism until recently was most often derived not from the Bible but from the 19th century Jewish prophet Karl Marx. The messianic ideal of a society which has realized the ideal of universal justice was forcefully articulated in secular form by Marx. In the 20th century there were a number of renowned Jewish libertarian socialist intellectuals (from Lukacs to Adorno) who were strongly influenced by their reading of Jewish messianism, as well as of Marx—they formulated a variety of secular versions of universal redemption (Loewy, 1988); their radical theories mirrored and fostered the social activism of the time, as did that of the Jewish Russian Marxist, Leon Trotsky. Walter Benjamin, who died—committed suicide—fleeing the Nazis, was perhaps the most influential explicitly messianic (left-wing) thinker–he had maintained a correspondence for years with his friend Gershom Scholem, the scholar of Jewish mysticism, and a cultural Zionist (Loewy, 1988). Martin Buber, among other Jews of conscience, combined the concept of a diaspora mission with cultural (not political) Zionism –a precarious combination that was extinguished by the growth of militarism and racism in the Israeli nation-state that was formally established by political Zionists in 1948.

The predominance of Jews in the social justice movements of the 20th Century is legendary—they constituted half the members of the Communist Party in the 1930s and over half of the whites who took part in the civil rights struggles in the early 1960s (Beit-Hallahmi, 1993, pp30-1). Jewish radicals, and non-Jewish radicals in the 1930s were inspired by the secular messianism of Marx, as interpreted by Lenin, Stalin or Trotsky. Jewish social activism seemed to be consonant with if not a direct expression of the universalist impulse of prophetic Judaism—even though there was only occasionally (e.g. Abraham Heschel's support for black civil rights movement) a direct inspiration. Yet one has to wonder about the impact of Martin Luther King's sermons upon the consciousness of secular Jewish activists. The 1960s student New Left, whose leaders were preponderantly Jewish, was influenced by many of the messianic neo-Marxists mentioned above; and by the end of the 1960s by more authoritarian Marxists, like Lenin and Mao. By the mid-1970s student activism was dead, or in hibernation—it had not outlasted the end of the war and the US surrender in Vietnam. Many Jews however continued to maintain a commitment to social change.

In the meantime another current was becoming stronger within the Jewish community. By 1967 after the Six Day War, as noted above, the state of Israel had become "the religion of the American Jews" and the Constantinian synthesis that developed led to the final disappearance of the ideal of prophetic Judaism as the foundation for Reform Judaism in the diaspora. Douglas Rushkoff ironically notes that those Jews who dedicated their lives to social justice were disdained by the Jewish religious community as "lapsed Jews" (see Rushkoff, 2003) He writes, "Though they had merely followed the same path as Moses toward unbiased compassion and selfless activism, they had seemingly abandoned all that was nominally Jewish" (p.43). The support of and vicarious identification with Israel became the substitute for the ideals of prophetic Judaism. In the collective imagination of Reform (and Conservative) Jewry even the luminosity of God had faded—and was replaced by military might and glory of the nation-state of Israel. Is it YHVH or the Israeli Defense Force (IDF) that is behind the burning bush in the Jewish collective imagination today? The universalist messianic mission that had inspired modern Judaism was replaced by an idolatry of the Israeli state that would have made Isaiah cringe in anguish.

The attempt to revitalize diaspora Jewish liturgy and social activism was undertaken in the 1980s by dissident Jews who formed the Jewish Renewal movement (Michael Lerner and Rabbi Arthur Waskow are among the most prominent figures), as well as Jewish feminists like Judith Plaskow and Susannah Heschel—Ellis aptly terms them "justice seeking Jews who integrate traditional Judaism and modern sensibilities" (2002,p.25). But Ellis finds there is something inauthentic about these innovations: "It is almost as if the argument for peace with the Palestinians, once made, becomes one among other issues for Jews... The new Jewish mysticism and politics of meaning tend to make peripheral the injustice that continues.... New meanings are ascribed to the Sabbath ritual and the moon is reincorporated into the Jewish calendar...Even peace marches in Jerusalem... attest to the wholeness of Jewish renewal. As it turns out, it is perfectly possible to celebrate one's Jewishness while another people is displaced and living in segregated and 'autonomous' areas" (2002, pp.25-6). For Lerner and Waskow the Palestinian issue is an issue for Jews to deal with among themselves. It is here as we will see that Ellis diverges radically from Jewish dissidents.

Thus despite the ephemeral triumph of the idea of the centrality of the Jewish prophetic mission within the diaspora in the 19th century and its hegemony albeit in an attenuated form among Reform Jews for a large part of the 20th Century, with the growth of the nation state of Israel it was gradually eclipsed, and was replaced among Jews in the last quarter of the 20th Century by the idea that Israel was the true home and spiritual center of the Jewish people. The Holocaust and Israel became the defining symbols of Jewish identity. Spiritual salvation no longer entailed the accomplishment of a universal mission; for the Jews it meant going "home," returning to Israel—not changing the world, not ending war, not establishing the spiritual foundation for the messianic age as described by Isaiah. One critic called this checkbook religion. Jews sent copious quantities of money to Israel but virtually no one emigrated—not to Israel. In fact Jews from all over, including Israel (the most dangerous place on the earth for a Jew) flocked to Brooklyn and Queens, leading Beit—Hallahmi to suggest that "New York City may be the real answer to the 19th Century 'Jewish Question'" (p.184). But Israel remains the holy shrine.

One cannot help but wonder: What would Reform Judaism look like had it remained faithful to its original mission? Well then of course it would spare no criticism today of those who Jews who commit injustice in the name of the people of Israel. The prophets of Judaism turned their moral weapons first upon their own people–as was appropriate for a people chosen by God to bring forth justice. As the Orthodox theologian Professor Yeshayahu Leibowitz wrote, "Nationalism and patriotism are not religious values. The prophets of Israel in the period of the first commonwealth...were for the most part 'traitors' from the perspective of secular nationalism and patriotism"(cited in Brownfeld, 2002). Had Reform Judaism remained faithful to its mission the synagogues would be chartering buses to go Washington D.C. to protest against Washington's support for Israel. Reform Judaism would be a fulcrum of resistance to the crimes committed in our name by the Jewish state backed by the American government. But American Jewry has sold its birthright for a mess of pottage. As Ellis wrote, "Some time ago I suggested we replace the Torah in the Ark of the Covenant with helicopter gunships. Since military power defines Jewish life, we should be honest about what we worship–power and might. At the most meaningful hour of worship, we bow before that which secures us. Once it was the covenant and the Torah; now it is helicopter gunships and the wall" (Ellis, 2003b,p.155).

Yoder's View:
The Exile, Jewish Mission, and the Christianization of Judaism

Besides Ellis one of the few theological critics of Zionism is not a Jew, but the late John Howard Yoder, the Mennonite (radical reformationist) theologian. Yoder argued that the Zionist triumph constituted the fall of Judaism—it represented Jews' acceptance of the Constantinian option. Yoder finds in the prophet Jeremiah an affirmation of the Diasporic mission and vision. The real mission of Jews, according to Jeremiah, is not to reconquer Israel by force but to settle into Babylon and seek to establish a righteous social order (Yoder, 2003, pp 190-1). As Yoder student Alain Epp Weaver put it, "Diaspora Judaism" was "an embodied critique of Constantinianism"(2002, p.11). Weaver argues that by demonstrating an alternative to the fusion of Christianity and empire Jews were at that time playing a significant role within salvation-history, as Yoder conceived it. Weaver writes succinctly, "In fact, God continued to reveal God's purposes for the world through the faithfulness of diaspora Jewish communities amidst the complicity of the Church with empire" (2002, p.11). Yoder wrote, "Occasionally privileged after the model of Joseph, more often emigrating, frequently suffering martyrdom nonviolently Jews were able to maintain identity without turf or sword, community without sovereignty. *They demonstrated pragmatically the viability of the ethic of Jeremiah and Jesus*" (Yoder, 2003, p. 81).

Even today Weaver and other prominent Christians (e.g. George Lindbeck) have noted Christians have the opportunity to learn anew from the history of diaspora Jewish communities—to learn "how to live faithfully in exile" (Weaver, 2002, p11). Of course the resurgence and coalescence of both Jewish Constantinianism and Christian Constantinianism (the "Christian Right") is a pernicious development that poses formidable new challenges for Jews and Christians of conscience who believe that empire building is not compatible with the calling of their respective faiths.

Yoder, as a Mennonite, affirms that "Judaism within Christiandom since Constantine has the shape which historians will later call 'radical reformation' or 'peace church.'"(Ibid, p.81). Or in other words, "[T]he Jews of the Diaspora were for over a millennium the closest thing to the ethic of Jesus existing anywhere in Christiandom" (Yoder, 2003, p. 81). Zionism, as Yoder saw it, was (ironically considering its contempt for Jewish assimilationists) itself a form of assimilationism—assimilation to the state, to military power, to secularism—and to Western colonialism, he might have added. Ultimately, *Zionism is an assimilation to Christianity in its dominant Western form!* It is in fact the substitution of the values of Constantine for those of Jeremiah and the Jewish diaspora. Rabbi Steven Schwarzschild wrote,"[W]hatever... theologians.... may say about Jewish theory with respect to violence, one thing I think is absolutely indisputable: namely, that two thousand years of actual Jewish history is quite unqualifiedly de facto the most extraordinary exemplification of persistent practiced pacifism in the history of the human race" (cited in Staub, 2002, p.142).

While Schwarzschild and Yoder were not quite right in their contention that European Jews were pacifists, modern scholarship demonstrates they were not far from the truth: Professor Daniel Boyarin's studies of Talmudic culture, provide edification. Boyarin writes that "we see at the foundation of the rabbinic value system the obverse of the 'manly' Roman values in the Masada foundation myth of Jewish heroism.... The Babylonian Talmud's Rabbi Yohanan prefers life and the possibility to serve God through the study of Torah over everything else...While the Josephan zealots proved themselves 'real men' by preferring death at their own hands to slavery, the Rabbis prefer slavery to death" (Boyarin and Boyarin, 2002, p.52). Rabbinic culture did not romanticize killing or "death with honor. " This was the ideal of European culture—the culture which Zionists envied and emulated. Boyarin comments, "The notion that dying with a weapon is more beautiful and honorable than dying without one is a surrender of Jewish difference to a 'universal' masculinist consensus. Modern Jewish culture (not only Zionist) has assimilated the macho male ethos of Western civilization. The result is the creation of the 'Muscle Jew' (Nordau) which divorces Jewish men from their emphasis on study, prayer and gentleness" (Boyarin and Boyarin, 2002, p.53).

Furthermore rabbinic Jews did in fact place their trust in God, as Yoder argues. They adopted the Jeremiac option. They did not dream of political sovereignty, but developed a more Godly orientation. Boyarin compares their ethos to that of Christian monks–with the difference that the Jews were not de-sexualized–who also created an alternative *counter-culture* antithetical to Constantinianism. Yoder argued that "[t]rust in Adonai is what opens the door to his saving intervention. It is the opposite of making one's own political military arrangements." Jeremiah's abandoning statehood for the future, Yoder wrote, is not so much abandoning an earlier hope than it is "returning to the original trust in YHVD" (cited in Weaver, 2003, p3). What could be further from this original trust than a quest for political sovereignty, of political domination? Thus it is not surprising that both Jews and monks–who sought to recover or cultivate their trust in God and placed God above the State in their tier of values—embodied what were considered *feminine* traits within the context of European society. Boyarin argues that "various symbolic enactments of femaleness" e.g. asceticism, submissiveness, retiring to private places– were "acts of resistance against the Roman culture of masculinist power-wielding" (Boyarin, 1997,p.6)–of seeking power in the framework of the state, power not to serve others, but to dominate them. In other words, I would submit, that the "feminine" traits that were adaptive in a religious counter-culture, be it rabbinic or monastic, would seem aberrant to the wider culture based on power-wielding, of idolatry of the state. Constantinian Christianity and Constantinian Judaism signified that the goal of surrender to God (represented by religion in its state of integrity) had been eclipsed by the satisfaction of gaining a share in the worldly power embodied in the State (the "hierarchies of office and gender," Ibid, p6)—the culmination of this Promethean endeavor required a mastery by the religious or Zionist authorities of the masculinist power wielding which is antithetical to the more receptive "feminine" quality of piety.

Boyarin does not claim that rabbinic culture escaped the sexism of Western society, although it arguably attenuated its most malignant aspects. He demonstrates however that rabbinic culture " defined ideal men as gentle, peaceful and nurturing" (1997, p.162) and that Jews tended to look down on those features that "in European society defined a man as manly: physical strength, martial activity and aggressiveness, and contempt for and fear of the female body" (1997, p.78). In Zionism the archetypal role model is transformed from the Torah scholar, the man of meekness and piety (weakness in Zionist eyes) into the Israeli soldier, the armored sabra (soldier) strong and "manly" enough to kill the "Canaanites," male or female or child and reconquer the promised land. Today "Israeli toughness and military prowess have become the model for right-wingers, machos and Rambos around the world. Israelis are admired because they are good fighters, and because, as such, they are very unlike Jews" (Beit-Hallahmi, 1993, pp.135-6). In every aspect, despite its reputation, Zionism was not an assertion of the Jewish ethos, but its repudiation—an assimilation to the values of Christiandom. Yoder put it aptly: "The culmination of the Christianization of Judaism, then, is the development of Zionism" (Yoder, 2003, p.154).

Many Jews have seen Israel as God's answer to the Jewish holocaust. They claim that Jewish empowerment dispels the religious difficulties the holocaust posed for Judaism–and for religion in general: "How could God allow this to happen? Does God exist?" Even Lerner and dissident Jews believe this: Israel is God's compensation for the holocaust, although in a more secular leftish-trendy vein they valorize the creation of Israel as an act of "national self-determination" (Lerner, 2003,p.38) and "a righteous act of affirmative action for Jews on the part of the world" (to quote Susannah Heschel, 2003). They also argue as we have seen that the post-1967 Occupation puts in jeopardy these claims. However it must be said that it beggars the imagination that the deliberate (Benny Morris in his latest incarnation leaves no doubt about the expulsions being a product of "design") expulsion in the1948 war of close to a million innocent Palestinian non-combatants and their consequent transformation into homeless refugees could be described by a progressive Jew as "righteous... affirmative action"– as if the consequences of the creation of a "purified" (or almost) Jewish state in an Arab land had no serious moral significance. As if the victims of the catastrophe never had any right to a say in the matter.

Furthermore the conviction that the establishment of Israel is God's compensation for Jewish suffering in the Holocaust (a common view among Jews) and thus resumes the broken thread of salvation-history or salvation meta-history is based upon a revival of the archaic narrative of the literal Jewish return from exile, "of innocence and redemption" which in its present form (rejected even by the Orthodox Neturei Karta) conflates military conquest and ethnic cleansing with messianic miracle, and thus perpetuates "the cycle of atrocities"(Ellis,1994) characteristic of civilization, while sacrificing the pacifistic and universalist aspirations that had become fused with the history of the (pre-state) people of Israel—as formulated by the prophets, as lived in the diaspora and reaffirmed by Judaism in its post-Enlightenment guises–and by the radical reformation which Yoder represents. No, this "solution" is unacceptable to Jews of conscience: the Israeli state poses a moral/religious problem for Judaism, as Rabbi Elmer Berger– and Norton Mezvinsky—and Neturei Karta had recognized from the start (e.g. Berger, 1988, pp.3-32). More recently Ellis stands alone (and ostracized by the Jewish religious establishment) as the only prominent American Jewish theologian to explore the extent to which the widespread Jewish support for Israel– a support which abides regardless of the policies Israel implements—constitutes an insurmountable moral and theological problem for the Jewish people, even if they refuse to recognize this fact.

Judaism is not a gnostic or world-rejecting religion that permits the abdication of individual responsibility for the collective, offering the individual mystical escape and consolation for the state of the world. As the renowned modern Jewish theologian and scholar Abraham Heschel wrote, "The presence of God in history... is the object of the prophet's longing. It is not mystical experience he yearns for in the night but historical justice. Mystical experience is the illumination of an individual; historical justice is the illumination of all men, enabling the inhabitants of the world to learn righteousness" (1962, Volume 1,p.175). Isaiah calls, "Hearken to me, you who pursue righteousness, you who seek the Lord" (51:1). Heschel asks rhetorically, "[W]hat greater praise is possible than is given by the juxtaposition of these [preceding] phrases?" (Ibid, p.207). To seek the Lord *is* to pursue righteousness. To shun righteousness is to abandon God.

But if the creation of the Israel state constituted a catastrophe for the Palestinians, if Israel's founders deliberately expelled the Palestinians from their land (as recent scholarship demonstrates to be so) and were oblivious to the suffering inflicted upon the Palestinians, how could Israel be "God's answer to the Holocaust"? To Jews who see Israel as a sign of redemption or God's intervention in history, Ellis asks "Can the question of God exist today for Jews without reference to Palestinians? Can it be that the presence of God is finally reasserted for Jews as the absence of God becomes clear for a people on the other side of Jewish power?.... To move forward is to understand that when redemption is a disaster for the 'other,' redemption cannot be claimed. Disaster for the other is, at the same time, disaster for the 'innocent'"(2002, p.59).

Ellis believes the Jewish establishment endeavors to "seal" the prophetic in the Hebrew Bible, while attempting to surreptitiously purge Judaism of its prophetic dimension—-the core of its identity; it is the prophets who reveal to the people the way to keep faith with God, to honor the covenant. The Jewish Establishment does not serve God or keep the covenant. It serves Israel. It serves the State. The Jewish critics of Israel speak the word of the prophet—they demand that Jews honor the covenant, they rebuke our people for seeking to substitute the might of Israel for the guidance of God, for substituting raison d'etat or egocentric satisfaction for the quest for justice for all people. That is the purpose of the covenant–to empower Jews to serve God, to serve humanity. Heschel wrote that prophetic inspiration is given to help Jews to maintain the integrity of the covenant. He stated, "The purpose of prophecy is to maintain the covenant, to establish the right relationship between God and man"(Ibid, p.202).

But now it is the very survival of the covenant that is at stake–the integrity of modern Jewry's relationship to God, which depends of course on our relationship to other human beings. Prophecy, exile, the covenant–each of these concepts is a Jewish/Christian archetype that Marc Ellis fashions into a metanarrative as an effort to expose—and evoke an alternative to—the Constantinian Jewish attempt to control history, to build empire, and to hide behind the post-Holocaust mythical status of Jewish martyrdom and innocence. Ellis asks, "For is the covenant present when a Palestinian is displaced or humiliated at Deir Yassin, in Lebanon, during the intifada, or with the Israeli death squads that have operated in parts of the West

Bank and Gaza over the decades? Is the covenant present when rabbis in Israel justify these actions...? Or when, through the language of suffering and innocence, rabbis in the United States and Europe refuse to acknowledge that these actions are taking place?" (1999, p.47). Dissident Jews like Lerner who appeal to the American Jewish establishment or the Israeli government to honor the values of Judaism have underestimated the hegemonic power of the state. "Religion in service to the state serves only the state" (Ellis, 2003b, p.143).

Ellis's Proclamation of the New Exile

For decades Ellis has been arguing with himself, appealing to other Jews— and affirming his solidarity with the Palestinians, in the name of humanity, but also in the name of the Jewish "covenant," in the name of the God of Abraham, Isaac and Jacob, as a more conventional Jew than Ellis would phrase it. Like the Jewish dissidents he evidently hoped at times that times that the Jewish religious tradition would influence the wielders of Jewish power. "For me an entire history of suffering and struggle, an ethical base from which to judge the world and establish...harmony...among peoples, is on the line" (2002, p28).

But Ellis reluctantly is forced to conclude that the Jewish tradition "as it has been known and inherited" has come to an end—Ellis repeats this over and again like a refrain in his later essays and books. This is a painful realization for Ellis- -he can not cultivate the kinds of hopes and illusions that sustain dissident Jews. "The realization that the community itself, the Jewish people as a people in history, will not embrace the covenant as a way towards ending suffering...evokes sadness. For does not the covenant speak of a people chosen among nations, with a destiny guided by God, particular and universal in significance, one of liberation and hope?" (1999, p.166). "In the displacement, torture and murder of Palestinians... the center of Jewish history has been turned inside out and gutted. A Jew in exile knows this at the deepest level of his being" (2002, p.35).

Ellis's formal abjuration of reform is not a retreat from political engagement. It is disengagement from a project based on the hope of reforming Constantinian Judaism—or even of reviving Judaism "as it has been known and inherited." But it is a reaffirmation of the Jewish diaspora–and a repudiation of Israel as the spiritual center of Judaism. It is the end of innocence about "my people" and all people, "including those I embrace in solidarity" (2002, p35). While a tradition has come to an end, at the same time a new diaspora, a new exile is forming. Ellis tells us that an image appears before his mind repeatedly–it is of Jews of conscience walking slowly into exile. Although many of these Jews see themselves as secular, Ellis notices that they are all carrying the covenant with them into exile! (see e.g. 2002, p.ix) Herein lies the hope.

They are not just thrust into exile. They are walking away—many from traditional bonds which sustained them ethically or spiritually. Others from the hope of creating and becoming part of a new enlightened Jewish establishment. Others are walking away as agnostics or atheists from a religious tradition they view as irrelevant, if not as corrupt as the modern state. (Both Finkelstein and Shapiro are atheists but neither has anything against religion per se, but rather with the state and state-religion.) All are walking away from—disengaging from—the state, and the religion which colludes with it–but in doing so they are unwittingly honoring the Jewish covenant. Even the Jewish atheists! Thus it is a remnant of the Jewish people which is faithful to the ethics of Judaism, who "struggle against the final assimilation to the state." Ironically, "this struggle is led by Jews without 'religion'...Jews like Noam Chomsky.... Is it any wonder that the most vehement critic of state power in the world is a religionless Jew..." (2003, p.151). (Ellis compares Chomsky's critique of the state to Marx and Freud, but Marx and Rosa Luxemburg or Trotsky or Buber would have been more accurate since they, contrary to Freud, rejected nationalism and preached the message of "universal human emancipation," as Isaac Deutscher noted)

By critiquing the state and the Constantinian synthesis, "[t]his remnant, though seemingly modern and without ties to the religious tradition of Judaism, is paradoxically embodying the most ancient of Jewish traditions, the refusal of idolatry" (2003,p.169). Ellis of course refers to the idolatry of the state of Israel, which in its scope and intensity surpasses anything in the history of Jewry. This rejection of the State enables the Jewish exile to separate itself from the Israeli nation-state and to prepare the ground for a revitalization of the diaspora and thus for a potential revival of the prophetic dimension of Judaism, *If the center of Jewish hope and prayer is demilitarized and divorced from the state, then the diaspora reality of Jewish history is reasserted* (2002, p107).

There is again a striking parallel here to the efforts made by radical reformation theologies to divorce Christian hope from the state and re-ground it within the Church. The radical Christian theologian Stanley Hauerwas writes in *Resident Aliens*: "The habit of Constantinian thinking is difficult to break. It leads Christians to judge their ethical positions, not on the basis of what is faithful to our peculiar tradition, but rather on the basis of how much Christian ethics Ceasar can be induced to swallow without choking" (Hauerwas and Willimon, 1993, p.72). Yoder argues that the Church ceases to serve God if it identifies with the "fallen" social order. It thus "denies the miracle of the new humanity in two ways: on the one hand by blessing the existing social structure that is part of the fallen order rather than a new miracle, and on the other hand by closing its fellowship to those of the outside or enemy class or tribe or people or nation" (1994, p.75). This of course is exactly what has happened in the last 50 years with Constantinian Judaism.

Ellis adds that a condition for fellowship and a new humanity is forgiveness. Jews as a people remain frozen in the past because they will not acknowledge the crimes they have committed against the Palestinians. Ellis cites Adi Ophir who wrote on Hannah Arendt's work: "The one who forgets cannot forgive, but the one who forgives (or is forgiven) is free to forget; forgiveness unties" (2003a, p.161). This is one of the reasons that Ellis emphasizes that the new exile must be based on solidarity with the Palestinians. The key to "moving forward"–a phrase Ellis often uses, implying a teleology immanent within the world itself, though dependent on human action for its actualization– is to accept one's frailties while honestly acknowledging one failings. "The freezing of memory, the inability to forgive and accept a new promise (as one is forgiven and welcomed back into the arena of promise as well) betrays the very structure of social existence...[I]t betrays the promise of life, for without forgiveness and promise there is no future" (Ibid, p163). For Ellis as for Yoder the new association must include the fellowship of former enemies, or putative enemies--a new humanity in embryo.

As Yoder sees it the Church in the Anabaptist model embodies the new values and thus discharges a modeling mission. "The church is called to be now what the world is called to be ultimately" (Yoder, 1984, p92). On the most general level the Radical Reformation model is based on prophetic Judaism, of which of course Jesus was an extraordinary exemplar. (The Anabaptists obviously make creedal statements about Jesus, but that is irrelevant to the point at hand.) Yoder wrote, "The work of God is the calling of a people, whether in the Old Testament or the New.... This creation of the one new humanity is itself the purpose that God had in all ages, is itself the 'mystery,' the gospel now to be proclaimed" (1994, p.74).

In Deuteronomy Israel is revealed as God's "chosen" people. But chosen for what? According to the prophets, most explicitly the Second Isaiah, Jews are chosen to bring God's truth to all the world's people. "I have given you as a covenant to the people, a light unto the nations, to open the eyes that are blind, to bring out the prisoners from the dungeon, from the prison those who sit in darkness" (Isaiah, 42:6-7). And to "bring forth justice to the nations" (Isaih, 42:1). In Isaiah the covenantal responsibility of other covenants has been broadened to include reaching out to other nations (Tarshish, pp77-8). This universalist nature of Israel's mission was emphasized by early Jewish Reform thinkers who minimized the significance of ritual dimensions of Judaism—in accord with the prophets. Thus in rejecting Constantinian Christianity, the radical reformers adopted a model of which the early prophets provided a prototype: Israel (or the Church, in the radical reformation view) is called to be a holy people set apart from the world—"resident aliens"– faithful to God and His commandments, so that they can bring justice to all the nations. It was that same model that was deliberately embraced by Reform Judaism at its inception, and that Ellis affirms with renewed fervor today—although outside the boundaries of institutionalized Judaism (in its Reform and other variants).

There are two fundamental and distinctive positions that are characteristic of Jews of conscience—of the new Jewish prophetic, as Ellis has also termed it. The first prototypical posture of Jewish exiles, Jews of conscience, is the refusal to sanction or seek cooperation with the Jewish state or with the Jewish Constantinian establishment in the United States; these Jews are involved as a matter of conscience in protesting state violence. They do not believe, as Lerner does, in the legitimacy (in the "righteousness") of the establishment of the "Jewish state"—although they may accept it as a temporary necessity (as Chomsky does), considering the world situation. Another equally important defining position of prophetic Jews–which is of course mutually implicated by the "first"—is the embrace of the Palestinian movement. The political rationale for this position has been established in this essay already, so I will not elaborate. Ellis provides a theological rationale starting from the premise that the crime committed against the Palestinians by Israel is not parenthetical in its religious significance *for Jews*—but that like the Holocaust itself is fraught with religious implications. Ellis asks rhetorically, "Could it be that in this era of empowerment, the only way to fulfill the covenant is to remember the victims of Jewish power, that is, to include the Palestinian people as part of Jewish history and destiny? Since they are already part of our biography, is it incumbent on Jews to embrace the Palestinian people as intimate to the covenant itself? Perhaps it is time to expand the covenant to include the Palestinian people, or perhaps it has already been expanded without Jewish acknowledgment"(1999, p.54). This is an astonishing and revolutionary revision of Jewish theology. The fact that it has gone theologically unnoticed—even un-attacked—is revealing of the Zionist prejudices of Jewish theologians.

Ellis posits that the Jewish covenant now includes Moslems, and (Palestinian) Christians. It is somewhat surprising that although Ellis asserts this theme repeatedly nowhere does he explore in depth the practical religious implications of this. How would or could this be operationalized in terms of spiritual practice and religious obligations and privileges for Palestinian Moslems and Christians? For Jews (particularly Israelis, presumably) Ellis tells us that at least it means confessing to Palestinians the horrific wrongs that have been done to them since they were first expelled from their homes in 1948. In fact Ellis points out the absurdity to which the Jewish pretense of innocence has reduced Judaism: On the Jewish day of atonement, Yom Kippur, Israel's oppression of the Palestinians is not even mentioned, "the central question facing us as a people becomes invisible. That invisibility is sanctioned by religious ritual" (2002, p130) Yet "[o]ne day we will ask them to forgive us" (2003a, p155).

Clearly there is no other Jewish theologian who is even thinking along the lines of Ellis. Furthermore Ellis realizes that most Jews of conscience are reluctant to speak today in religious terms, let alone to think theologically–as they tend to identify religion with hypocrisy and the legitimation of the state. And for that matter there are few—if any—religious Jewish authorities, other than Ellis, who are in *solidarity* with the Palestinians. Thus Ellis tends to focus on the political and moral responsibilities of Jews of conscience–he does not call for a Jewish prophetic version of Vatican Two to spell out a program of religious and ecumenical action. (Although it strikes me that a Jewish-Islamic-Christian conversation around ecumenical issues based on Jewish repentance would in fact give rise to creative exchanges and new and promising hybrid theological perspectives. One might even imagine novel liturgical practices.)

There are small but growing groups of Jews all around the United States who have come together for political action to protest Israel's treatment of Palestinians– and this is what is evidently of primary concern to Ellis as a political activist and moral philosopher. They do not accept the more moderate and Zionist position of the Tikkun groups, though they often enter into alliances with them, as well as other groups that oppose the Occupation or US imperialism in general. Unlike Jewish dissidents, Jews of conscience in America do not preface every criticism of Israeli policies with an avowal of their "love" for the state of Israel. Although concerned for the people of Israel, Jewish radicals' priority is standing in solidarity with the victims of Israeli power, the Palestinians. Ellis writes "Those Jews who search out the new diaspora "refuse the borders of Israel as the boundaries of Jewish destiny." They have–"at this very moment"– "crossed over into solidarity" with the Palestinians (2003a, p.145).

The primary purpose of the new exile is to act as witnesses. In the light of Jews of conscience's obvious political impotence in the short term, to speak in more strategic terms of influencing the Empire would be jejune. Clearly these Jews do not have the clout to influence the American government to pressure Israel to make concessions to the Palestinians. In the short term Jews of conscience can claim at most to be witnesses. Practicing exile is an affirmation of a future beyond the cycle of atrocity, beyond empire "pursued in the name of Jewish history and the Jewish people." (2003, p170)."This witness is bound to fail in our time, so *it is fidelity to the past and future of conscience and justice embodied in the world that the practice of exile speaks to*" (2003, p.170, emphasis added). This is a feature of those who bear the prophetic–they persist in spite of failure, and seeming impotence. "I obey nonetheless" is Isaiah's response to God according to Daniel Berrigan, and Ellis add that it must be "in response to and in spite of God *and* humanity" (2002, p.152).

But it would be disingenuous to end on this note for as I have demonstrated in another essay (Farber, 2003) despite the somber and lugubrious tone of Ellis's recent work—influenced obviously by the increase in the extent and intensity of Israel's violence against the Palestinians, as well as the particularly aggressive policies of the Bush Administration—his 1999 book is suffused by a hopefulness that rises to Biblical heights of lyrical messianic affirmation. And messianic motifs and images are dispersed throughout all his works. Thus one frequently finds the assertion or insinuation that the act of Jewish solidarity with the Palestinians has messianic implications. Even in his most recent book Ellis wonders again if Jewish solidarity with Palestinians is not a "counter-testimony to Auschwitz" that may "initiate a restoration of the image of God [in man] so desecrated in the Holocaust" (2003,p30)—clearly a messianic ideal. Although in *Out of the Ashes* the messianic is mostly eschewed and he cautions readers that realistic idealism can only validate the vision of the co-existence of community and empire, Ellis expresses the hope, the faith, that the remnant of Jews, not Jewish dissidents but Jews of conscience (perhaps a couple of thousand at most in the United States) who choose exile and community (as opposed to empire or reform) and thus political impotence and ostracism, will have the last word. "Those who carry the memory of Jewish suffering and act in solidarity with the Palestinian people may ultimately decide the future of the covenant and the Jewish people" (1999, pp. 71-2) " They are in exile preparing the future of Jewish life, a future that can arise when the land of Israel and Palestine are shared." (2003, p.145).

Appendix

Essential Websites

Jews Against the Occupation—www.jato.org

The Palestine Right to Return Coalition—www.al-awda.org

Jewish Voice For Peace—www.jewishvoiceforpeace.org

American Council for Judaism—www.acjna.org

The Palestine Chronicle Weekly Journal—www.palestinechronicle.com

Z Magazine—www.zmag.org

Counterpunch—www.counterpunch.org

Tikkun Magazine—www.tikkun.org

The Link—www.ameu.org

Gush Shalom (Israeli peace group)—www.gush-shalom.org

International Solidarity Movement—www.palsolidarity.org

Institute of Islamic Political Thought—www.ii-pt.com

Council on Islamic-American Relations—www.cair-net.org

References

References—Preface

Beinin, J. (2004), "The New McCarthyism" in *Race and Class*, Vol. 46, No. 1.

Brenner, Lenni (1983), *Zionism in the Age of Dictators* (Westport, Connecticut: Lawrence Hill).

Ellis, Marc (1990), *Beyond Innocence and Redemption: Confronting the Holocaust and Israeli Power* (San Francisco: HarperCollins).

Ellis, Marc (1997), *Unholy Alliance: Religion and Atrocity in Our Time* (Minneapolis: Fortress Press).

Ellis, Marc (1999), *O, Jerusalem: The Contested Future of the Jewish Covenant* (Minneapolis: Fortress Press).

Ellis, Mark (2000a), *Revolutionary Forgiveness: Essays on Judaism, Christianity and the Future of Religious Life* (Waco: Baylor University Press).

Ellis, Mark (2000b), "On the Future of Judaism and Jewish Life" (Birmingham, England: University of Birmingham and the Center for American and Jewish Studies).

Ellis, Marc (2002a), *Practicing Exile: The Religious Odyssey of an American Jew* (Minneapolis: Fortress Press).

Ellis, Marc (2003), *Israel and Palestine*: *Out of the Ashes: The Search for Jewish Identity in the 21st Century* (London: Pluto Books).

Evron, Boas (1995), *Jewish State or Israeli Nation* (Bloomington: Indiana University Press).

Feuerlicht, Roberta (1983), *The Fate of the Jews* (New York: New York Times Books).

Finkelstein, Norman G. (2003), Preface to the German Edition (English translation) of *The Rise and Fall of Palestine (Germany*: Hugendubel) *at* www.normanfinkelstein.com.

Finkelstein, Norman G. (1995), *Image and Reality of the Israel-Palestine Conflict* (London: Verso).

Frye, Northrop (1971), *Anatomy of Criticism* (Princeton: Princeton University Press).

Ginsberg, T. (2005) Academic Integrity: Travestied at Columbia Middle East Studies Conference at www.zmag.org, March 14, 2005.

Grinberg, Lev (2002a), "State Terrorism in Israel," *Tikkun*, May-June, 2002.

Grinberg, Lev (2002b), "Trapped by the USA," *Tikkun*, November-December, 2002.

Lerner, Michael (2002b), "The Great Denial in America and Israel," *Tikkun*, Sept/Oct 2002.

Lustick, Ian (2002), "Through Blood and Fire Shall Peace Arise," *Tikkun*, May-June, 2002.

Margolit, Avisha (2002), "The Suicide Bombers," *The New York Review of Books*, January 16, 2003.

References— Introduction

Chomsky, Noam (2003), *Middle East Illusions* (New York: Rowman and Littlefield Publishers).

Cohen, Aharon (1976), *Israel and the Arab World*, (NY: Beacon Press).

Kohn, Hans (1958), "Zion and the Jewish National Ideal" printed in Khalidi, Walid (ed) 1971, *From Haven to Conquest*, (Washington, D.C.: Insitute for Palestinian Studies).

Lockman, Zachary (1996), *Comrades and Enemies: Arab and Jewish Workers in Palestine, 1906-1948*, (Berkeley: University of California Press)

References—Chapter 5

Chomsky, Noam (2003), *Middle East Illusions* (Rowman and Littlefield, New York).

Evron, Boas (1995), *Jewish State or Israeli Nation* (Bloomington: Indiana University Press).

Finkelstein, Norman G. (1988), *From the Jewish Question to the Jewish State: An Essay on the Theory of Zionism*, unpublished dissertation.

Finkelstein, Norman G. (1995), *Image and Reality of the Israel-Palestine Conflict* (London: Verso).

Finkelstein, Norman G. (1996), *The Rise and Fall of Palestine*, (Minneapolis: University of Minnesota

Press)

Finkelstein, Norman G. (2000), *The Holocaust Industry: Reflections on the Exploitation of Jewish Suffering* (London: Verso).

Finkelstein, Norman G. (2002) "An Introduction to the Israel-Palestine Conflict," (Finkelstein website).

Flapan, Simha (1987) *The Birth of Israel*, (London: Croom Helm).

Heschel, Susannah (2003) "Whither the Zionist Dream?", *Tikkun,* May/June 2003.

Hirst, David (1984) *The Gun and the Olive Branch*, (London: Faber and Faber).

Masahla, Nur (1992) *Expulsion of the Palestinians: The Concept of Transfer in Zionist Political Thought*, (Washington, D.C.: Institute for Palestinian Studies).

Masahla, Nur (2000) *Imperial Israel and the Palestinians*, (London: Pluto Press).

Palumbo, Michael (1988), 1987, *The Palestinian Catastrophe: The 1848 Expulsion of a People from their Homeland*, (London: Faber and Faber,1987).

Schoenman, Ralph (1988) *The Hidden History of Zionism* (Santa Barbara: Veritas Press).

Rodin, Maxime (1973) *Israel: A Colonial-Settler State?* (New York: Monad Press).

Will, Donald (1975) "The UN, Zionism and Racism," *The Link*, Vol.8, 5.

Zoughbi Zoughbi (1999) "Native Americans and Palestinians-The Visit," *The Link,* Vol. 32, 5.

References—Chapter 8

Boyarin, Daniel (1997), *Unheroic Conduct: The Rise of Heterosexuality and the Invention of the Jewish Man* (Berkeley: University of California Press).

Boyarin, Daniel (2002), "Tricksters, Martyrs, and Collaborators" in Boyarin, J. and Boyarin, D. (Eds) *Powers of Diaspora*, (Minneapolis: University of Minnesota Press)

References—Conclusion

Almog, Shmuel et al, Eds. (1998) *Zionism and Religion* (Hanover, N.H.: University Press of New England).

Beit-Hallahmi, Benjamin (1993), *Original Sins*, (New York: Olive Branch Press).

Berger, Elmer (1988), "Zionist Ideology: Obstacle to Peace" in Tekiner, Rochelle, Mezvinsky, Norton, and Abed-Rabbo, Samir (eds), *Anti-Zionism: Analytical Reflections* (Brattleboro, Vermont: Amana Books).

Boyarin, Daniel (1997), *Unheroic Conduct: The Rise of Heterosexuality and the Invention of the Jewish Man* (Berkeley: University of California Press).

Boyarin, Daniel (2002), "Tricksters, Martyrs, and Collaborators" in Boyarin, J. and Boyarin, D. (Eds) *Powers of Diaspora*, (Minneapolis: University of Minnesota Press)

Brenner, Lenni (1983), *Zionism in the Age of Dictators* (Westport, Connecticut: Lawrence Hill).

Brownfield, Allan, (1998) *The Washington Report on Middle Eastern Affairs,* July/August 1998.

Brownfield, Allan, (2002) "Religion and Nationalism," *Issues of the American Council of Judaism*, Spring, 2002.

Ellis, Marc (1992), "Beyond the Jewish-Christian Dialogue: Solidarity with the Palestinian People" *The Link,* February, 1992.

Ellis, Marc (1999), *O, Jerusalem: The Contested Future of the Jewish Covenant* (Minneapolis: Fortress Press).

Ellis, Mark (2000a), *Revolutionary Forgiveness: Essays on Judaism, Christianity and the Future of Religious Life* (Waco: Baylor University Press).

Ellis, Marc (2002), *Practicing Exile: The Religious Odyssey of an American Jew* (Minneapolis: Fortress Press).

Ellis, Marc (2003a), *Israel and Palestine: Out of the Ashes: The Search for Jewish Identity in the 21st*

Century (London: Pluto Books).

Ellis, Marc (2003b), "Jew vs. Jew: On the Jewish Civil War and the New Prophetic," in Kushner, Tony and Solomon, Alisa (eds.) *Wrestling With Zion: Progressive Jewish-American Responses to the Israeli-Palestinian Conflict* (New York: Grove Press)

Ellis, Marc (2003c), "The 11th Commandment" An address presented at the American Muslims for Jerusalem Annual Convention.

Ellis, Marc, (2003d), "Jews and Palestinians: The Search for Justice and Reconciliation" unpublished essay.

Ellis, Marc (19994), *Ending Auschwitz* (Knoxville: Westminister/John Know Press).

Evron, Boas (1995), *Jewish State or Israeli Nation* (Bloomington: Indiana University Press).

Farber, Seth (2003), "Jewish Solidarity With the Palestinian Liberation Movement," in *Crosscurrents*, Volume 53, No 1.

Hauerwas, Stanley and Willimon, W. (1993), *Resident Aliens*, (Nashville: Abingdon Press).

Heschel, Abraham (1962), *The Prophets*, Volume 1, (New York: Harper Torchbooks).

Heschel, Susannah (2003) "Whither the Zionist Dream?", *Tikkun,* May/June 2003.

Kee, Alistair (1982), *Constantine vs. Christ*, (London: SCM Press).

Lerner, Michael Rabbi (2003), *Healing Israel/Palestine* (San Francisco: Tikkun Books).

Loewy, Michael (1988), *Redemption and Utopia*, (Stanford: Stanford University Press).

Masalha, Nur (1992), *Expulsion of the Palestinians: The Concept of Transfer in Zionist Political Thought, 1882-1948*, (Washington, D.C., Institute for Palestinian Studies)

Mezvinsky, Norton (1988), "Reform Judaism and Zionism" in Tekiner, Rochelle, Mezvinsky, Norton, and Abed-Rabbo, Samir (eds.), *Anti-Zionism: Analytical Reflections* (Brattleboro, Vermont: Amana Books).

Pagels, E. (1988), *Adam, Eve and the Serpent.* (New York: Random House.)

Rushkoff, Douglas (2003), *Nothing Sacred: The Truth About Judaism.* (New York: Crown Publishers).

Scriven, Charles (1988), *The Transformation of Culture*, (Scottsdale, 1988).

Schonfeld, Moshe (1982), *The Holocaust Victims Accuse* in Weizfeld, Ebie (ed.), *The End of Zionism.*

Shahak, Israel (1988) "Zionism as a Recidivist Movement" in Tekiner, Rochelle, Mezvinsky, Norton, and Abed-Rabbo, Samir (eds), *Anti-Zionism: Analytical Reflections* (Brattleboro, Vermont: Amana Books).

Staub, Michael E. (2002), *Torn at the Roots: The Crisis of Jewish Liberalism in Postwar America* (NY: Columbia University Press).

Tarshish, Allan (1952), *Not By Power: The Story of the Growth of Judaism* (New York, Bookman Associates).

Tekiner, Rochelle, Mezvinsky, Norton, and Abed-Rabbo, Samir (1988), (eds.) *Anti-Zionism: Analytical Reflections* (Brattleboro, Vermont: Amana Books).

Weaver, Alain Epp (2002), "Constantinianism, Zionism, Diaspora: Toward a Political Theology of Exile and Return" *Occasional Papers #28*, (Akron, Pa: Mennonite Central Committee).

Weaver, Alain Epp (2003), "On Exile: Yoder, Said and a Theology of Land and Return," Crosscurrents, Volume 52, No 4.

Yoder, John Howard (1982), *The Priestly Kingdom: Social Ethics and Gospel*, (Notre Dame: University of Notre Dame Press).

Yoder, John Howard (1994), *The Royal Priesthood*, (Pennsylvania: Herald Press).

Yoder, John Howard (2003), *The Jewish-Christian Schism Revisited*, (Grand Rapids, Michigan: Wm Eerdmans Publishing Company).

About the Author

Dr. Seth Farber became a political radical as a youngster—in 8th grade—motivated largely by his sympathy for the "underdog." In high school he became an activist against the war in Vietnam. Farber received his Ph.D. in counseling psychology in 1985 from the California Institute of Integral Studies, and completed post-graduate training as a family therapist. In 1987 Farber co-founded a patients rights organization with leaders in the mental patients liberation movement. He appeared on numerous television shows, including Oprah Winfrey and William F. Buckley, Jr. His first book, *Madness, Heresy and the Rumor of Angels* (1993), contains a forward by Dr. Thomas Szasz. He also has an interest in various religions and has been at different times a practicing Jew, a Buddhist, a member of the Eastern Christian Church and a student of Hindu thought. He is now a member of Jews Against the Occupation. This book reflects both his commitment to justice and his faith in prophetic Judaism as a medium of spiritual/ social transformation. His latest book on psychology is *Lunching With Lunatics: Adventures of a Maverick Psychologist.*